Changing Ideas in a Changing World

Changing Ideas in a Changing World: The Revolution in Psychoanalysis

ESSAYS IN HONOUR OF ARNOLD COOPER

Edited by
JOSEPH SANDLER,
ROBERT MICHELS,
and
PETER FONAGY

KARNAC

London
New York

Production Editor: Robert D. Hack

This book was set in 11 pt. Berkeley Book by Alpha Graphics of Pittsfield, New Hampshire.

Copyright © 2000 with Joseph Sandler, Robert Michels, and Peter Fonagy for overall arrangement; copyright © 2000 with individual contributors for their chapters.

10 9 8 7 6 5 4 3 2 1

Published by H. Karnac (Books) Limited, a subsidiary of Other Press LLC, 58 Gloucester Road, London. All rights reserved, including the right to reproduce this book, or parts thereof, in any form, without written permission from Other Press, LLC except in the case of brief quotations in reviews for inclusion in a magazine, newspaper, or broadcast. Printed in the United States of America on acid-free paper. For information write to Other Press, LLC, 377 W. 11th Street, New York, NY 10014. Or visit our website: www.otherpress.com.

ISBN 1-892746-73-5

A CIP record for this book is available from the British Library.

Contributors

EDITORS

Joseph Sandler, Ph.D., M.D., was born in Cape Town, South Africa. He did his doctoral research in psychology at the Institute of Psychiatry, London. Subsequently he pursued medical studies at University College London. He was a Training Analyst at the British Psychoanalytical Society and Past President of the International Psychoanalytical Association and of the European Psychoanalytical Federation. He was Editor in Chief of the *British Journal of Medical Psychology*, the *International Journal of Psycho-Analysis*, and the *International Review of Psycho-Analysis*. He published numerous papers and books on psychoanalysis and allied topics and was awarded the Sigourney Award for outstanding contributions to psychoanalysis.

Robert Michels, M.D., is the Walsh McDermott University Professor of Medicine and University Professor of Psychiatry at Cornell University. He is also a Supervising and Training Analyst at the Columbia University Center for Psychoanalytic Training and Research, where he is a member of the Executive Committee. He is the author of more than 200 scientific articles, and is or has been a member of several editorial boards including *The American Journal of Psychiatry, The New England Journal of Medicine, Journal of the American Psychoanalytic Association, Psychiatry, The International Journal of Psycho-Analysis, The American Journal of Drug and Alcohol Abuse,* and *The Journal of Psychotherapy Practice and Research.*

Peter Fonagy, Ph.D., is Freud Memorial Professor of Psychoanalysis and Director of the Sub-Department of Clinical Health Psychology at University College London. He is Director of the Menninger Clinical Outcomes Research and Effectiveness Centre and the Child and Family Centre, both at the Menninger Foundation, Kansas. He is also Director of Research at the Anna Freud Centre, London. He is a clinical psychologist and a Training and Supervising Analyst at the British Psycho-Analytical Society in child and adult analysis. He has published over 200 chapters and articles and has authored or edited several books, including most recently *What Works for Whom: A Critical Review of Psychotherapy Research* (1996) and *Psychoanalysis on the Move: The Work of Joseph Sandler* (1999).

CONTRIBUTORS

Salman Akhtar, M.D., is Professor of Psychiatry, Jefferson Medical College, Lecturer on Psychiatry, Harvard Medical School, and a Training and Supervising Analyst, Philadelphia Psychoanalytic Institute. He is the author of *Broken Structures* (1992), *A Quest for Answers* (1995), *Inner Torment* (1999), and *Immigration and Identity* (1999), as well as the editor or co-editor of fifteen other books in psychiatry and psychoanalysis. He has also published five volumes of poetry.

Elizabeth L. Auchincloss, M.D., is Associate Chairman for Graduate Medical Education and Director of Residency Training, Department of Psychiatry, Weill Medical College of Cornell University. She is a Training and Supervising Analyst at the Columbia University Center for Psychoanalytic Training and Research where she chaired the Center curriculum committee from 1991–1997.

Jorge Canestri, M.D., is a Training and Supervising Analyst at the Italian Psychoanalytical Association and the Argentinean Psychoanalytic Association. He is a Full Member of the International Psychoanalytical Association and is trained in linguistics and epistemology. He has published numerous psychoanalytical papers and has written (with Jacqueline Amati Mehler and Simona Argentieri) *The Babel of the Unconscious: Mother Tongue and Foreign Languages in the Psychoanalytic Dimension* (1993).

Marcia Cavell, Ph.D., is a Visiting Associate Professor of Philosophy at the University of California, Berkeley, and author of *The Psychoanalytic Mind:*

From Freud to Philosophy (1993). She is an Academic Associate of the American Psychoanalytic Association, an Interdisciplinary Member of the San Francisco Psychoanalytic Association, and a Candidate of the San Francisco Psychoanalytic Institute.

Allan Compton, M.D., is a Training and Supervising Analyst with the Los Angeles Psychoanalytic Society and Institute. He is Treasurer of the American Psychoanalytic Association (APsA); Chair of the Task Force on Psychoanalytic Science, ApsA; Chair of the Investment Oversight Committee, IPA; and Treasurer of the Los Angeles Psychoanalytic Foundation. His most recent publications include *Psychoanalytic Process* (1990), and *The Psychoanalytic View of Phobias, I-IV* (1992).

Katherine Dalsimer, Ph.D., is on the faculty of the Columbia University Center for Psychoanalytic Training and Research, and is Consulting Psychologist at the Columbia University Mental Health Service. She has taught at Columbia College and, as Visiting Professor, at Mount Holyoke College. She is the author of *Female Adolescence: Psychoanalytic Reflections on Literature* (1987).

Glen Gabbard, M.D., is Bessie Walker Callaway Distinguished Professor of Psychoanalysis and Education in the Karl Menninger School of Psychiatry at the Menninger Clinic; Director and Training and Supervising Analyst, Topeka Institute for Psychoanalysis; and Clinical Professor of Psychiatry, University of Kansas School of Medicine, Wichita. He is the author of *Psychodynamic Psychiatry in Clinical Practice* (3rd ed) (1995) and *Love and Hate in the Analytic Setting* (1996).

Peter Gay, Ph.D., is Sterling Professor of History Emeritus at Yale University and Director of the Center for Scholars and Writers, New York Public Library. He is the author of many books, including *Freud: A Life for Our Time* (1988) and the five-volume *The Bourgeois Experience: Victoria to Freud* (1984–1998).

Arnold Goldberg, M.D., is the Cynthia Oudejans Harris Professor of Psychiatry at Rush-Presbyterian-St Luke's Medical Center of Chicago, and a Training and Supervising Analyst at the Chicago Institute for Psychoanalysis. He is the author of over fifty articles and books in psychiatry and psychoanalysis, a member of the editorial board of several psychiatric and psychoanalytic journals, and a six-time winner of the Benjamin Rush Award for excellence in teaching.

Theodore Jacobs, M.D., is Clinical Professor of Psychiatry, Albert Einstein College of Medicine, and a Training and Supervising Analyst at New York and New York University Psychoanalytic Institutes. He is the author of *The Use of the Self: Countertransference and Communication in the Analytic Situation* (1991).

Otto F. Kernberg, M.D., is Director of the Personality Disorders Institute, The New York Hospital-Cornell Medical Center, and Professor of Psychiatry, Cornell University Medical College. He is a Training and Supervising Analyst, Columbia University Center for Psychoanalytic Training and Research, and President of the International Psychoanalytical Association. He is the author of seven books and co-author of five others. He is also Guest Editor of a volume on the Narcissistic Personality Disorder of the Psychiatric Clinics of North America. His most recent book is *Ideology, Conflict, and Leadership in Groups and Organisations* (1998).

Eva P. Lester, M.D., is Professor, Department of Psychiatry, McGill University; Training and Supervising Analyst, Canadian Institute of Psychoanalysis (CIP); Former Director of CIP (1982–1985); and Former President of the Canadian Psychoanalytic Society (1985–1987). She is Editor in Chief of the Canadian Journal of Psychoanalysis/Revue Canadienne de Psychanalyse. In 1999, she received the Mary S. Sigourney Award for Outstanding Contribution to Psychoanalysis.

Lester Luborsky, Ph.D., completed his degree in Psychology in 1945 and his psychoanalytic training in 1958, and has split his time equally between psychoanalysis and psychoanalytic research ever since. He has published over 400 articles and books and has received several awards: the Sigourney Award for research in psychoanalysis (1997); the Gold Medal Award for lifetime achievement from the American Psychological Foundation (1999); and the American Psychoanalytic Association Award for distinguished psychoanalytic therapy research (1999).

Patrick J. Mahony, Ph.D., is a Training and Supervising Psychoanalyst, Canadian Society of Psychoanalysis; Fellow of the Royal Society of Canada; and Professor Emeritus, Université de Montréal. He is the author of six books and over 100 articles.

George J. Makari, M.D., is Director of the Institute for the History of Psychiatry and Associate Professor of Psychiatry at the Weill Medical College of Cornell University. He is on the faculty of the Institute for Psychoanalytic Training and Research at Columbia University. He has published extensively on the origins and history of psychoanalysis.

Barbara Milrod, M.D., is Assistant Professor of Psychiatry at Cornell University Medical College. She is the principle investigator of an outcome study of psychodynamic psychotherapy for panic disorder, and author, with Arnold Cooper, of the *Manual of Panic-Focused Psychodynamic Psychotherapy*. She has received several grants in support of her work on panic disorder, and recently received an NIMH K award for a randomized controlled trial of the treatment. Dr. Milrod is the recipient of the Heinz Hartmann award for recent graduates of psychoanalytic training programs.

Edward Nersessian, M.D., is a Training and Supervising Psychoanalyst, New York Psychoanalytic Institute; Clinical Associate Professor of Psychiatry, Joan and Sandford Weill School of Medicine, Cornell University; Chair of the Educational Committee of the New York Psychoanalytic Institute; past Assistant Chairman of the Arnold Pfeffer Center for Neuro-Psychoanalysis of the New York Psychoanalytic Institute; and President of the Board of the New York Psychoanalytic Foundation. He is co-editor of the journal *Neuro-Psychoanalysis*, and the books *Textbook of Psychoanalysis* (1996) and *Controversies in Contemporary Psychoanalysis* (1999).

Robert A. Paul, Ph.D., is Charles Howard Candler Professor of Anthropology, Director of the Graduate Institute of Liberal Arts, and Coordinator of the Psychoanalytic Programme at Emory University. He is Associate Professor in the Department of Psychiatry and Behavioral Sciences, and is on the teaching faculty of the Emory University Psychoanalytic Institute. He is also an analyst in private practice. His last book, *Moses and Civilization: The Meaning Behind Freud's Myth* (1996), received the Heinz Hartmann Award, the L. Bryce Boyer Award in Anthropology, and the National Jewish Book Award.

Ethel Spector Person, M.D., is Professor of Clinical Psychiatry at the College of Physicians and Surgeons, Columbia University, and a Training and Supervising Analyst at the Columbia University Center for Psychoanalytical Training and Research, where she was the Director from 1981–1991. She is the editor of the IPA monograph series, the most recent volume of which is *On Freud's "A child is being beaten"* (1997) and is the author of *The Sexual Century* (1999).

Mervyn M. Peskin, M.D., is Clinical Associate Professor of Psychiatry, Cornell University Medical College, and is on the Faculty of New York

Psychoanalytic Institute. He is a former student of the anatomist and palaeontologist Philip Tobias and of Arnold Cooper, and has a psychoanalytic practice in New York.

Allan D. Rosenblatt, M.D., is a Training and Supervising Analyst at the San Diego Psychoanalytic Institute. He is Clinical Professor of Psychiatry at the University of California at San Diego and is in private practice in La Jolla, California. He is author and co-author of numerous publications, including the book *Modern Psychoanalytic Concepts in a General Psychology* (1978).

Douglas L. Rothman, Ph.D., is Associate Professor of Diagnostic Radiology and present Director of the Magnetic Resonance Center at Yale University School of Medicine. The focus of his research group is the development of noninvasive MRS methods to image glutamate and GABA neurotransmitter systems in the human brain and to understand their biochemical regulation.

Roy Schafer, Ph.D., is Training and Supervising Analyst at the Columbia University Center for Psychoanalytic Training and Research. His recent books include *Retelling a Life* (1992), *The Contemporary Kleinians of London* (1994), and *Tradition and Change in Psychoanalysis* (1997). He has a private practice in New York City.

Herbert J. Schlesinger, Ph.D., is Alfred J. and Monette C. Marrow Professor of Psychology, Emeritus at the Graduate Faculty of New School University; Professor of Clinical Psychology in Psychiatry at the College of Physicians and Surgeons of Columbia University; Adjunct Professor of Psychology in Psychiatry at Weill Medical College of Cornell University; and Attending Psychologist at New York-Presbyterian Hospital.

Theodore Shapiro, M.D., is Professor of Psychiatry and Professor of Psychiatry in Pediatrics, Weill Medical College of Cornell University, and a Training and Supervising Analyst in New York Psychoanalytic Institute. His main scholarly and investigative interest concerns the interface of linguistics and psychoanalysis. He is a past editor of the *Journal of the American Psychoanalytic Association*, and was Program Chair for the 1999 41st IPA Congress in Santiago, Chile.

Robert G. Shulman, Ph.D., is Sterling Professor of Molecular Biophysics and Biochemistry at Yale University School of Medicine. Dr. Shulman's laboratory has pioneered the development of NMR techniques to understand the basic biochemistry of metabolism in vivo in humans and animals. More recently, his laboratory has been studying the regional activation of the brain during sensory stimulations such as seeing and hearing and during cognitive tasks.

Elizabeth Bott Spillius, Ph.D., trained originally as a social anthropologist, becoming a psychoanalyst in 1964. She has been a Training Analyst of the British Institute of Psycho-Analysis since 1975. As well as publishing analytic papers, she has edited the two-volume *Melanie Klein Today* (1988), and from 1988 to 1998 was Series Editor of the New Library of Psychoanalysis, published by Routledge in association with the British Institute of Psycho-Analysis.

George Stade, Ph.D., has taught at the Department of English and Comparative Literature at Columbia University since 1962. He has published over 100 essays and reviews, edited over 100 volumes of American and European literature, and is the author of the novel *Confessions of a Lady-Killer* (1979).

David Tuckett, M.Sc., is Editor in Chief, *International Journal of Psychoanalysis*; President, European Psychoanalytic Federation; Visiting Professor and Programme Director, Psychoanalysis Unit, University College London; Training and Supervising Analyst, British Psychoanalytical Society, and Founding Editor, the *New Library of Psychoanalysis*.

George E. Vaillant, M.D., is Professor of Psychiatry at Harvard Medical School; Director of Research for the Division of Psychiatry, Brigham and Women's Hospital; and Director of The Study of Adult Development at the Harvard University Health Service. Dr. Vaillant's most recent award was the research prize of the International Psychogeriatric Society, and his recent publications include *The Wisdom of the Ego* (1993) and *The Natural History of Alcoholism Revisited* (1995).

Milton Viederman, M.D., is Professor of Clinical Psychiatry at the Weill Medical College of Cornell University and Training and Supervising Analyst at Columbia Psychoanalytic Center for Training and Research. Dr. Viederman's publications include "Models for Adaptation to Physical Illness," "Brief Interventions in Crisis Situations," "Personality Change in the Context of Life Experience," "Applied Psychoanalysis in the Area of Painting," and "The Role of the Analyst in the Process of Psychoanalytic Change."

Daniel Widlöcher, M.D., is a Training and Supervising Analyst for the French Psychoanalytical Association. He is also Emeritus Professor of Psychiatry at the University of Paris VI and Honorary Chief of the Department of Psychiatry of the Hôpital de la Salpêtrière. He is President-elect of the International Psychoanalytical Association. His most recent publications include *Métapsychologie du Sens* (1986) and *Les Nouvelles Cartes de la Psychanalyse* (1996).

Contents

Foreword *Peter Fonagy*	xvii
Acknowledgments	xxv
Introduction *Robert Michels*	xxvii

Part I: Perspectives on the Change in Psychoanalysis

On Insight and Engagement *Theodore J. Jacobs*	3
On Becoming a Psychoanalyst *Barbara Milrod*	11
From Bellowing to Mellowing: My Changing Views on Psychoanalysis *Allan D. Rosenblatt*	17
Current Views on Psychoanalytic Practice *Allan Compton*	25
The Development of My Ideas about Psychoanalysis *Roy Schafer*	33

The Elusive Wisdom of the Analyst   41
   Arnold Goldberg

Musings about My Intellectual Development   49
   Herbert J. Schlesinger

A Psychoanalytic Stance   57
   Milton Viederman

Psychoanalytic Curriculum: A Study in Change and   65
   "The Anxiety of Influence"
   Elizabeth L. Auchincloss

Part II: The Changing Ideas in Psychoanalysis

Change Moments in Therapy   77
   Ethel Spector Person

Normal and Pathological Narcissism in Women   87
   Eva P. Lester

"Mourning and Melancholia" Eighty Years Later   95
   Otto F. Kernberg

The Role of Curiosity in Psychoanalysis: Changes   103
   in My Technique in the Past Fifteen Years
   Edward Nersessian

The Shy Narcissist   111
   Salman Akhtar

On Abstinence   121
   Daniel Widlöcher

Coming of Age   129
   Katherine Dalsimer

Part III: The Changing World Outside Psychoanalysis

Are the Freuds' Ego Psychology, Klein's Object Relations,   139
   Kohut's Self Psychology, and Beck's Cognitive Psychology
   All Alive and Well and Living in the Same Brain?
   George E. Vaillant

Psychoanalysis and Empirical Research: A Reconciliation   149
   Lester Luborsky

The Integration of Psychoanalytic and Neuroscientific   155
Thought in the Realm of Personality
   Glen Gabbard

Freud's Theory of the Mental and Modern Functional   163
Imaging Experiments
   R. G. Shulman and D. L. Rothman

Normative Sexuality in Contemporary Evolutionary Perspective   171
   Robert A. Paul

Totem and Taboo and Professional Correctness   179
   Elizabeth Bott Spillius

Words, Ideas, and Psychoanalysis   189
   Theodore Shapiro

Notes on Linguistic Activity and Psychoanalysis   197
   Jorge Canestri

Reasons, Causes, and the Domain of the First-Person   207
   Marcia Cavell

Oedipus Reckoned   215
   Patrick J. Mahony

An Indiscretion on Psychoanalytic Fiction   223
   George Stade

Part IV: Setting the Frame for the Future

Through the Looking Glass – Psychoanalysis,   229
Conceptual Integration, and the Problem of the Innate
   Mervyn M. Peskin

Theoretical Pluralism and the Construction   237
of Psychoanalytic Knowledge
   David Tuckett

Against Post-modernism   247
   Peter Gay

Change in Psychoanalysis: Science, Practice,
and the Sociology of Knowledge 255
George J. Makari

References 263

Foreword

PETER FONAGY

Psychoanalysis has changed. The process of change in this discipline, however, has been an intensely personal one. Behind the shifts in theories, techniques, and application are individuals whose sense of identity and ways of viewing the world have profoundly altered. Relatively few individuals created the social environment within which innovation and these personal transformations became possible. There were only a handful, and Arnold Cooper is perhaps the foremost amongst them. As a professional leader, a mentor, and a friend to the contributors of this volume, he has created a context where change became possible, where new ideas could be safely thought about, where suggestions for productive and sensible modification to widely held preconceptions could be sympathetically considered. Robert Michels describes this career, in the Introduction to this book, and summarises with his usual integrative flair Arnold Cooper's remarkable contribution to the changes we have witnessed.

The main part of the volume is divided into four sections. In the first section, many of those most active in this change process provide a personal narrative of how the "global warming" of psychoanalysis (to use the phrase quoted by Compton) took place over the last thirty years. As one might expect, these participant observers of the change process tell somewhat different stories, highlight different facets, and yet the body that they are aiming to describe – the revolution in psychoanalysis – remains clearly discernible throughout. They describe an increasing interest in the relationship aspect of clinical work, a growing openness to other disciplines, the questioning of our assumptions concerning training, a greater emphasis on empirical in addition to clinical research, as well as a change in the identity of the analyst, perhaps most clearly discerned in the move towards increasing informality in the clinical stance of the analyst. In Arnold Cooper's view, this change in theory and practice was a response to the "philosophical debate concerning the nature of history, veridicality, and narrative. . . . The analytic task [becomes] interpretation, *with* the patient, of the events of the analytic situation, usually broadly labelled transference – with a construction rather than a reconstruction of the past" (1987a, p. 83).

Theodore Jacobs uses the change of attitude towards countertransference enactments as an illustration of the revolution in psychoanalysis. This ubiquitous aspect of clinical work, which could somehow remain relatively neglected until the late 1960s, could become part of "real analysis" once the broad, integrative, and flexible approach that Arnold Cooper represents was more generally adopted. Along similar lines, Allan Rosenblatt intriguingly highlights how the move from the motivational system of drives to a systemic model came to shift emphasis in clinical work from explicit communication from the analyst via interpretation to implicit information communicated by the nature of the therapeutic relationship. Roy Schafer's contribution to the move away from what is sometimes called the "classical" view was colossal. His action language for psychoanalysis acted as a bulwark against reification; his emphasis on narration created the potential of a unique epistemology for psychoanalysis, and his integration of Kleinian ideas made a major contribution to the globalisation of the discipline. Herb Schlesinger describes a similar professional journey to Roy Schafer – a move away from research and towards an ever sharpening focus on the nature of the dialogue between patient and analyst. Arnold Goldberg highlights the risks of such enhanced sophistication – wisdom is something we perceive in others and strive for, yet at the core of wisdom can be complacency and the inability to see what is genuinely unfamiliar. Milton Viederman, in contrast, describes a clinical journey towards a more active, spontaneous stance. Working with physically ill patients, he recognized the opportunities for change offered by crisis situations, and by increasing the sense of his "presence" in his patients' minds.

Elizabeth Auchincloss in her chapter explores the transformation of psychoanalysis through its projected image on the psychoanalytic curriculum. She outlines the battle between seeing research as a potential aid to psychoanalytic theory building, and seeing the dangers that reductionism can represent. Barbara Milrod describes the same battle, although her position is very close to that of Arnold Cooper's. Her scientific agenda is the empirical demonstration of facts that analysts have previously accepted on a clinical and anecdotal level. Allan Compton emphasizes another aspect of science, in addition to empirical research – that of scholarship and scrutiny. He eschews the adoption of new ideas on the basis of intellectual fashion and, while welcoming a broad psychoanalytic education in the arts as well as the sciences, sees the responsibility of health professionals as unequivocally to strive for a science-based practice.

The changing ideas described globally in the first section of the volume are treated in greater depth in the second. Authors in this section identify specific elements of the theoretical and clinical psychoanalytic corpus, and illustrate how these have developed as part of the revolutionary process. Ethel Person explores changing views on psychic change, views that now more readily than before can admit the possibility that most critical change is sudden rather than gradual. Her comments echo strongly the theoretical work of Daniel Stern, Ed Tronick, and the Boston group, who have arrived at similar conclusions through the integration of developmental research and clinical work. Eva Lester explores changes to the concept of narcissism and also integrates findings from infancy research with the clinical understanding of narcissistic and borderline personality disorder. In an intriguing essay, she offers challenging ideas about the roots of the marked gender differences in these diagnoses. Salman Akhtar profiles a special form of narcissism: the shy narcissist. Linking his ideas to those of many of the major contributors, he at once offers an eloquent psychoanalytic model and a critique of diagnostic systems exclusively focused on manifest symptomatology.

Otto Kernberg revisits the clinical manifestations of depression in the light of recent advances in neurobiology, brilliantly exemplifying Cooper's integrationist agenda. He offers a compelling demonstration of how the unconscious motivational forces described by Freud may be coherently integrated with an object relations perspective and neuro-biological findings by means of a clinical approach that focuses on the determinants and vicissitudes of affects. Katherine Dalsimer takes a developmental perspective and revisits the concept of adolescence, taking on board epidemiological findings that adolescence is not necessarily a time of turmoil. She demonstrates that a break with parental ties is by no means inevitable at this stage; at the core of this phase is the discovery of continuity between the self and the parent, learning to value something from the previous generation. Daniel Widlöcher's timely reconsideration of abstinence explores the boundary between psychoanalysis and psychotherapy. While psychoanalysis is frequently defined in terms of the intensity of the treatment, the theoretical grounds for justifying this intensity are frequently overlooked. For Widlöcher, intensity links directly to abstinence in the patient; the continuing relevance of the abstinence rule for the patient is as an expression of deep commitment to a process that should never become commonplace. Edward Nersessian reexplores another aspect of the patient's clinical attitude – that of curiosity. He sees curiosity as at the root of self-reflection, which may be acquired in the course of treatment through an identification with the analyst. He proposes that genuine self-enquiry cannot take place without such an identification.

In the third section of the book, contributors provide evidence for the type of interdisciplinary synthesis that Arnold Cooper encouraged, both explicitly and also implicitly through example, throughout his career. The chapters in this section explore psychoanalytic issues from the standpoint of cognitive psychology, neuroscience, anthropology, linguistics, philosophy and literature. The value of this approach is still controversial within psychoanalysis, yet the examples in this section clearly suggest that psychoanalysis should repudiate its isolationist stance. It both benefits from and can directly benefit neighbouring disciplines.

George Vaillant celebrates Cooper's commitment to integration and synthesis by bringing together cognitive behaviour therapy, self psychology, Kleinian object relations theory, and Freudian metapsychology. The common currency is the clinical phenomena, upon which all these theoretical structures were built. Conflict is ubiquitous, because desire, conscience, people, and reality pull the individual in different directions. Defensive operations are what permit the self to adapt to these conflicting demands. Vaillant suggests, in sympathy with Schafer, that terms such as defence mechanisms are reifications, and the alternative "unconscious regulatory processes" may be far more descriptive. In a similar effort to tie theory firmly to clinical practice, Lester Luborsky summarises the six principles of psychoanalytic practice, which have been robustly confirmed by empirical research on psychoanalytic psychotherapy. Many of these are quite familiar to analysts; for example, that the depth and quality of insight into conflict predicts improvement in treatment. Other principles, such as the predictability of recurrent symptoms from prior psychoanalytic material, might have been hard to establish on the basis of anecdotal observations alone. Luborsky's thesis is that empirical work is necessary to prune the overgrown theoretical tree of psychoanalysis, a point powerfully made by Arnold Cooper in his own explorations of the epistemology of psychoanalysis.

Glen Gabbard also follows in Arnold Cooper's footsteps, integrating neuroscience and psychoanalysis, in the study of personality disorder. Gabbard demonstrates the complementarity of a biological and a psychoanalytic perspective in clinical treatment. He argues that the recognition that biological temperament plays a role in personality and pathology in no way diminishes the value of psychoanalytic approaches, but rather enables more targeted strategies. For example, medication may be essential, in order for the patient to become accessible to help through a talking cure. Drs. Shulman and Rothman take this approach a step further in their examination of the possible links between functional imaging studies and Freudian models of the mind. They highlight the limitations of imaging techniques and point to a potential for misunderstanding if changes in levels of the imaging signal are directly equated with the mental process of a particular functional module, as cognitive theory suggests. They argue for a more holistic interpretation of functional imaging experiments, an interpretation that would investigate the role for such nonmodular concepts as subjectivity and the unconscious.

Robert Paul takes a fascinating sociobiological perspective and reconsiders the classical psychoanalytical approach to sexuality. He suggests that observational studies of chimps and bonobos provide an evolutionary explanation for the pervasiveness of conflict and inhibition in relation to human sexuality. Like bonobos, humans have sex for nonreproductive reasons, but like chimps, male-to-male competition is a ubiquitous threat to stable social organization. The adaptation of diverting sexuality from reproductive uses into prosocial erotic bonds with other men and with the group as a whole achieves relative social harmony at the cost of placing conflict at the heart of sexuality. As all compromise, this evolutionary adaptation cannot be entirely successful. Elizabeth Spillius has also chosen an anthropological perspective and examined the reactions of anthropologists to Freud's *Totem and Taboo*. The current neglect of the work by modern psychoanalysts kindled her interest. Her epistemological study illustrates how the broad multidisciplinary perspective of Freud clashed with the empirical concerns of anthropologists, with the notion of inherited memory and conjectural reconstructions of an imaginary history jarring particularly with modern perspectives, both in social science and in modern psychoanalysis.

Two chapters pursue the application of recent work in linguistics to psychoanalysis. Theodore Shapiro takes as his starting point the psychoanalyst's belief in the power of words. He points to the strong parallel between Freud and Chomsky in hypothesizing deep structures (unconscious fantasy or grammar), which appear to be universal algorithms determining infinite permutations of surface manifestations. He makes two further links identifying a strong association between the discipline of semiotics (the science of signs) and psychoanalysis, where what is represented exists outside of awareness. Further, he forges an imaginative link between pragmatics and the interpersonal aspects of the analytic situation, particularly countertransference and intersubjectivity. He offers linguistic science as a tool to replace the outmoded psychological concepts of classical psychoanalytic theory. Jorge Canestri suggests a somewhat different bridge between psychoanalysis and the study of language. Taking his starting point from Cooper's statement in *Psychoanalysis: Toward the Second Century* (1989) that psychoanalysis may be seen as a set of transformational rules for decoding unconscious meanings, Canestri presents the new pragmatic paradigm in linguistic theory. Psychoanalysts, according to Canestri, work with specific philosophies of language, and such philosophies may be helpful in distinguishing different psychoanalytic orientations. He recommends the careful study of psychoanalytic discourse: its rules, its structures, and its codifications. The discourse of patients about psychoanalysis may be a further important area of study.

Marcia Cavell's intriguing contribution explores the nature of explanation of human action, tackling the philosophical dichotomy of causes and reasons. The language of mind cannot be adequately replaced by the language of neurophysiology and, even within a psychological language, the first-person point of view can never be fully translated into the point of view of the third. Both these irreducibilities might be considered as challenges to the world view traditionally held by psychoanalysts. Patrick Mahony pursues another aspect of Cooper's interest, literature. In a challenging essay, Mahony explores Freud's passages in the Dreambook on Oedipus Rex and Hamlet, concentrating on three particular foci: the thematic consideration of knowledge, the performative textuality of Freud's text, and the issue of translation. While Mahoney is concerned with literary criticism in relation to the oedipal organization in the human psyche, George Stade examines the entire enterprise of the psychoanalytic exploration of literature. He identifies three types of psychoanalytic literary criticism: the first, which reconstructs the author's psyche through the text read as symptom; the second, which applies the same analytic knowledge to the characters depicted within a text; and the third, which reads texts as allegories of psychoanalytic doctrine. But he sees psychoanalysis itself as a form of literature that can be examined by critics, perhaps as much as it can itself provide a framework for examining literature. Further, it provides a critical method for examining the psychoanalyst's obsession with literature.

In the final section of the book we take an even broader view. Four authors look at epistemological, conceptual, and theoretical perspectives that may set the frame for psychoanalysis in the twenty-first century. Mervyn Peskin provides a virtuoso examination of the possibility and dangers of integrating evolutionary biology and psychoanalysis. He explores in depth the implications of the integrationist stance advocated by Arnold Cooper. His sophisticated scrutiny of the literature finds flaws with this enterprise, particularly in the readiness with which incompatible psychoanalytic propositions may find support by leaning on sociobiological constructs. David Tuckett tackles head on the most central concern of modern psychoanalysis: pluralism. He takes a sociological perspective on the development of psychoanalytic knowledge and draws our attention to the pervasiveness of oligarchy, prescription, politicisation, and the recourse to authority. He points to the risk of prejudice in characterizing the belief systems of groups other than our own because of our ignorance of the subtleties of these views. Peter Gay offers a scrutiny of the postmodernist movement in psychoanalysis. He offers powerful arguments against the "deep shallowness" of postmodernist writers and considers these as distractions from the essential business of psychoanalysis. Borrowing from Samuel Johnson, he concludes that what is true in postmodernism is not new, and what is new is certainly not true. Finally, George Makari considers various views of the epistemic status of psychoanalysis as a science. He rejects both extremes – psychoanalysis doesn't meet Popperian criteria, but nor does physics. Nor is psychoanalysis a cultural phenomenon. It is an attempt to resolve a deep paradox – an attempt to create an objective science of subjectivity. A hope for a resolution of this dialectic is foolhardy. Both objective and subjective must be pursued by distinguishing the claims that we make in an empirical register from those that are more appropriately contextualised historically. Only in this way will we acquire a better understanding of the way the subject has evolved, is evolving, and shall evolve.

As this brief introduction should make clear, this volume brings together a unique collection of perspectives on the dramatic change that has occurred in psychoanalysis, as well as the challenges it faces in the future. Almost without exception, the contributors to this volume are at the cutting edge of their field. That there are so many cutting edges is both our problem and our greatest promise. This book cannot and does not attempt to offer a solution to the difficulties that psychoanalysis faces, now that the discipline has all but totally shed its classical skin. Nevertheless, what emerges from these chapters is a somewhat vulnerable, perhaps even fragile creature, which, having discarded its armour – the illusion of certainty – is now ready to face the world in a far broader, more open-minded way than perhaps ever before in its distinguished history. The fundamental questions for psychoanalysis, addressed by the authors of these chapters, have arisen in this form because of the revolutionary changes brought about by giants like Arnold Cooper and other open-minded clinician-thinkers of his generation. Cooper and those working alongside him have helped to open our eyes, not only to the problems we have created for ourselves but also to the tremendous possibilities available to us, if we step beyond these problems. The contributors to this volume, through the brilliance with which they have tackled the questions they set themselves, have paid appropriate homage to a man to whom the profession will forever be indebted, for leading it through turbulent times into the open vistas of the new century.

Acknowledgments

This book was the idea of Joseph Sandler who, with his customary originality and flair, thought of its theme and oversaw the early stages of its development. Robert Michels and Joseph Sandler commissioned the authors and drew up the plan for the book. Sandler's untimely death, in October 1998, left the project without its leader. Dr. Michels asked Peter Fonagy to join with him in putting the final touches to the manuscript, an honour which he willingly accepted. Kathy Leach, Editorial Assistant in the Psychoanalysis Unit at University College London, the unit Dr. Sandler founded, did much of the editorial work on the manuscript. Hence, the final product is the culmination of all our efforts, the work of a team rather than the work of a single individual. And appropriately so. The psychoanalyst whose contributions this book celebrates, Arnold Cooper, is an individual who throughout his rich career has been able to bring people together to work with a common aim, for a joint purpose. His corpus speaks to the importance Dr. Cooper has always attached to collaboration, not just among psychoanalysts, but also among those from different disciplinary backgrounds whose commitment is to the study of the human mind. The contributors to this volume and the editors pay homage to his contribution, not just by saying what he did, but also by doing as he said.

Introduction

ROBERT MICHELS

Arnold Cooper was born in New Jersey on March 9, 1923. He attended Columbia College, from which he graduated in 1943 and where his love of literature, great books, and great thinking began. He wrote that when he first read Freud, "I experienced a sense of instant revelation into myself . . . my friends . . . my world of politics and literature. . . . Things seemed clearer. . . . I asked a friend what one had to do to become a psychoanalyst . . . I had never thought of going to medical school" (1998, p. 2). He attended the University of Utah School of Medicine (only to discover that they had no Department of Psychiatry!), and received his M.D. there in 1947. He then spent a year as a fellow at Harvard and Boston City Hospital's Thorndike Memorial Laboratory, beginning a commitment to research that was to continue throughout his career. By the time he had finished his medical internship at Presbyterian Hospital in New York, he had published five papers, three in the prestigious *Journal of Clinical Investigation*. They described studies of urinary amino acids in Wilson's Disease and the treatment of cirrhosis of the liver (Cooper, Eckhardt, Faloon, & Davidson, 1950; Faloon, Eckhardt, Cooper, & Davidson, 1949a; Faloon, Eckhardt, Davidson, Murphy, & Cooper, 1949b).

During his research fellowship he had his first experience in psychoanalysis, with a recent graduate of the Boston Institute. It lasted for eight months, and years later he recalled it as extraordinarily painful: "Each session was excruciating. I found myself tongue-tied and he was entirely silent" (1998, p. 3). The following year, during his internship, he entered analysis with Leonard Blumgart, who had himself been analysed by Freud. Cooper found this experience quite different: "this man was responsive and talkative . . . I began to have some idea that perhaps psychoanalysis consisted of more than abstinence" (1998, p. 4). He entered psychiatric training at New York's Bellevue Hospital in 1950, and two years later psychoanalytic training at Columbia, which accepted his ongoing analysis as a training analysis. He was quickly engaged in the Columbia faculty's struggles to sort out the core clinically relevant concepts of psychoanalysis from the burdens of an overly elaborate, scientifically outdated, and clinically irrelevant metapsychology, a theme that has persisted in his work.

Cooper came to know Edmund Bergler while still a candidate, and was greatly influenced by Bergler's thinking. His interest in masochism, narcissism, the importance of pre-oedipal themes in character development, and the significance of both the actual behaviour of the patient and the interaction of analyst and patient can be traced to Bergler. A second formative experience was a course he started teaching shortly after graduating from Columbia Psychoanalytic in 1956, reviewing what were then called dissident schools – Jung, Adler, Horney, Klein, Sullivan, and others. It marked the beginning of his interest in the study of theoretical pluralism. Cooper became a training analyst at Columbia in 1961, rose in faculty rank to Clinical Professor in 1971, and was active in teaching at the Columbia psychiatric residency, and the Psychoanalytic Center through those years.

In 1957 he was invited to deliver the University Lectures on Psychoanalysis, "Twenty Years after Freud," at his alma mater, Columbia College. These evolved into the Seminars on Psychoanalytic Thought and Literature, and then the Columbia Programme in Psychoanalytic Studies, one of the first such programmes in the world, which began under his direction in the early 1960s. Cooper's introductory course was the prerequisite for seminars on subjects such as Literature, Philosophy, Art History, and Sociology. The programme was enormously popular and provided an introduction to the field for a number of future psychoanalysts.

Cooper's psychoanalytic writing is marked by its extraordinary breadth. He has reported the results of systematic psychoanalytic research, discussed the vital significance of research for the profession, written about psychoanalytic theory and the role of theory in clinical work, the evolution of core concepts in psychoanalysis, psychoanalytic education, technical aspects of the analysis of character pathology, the narcissistic masochistic character, social implications of psychoanalysis, psychoanalytic studies of literature, the relationship between psychiatry and psychoanalysis,

psychoanalysis and the university, and the future of the profession. His ability to dissect and formulate critical issues in the field has been demonstrated by his discussions of the works of Bergler, Fairbairn, Kohut, Schafer, Kernberg, Loewald, Sandler, and others.

His first psychoanalytic publications (1962; 1964; 1966) continued his interest in research that had led to his studies of metabolism twelve years earlier. Together with Aaron Karush, B. Ruth Easser, and Bluma Swerdloff, he developed the Adaptive Balance Profile, "a technique which bring[s] some increased measure of objectivity to the procedures which psychoanalysts use in making assessments of the patient's psychological strength and weakness" (1966, p. 183), demonstrated its reliability, and applied it to the prediction of behaviour in treatment. He believes that ultimately psychoanalysis will progress by the systematic study and assessment of what psychoanalysts do.

This theme continues in his current work. Together with Fred Busch, Barbara Milrod, and Ted Shapiro, he has recently studied panic-focused psychodynamic psychotherapy, and demonstrated the feasibility of systematic research in psychodynamic psychotherapy while making important contributions to the integration of biological and psychodynamic perspectives on panic disorder.

Cooper's academic and professional responsibilities broadened as he became Professor of Psychiatry and Associate Chairman for Education at the New York Hospital-Cornell Medical Center in 1974, President-elect and then President of the American Psychoanalytic Association from 1979–1982, and Vice-President and then North American Secretary of the International Psychoanalytical Association from 1985 to 1993. At the same time, he became increasingly interested not only in the conduct of psychoanalytic research, but also in the intellectual and organizational barriers to the advancement of research in the profession. In his 1982 Presidential Address to the American Psychoanalytic Association (1984b) he discussed the history of major scientific developments, along with the frequent resistance that emerges in response to revolutionary new discoveries. He argued that "Freud was correct in his insistence on establishing psychoanalysis as a movement of adherents to his new ideas, rather than allowing as Bleuler wished for free scientific interplay" (p. 252). However, he added that today "Psychoanalytic ideas are too important for our research to remain a cottage industry . . . we must create new structures for the education and support of those rare persons who have research passion" (p. 259). In 1986, addressing the American Academy of Psychoanalysis (1987b), he observed that "the dominant attitude of analysis, for many years, was hostile to research that was not done on the couch. It is still the case that the training of psychoanalytic researchers has a very low priority within most analytic institutes . . . [however] the research yield has already been great . . . our analytic thinking and technique have been profoundly altered by our new views of the infant" (p. 287). For Cooper, research is not only the source of new knowledge, but also the best treatment for pedagogic narcissism: "Psychoanalytic teaching has probably been influenced by not only our new views of the baby but also by the growing recognition of the discrepancy between belief and evidence" (1987b, p. 287).

Cooper's interest in the maturation of psychoanalysis as a science based profession has led to studies of psychoanalytic theory, technique, education, and the structure of the profession. He has regularly been selected to review where we have been, formulate current challenges, and suggest where we might go next. The titles of his publications reflect this recurrent theme:

> Psychoanalysis at One Hundred (1984b)
> A Historical Review of Psychoanalytic Paradigms (1985b)
> The Changing Culture of Psychoanalysis (1987b)
> Our Changing Views of the Therapeutic Action of Psychoanalysis (1988b)
> The Future of Psychoanalysis: Challenges and Opportunities (1990a)
> Psychoanalysis: The Past Decade (1991a)

He brings to these papers his familiarity with and interest in literature, art, philosophy, and the history of science, as well as his knowledge of psychoanalysis. Several themes are prominent. Psychoanalysis is alive, different now from what it was at its beginning, and will become different in the future from what it is now. The social context of psychoanalysis is changing as well – philosophers have quite different views of science now than they did 100 years ago (Cooper describes science as "that quivering, imaginative, uncertain enterprise of the human observer entwined with the observed in a pursuit of new knowledge that can be validated" 1983a, pp. 32–33); neurobiology has advanced greatly, medicine and psychiatry have changed, the general culture reflects different attitudes and different values. Tradition and authority are to be understood and respected, but they must always defer to experience, both personal experience in the clinical setting and the systematic study of experience in scientific research. Theory is important – one cannot listen or understand without theories to organize experience, and furthermore, theory is worthy of study – "It is desirable . . . for the psychoanalyst to know what his theory is" (1985b, p. 5). However, theory is always tentative, open to challenge, modification, and growth. Theories are good not because they explain something, but because they lead to new experiences and, eventually, better theories. Theories have clinical consequences and therefore theoretical pluralism is valuable in part because it engenders alternative clinical strategies and the possibility of empirical comparative study, new knowledge, and improved technique. Conflicting ideas are to be encouraged, for they may lead to critical tests. "We can learn something new by the strategy of emphasizing differences rather than similarities" (1980, p. 23). The goal is not to refine our answers to old questions so much as to generate new and more interesting ones. The process is revered more than the current state of understanding. The very definition of psychoanalysis can grow and evolve, "Its limits are yet to be determined and should be discovered from the study of our successful techniques rather than dictated by *a priori* definition" (1980, p. 11). Psychoanalysis is important, young, strongly linked to other areas of knowledge from which it has much to learn and to which it has much to contribute, fundamentally based on its clinical foundation, of immense human significance but often only modest therapeutic effectiveness, and one of the most fascinating and exciting intellectual pursuits that exists today.

Cooper's interest in the future of the profession is closely linked to his interest in education. He has taught undergraduates, medical students, residents, and psychoanalytic candidates, developed the curriculum of the Columbia Psychoanalytic Center, and for many years led one of the largest and most prominent psychiatric residency programs in the world. He has argued that medical education is vital for psychiatric training, but neither medicine nor psychiatry are essential for psychoanalysis and has discussed both training analyses and supervision (1985a; 1986c). However, the most powerful theme that recurs in his writing on education is that we must emphasize "education for a life of new learning," rather than "training for an art or craft" (1983b, p. 10), openness to new ideas rather than reverence for old ones, curiosity about the unknown rather than a restricted focus on what we believe we already understand. This is further reflected by his interest in teaching "alternative" schools, in studying the impact of "outsider" theorists, and above all in advocating a university-like model for psychoanalytic institutes and psychoanalytic education.

Of course, his writing on teaching is only a pale reflection of his personal impact as an educator. He is revered as a supervisor, mentor, and role model. His former and current students have regularly found that their work with him not only taught them about psychiatry and psychotherapy, but changed the way in which they understood themselves, their worlds, and their work.

In recent years Cooper's teaching and writing have led to major editorial responsibilities as Deputy Editor of the *American Journal of Psychiatry* and the North American Editor of the *International Journal of Psycho-Analysis*. His unusual ability to formulate and organize complex ideas has been reflected by his leadership of their editorial boards, his impact on their many contributors, and their expanding influence on the profession.

Very much a psychiatrist as well as a psychoanalyst, Cooper has addressed the interface of these disciplines in a number of papers over the years. His discussions of *DSM-III* from a psychoanalytic perspective (written with Allen Frances) (1980; 1981) and his reviews of *DSM-III* (1981) and *DSM III-R* (1988), written with me, were influential both in introducing the new nosology to the psychoanalytic profession and in formulating the importance of dynamic thinking in the development of nosological concepts. His 1985 paper "Will Neurobiology Influence Psychoanalysis?" has been immensely influential in mapping the boundaries of modern neurobiology, modern clinical psychiatry, and modern psychoanalysis. He argued that "Knowledge of the brain will not fundamentally alter our mode of inquiry about the mind . . . what is to be sought is congruence and limit setting on both sides" (1985c, pp. 1401–1402). His clinical discussion in the same paper illustrated the value of recognizing and treating psychiatric disorders that become apparent in the course of psychoanalysis, and was instrumental in opening the dialogue concerning the combined treatment strategies that have today become commonplace.

His interests in the evolution of psychoanalysis, in the relation of theory to technique, and in education are combined in his studies of key concepts in the field. In 1986 he discussed psychic trauma, arguing for a return to Freud's original limited definition (1986d). The following year he published his Sandor Rado Lecture on transference and transference interpretation (1987a), arguing for a modernist view, one that is based on synchronic rather than diachronic thinking, that recognizes early experiences as repeatedly transformed in the course of development and that is responsive to modern views of the clinical process. In 1987 he discussed transference neurosis, and suggested that we retire the concept, which, although of great historical interest, was no longer of theoretical value and had become a source of clinical mischief (1987c). In 1988 he wrote of our changing view of therapeutic action, discussing the shift from Strachey's interest in structural theory to Loewald's concern with object relational and interpersonal frames of reference (1988b). Finally, in a 1990 talk at a Columbia Psychoanalytic retreat, he addressed "reconstruction," its relation to "truth," and redefined it in keeping with his reformulations of psychoanalytic technique – "it guides our questions and it gives the patient possibilities that otherwise would be neglected" (1990b, p. 17).

Cooper's discussion of the narcissistic-masochistic character is one of his most well-known clinical contributions. He highlights the essential link between masochistic pleasure and narcissistic triumph, and traces the pre-oedipal dynamics of this constellation, building on his early interest in Edmund Bergler. In Cooper's words, "early frustrations of narcissistic strivings lead to reparative attempts to maintain omnipotent fantasies, despite the helpless rage experienced by the infant in the course of ordinary failures of maternal care. One of these defensive efforts involves the attempt to master feelings of rage, frustration, and helplessness by the intrapsychic shift from pride in providing one's self with satisfactions to pride in the fantasy of control over a "bad mother" (1986a, pp. 139–140). The clinical picture that results is that of the "injustice collector" (p. 140). Treatment must address both narcissistic and masochistic themes. He has also explored the relationship between masochism and depression, and the significance of depressive and masochistic dynamic patterns in the construction of descriptive diagnostic categories. Through a series of vignettes, and in his discussion of the unusually painful analysis (1984c), he has described the technical challenges presented by narcissistic-masochistic patients and suggested some strategies for dealing with them.

His early interest in literature has been continued in a series of papers on applied psychoanalysis (1976; 1981b; 1982b). They are marked by his obvious love of literature and his respect for the need to adapt the method to the task: "Surely it is not validation by positivist scientific credos, but it is validation in an important creative and scientific sense, if both analyst and scholar of the applied fields discover new themes, new ways of understanding and new potential explanations for puzzles by such techniques" (1981b, p. 43). His personal interest extends to music as well as literature – if he has a cultural passion that is stronger than psychoanalysis it is certainly playing the clarinet. His early involvement in politics and social issues also became intertwined with his psychoanalytic work. He has discussed value systems (1972), social research, and particularly, the attitudes of psychoanalysis, psychiatry, and general society toward homosexuality. His approach has always been open-minded, liberal, curious, and searching for opportunities to learn more in order to inform social discourse.

Cooper's contributions as a psychoanalytic scholar, teacher, writer, and editor notwithstanding, his core identity is as a practitioner of psychoanalysis and psychotherapy. He is the supervisor and consultant sought out by colleagues for their difficult clinical problems, their loved ones, and themselves. He has been spectacularly successful as the clinician whose work demonstrates the value of psychoanalysis to psychiatrists, physicians, and academics who have had little contact with it. His quiet and largely invisible role in consulting and referring members of those communities for psychoanalytic treatment has probably been as influential as his more public teaching and writing about the applications of psychoanalytic thinking.

In 1986 Cooper wrote of problems in being a psychoanalyst: the "burn-out syndrome" (1986b). He spoke of the analyst's character, theory, and values. However, he concluded by pointing out that the gratifications of the profession far outweigh its difficulties. His summary tells us much about his own career:

> Many of us are unable to imagine anything else as interesting, exciting, important, challenging, or gratifying. No other profession provides us the opportunity to know human beings so well, to touch their suffering so closely, to have the opportunity to help. To realize that we have at least been a factor in bettering lives and perhaps releasing creativity and joy where none existed before are great satisfactions and privileges. There is even the opportunity to add to the sum of human knowledge. I also believe that doing psychoanalysis is good for the mental health of the not-too-neurotic psychoanalyst. [1986b, pp. 596–597]

Cooper himself has gone further – his contributions have done much good for the scientific and intellectual health of the not too neurotic profession of psychoanalysis.

Part I

Perspectives on the Change in Psychoanalysis

On Insight and Engagement
THEODORE J. JACOBS

Psychoanalysis in America is just catching up with Arnold Cooper. Anticipating current developments in our field, from early in his career, Cooper advocated a broad, integrative, and flexible approach to psychoanalysis theory and technique. Consistently emphasizing the link between mind and brain, he was one of the first to recognize the important contributions that neuroscience and psychoanalysis could make to each other. These views made Arnold Cooper a "modern" psychoanalyst many years ago. In fact, one might say that Cooper is an analyst whose time has come.

The view of analysis that characterizes Cooper's work, however, was not one much appreciated by most of my teachers. At the New York Psychoanalytic Institute in the early sixties, colleagues like Cooper, trained at the camp of the much disparaged Sandor Rado, were regarded as ersatz analysts, that is, psychotherapists who held themselves out to be, but clearly were masquerading as, psychoanalysts.

This was a time in which concern about the assimilation, dilution, and ultimate erosion of Freudian analysis was at its height in traditional institutes. Any departure from classical approach was dismissed as being of little value, and deliberately omitted from the curriculum. Freudian theory, and pretty much only Freudian theory, was taught, and truths about the human mind and its disorders were thought to reside solely in classical analysis and the drive-defence model of mental functioning.

The analyst's psychology was viewed as a factor of little importance in the analytic process. In case conferences countertransference was almost never mentioned. In a setting that fostered conformity, no student dared to bring up the subject and to reveal that such personal responses were influencing his or her work. While the analytic work reported in these conferences and study groups was often of a high calibre, technically correct, and productive of insights, in not a few cases this skillful technique did not lead to change in the patient.

On the basis of what was omitted from the presentation as well as from hints in the material, it seemed to me that the central problem in many of these cases lay in unrecognized and unresolved transference–countertransference interactions; interactions that, most often, were expressed in indirect, covert, and subtle ways. In this unconscious exchange of messages, the analyst's subjective experiences, and especially his unexplored countertransference responses, were clearly playing a major role. Yet the analyst's contributions to the treatment and to the difficulties that developed were rarely mentioned. Listening to the presentations and discussions, one had the impression that, unconsciously, a collusion was taking place between the participants – a collusion aimed at keeping out of awareness essential, if troubling, aspects of the analytic work.

My own experience with patients was so different – I kept bumping up against countertransference in every phase of the treatment – that I found myself searching for colleagues with whom I could explore this difference, compare notes, and talk openly about the subjective reactions that I was having in analytic hours.

Others, too, I discovered, shared this need, and in the mid-70s I joined with four friends and colleagues, Sander Abend, Michael Porder, Martin Willick, and Albert Sax, to form a study group for the purpose of discussing case material and, particularly, our personal responses to the patients whom we were treating. With the support of these colleagues, as well as teachers such as Charles Fisher and Annie Reich, who had a keen interest in communication and the transmission of covert messages in analysis, I began a project of recording my inner experiences, verbal and nonverbal, as they arose in sessions in an effort to understand how these interdigitated with the patient's material and affected the analytic process.

In time, I began to publish some observations on the effects that my countertransference reactions were having on the analytic process (Jacobs, 1973; 1980; 1986). In doing this, I was following the lead of Heinrich Racker (1968), who was a pioneer in studying and elucidating the range of countertransference phenomena that, typically, may occur in sessions. What I found missing from the literature on this subject, however, even in Racker's valuable studies, were concrete examples that explored the childhood roots of countertransference reactions and demonstrated how the patient's material resonated with, and could be illuminated by, aspects of the analyst's personal history.

I discovered, for instance, that often embedded within quite proper – and current – technique were concealed countertransference enactments. The strong empathy that I felt for a female patient who was experiencing marital difficulties, useful as that feeling was, contained within it the living out of certain aspects of my relationship in adolescence with my own mother. And when I found myself listening too carefully and well to a businessman describe his workplace in a way that pictured every nook and cranny in his office, I came to understand that, unconsciously, I was enacting a familiar scenario: myself as a boy listening at the dinner table to my father, the storyteller, spin yarns about the day's activities.

I decided, therefore, in my own clinical illustrations, to be as specific as possible, and, where feasible, to demonstrate how my own memories and imaginations, stimulated by the material of the hour, affected my understanding of that material. It seemed to me that if one was going to say anything meaningful about the question of countertransference, it was essential to provide as much data as possible and not simply to allude in general ways to the personal experiences that lay behind one's countertransference responses.

Initially my papers came in for a great deal of criticism from my colleagues, who strongly opposed self-disclosure of any kind. In addition, some colleagues believed me to be advocating a way of listening that focused as much, or more, on the analyst as it did on the patient.

In fact, what I was trying to convey was the very opposite view. In my opinion it is a mistake for the analyst, while listening, to pay more than occasional or momentary attention to his or her subjective experiences. In order for his unconscious to resonate with that of the patient and for the thoughts, sensations, and imaginations that arise from within to be meaningfully related to the patient's communications, it is essential for the analyst to give him or herself over quite totally to the patient. Listening in an open-ended and fluid way that allows for some regressive movement in the mind, for the emergence of resonant thoughts, imaginations, and memories, and for the employment of a freely flowing and creative responsiveness, the analyst must lose himself in the patient's material. Like a reader absorbed in a novel, he imagines himself into the patient's life, and vicariously, like Joyce walking in Bloom's shoes, lives in his skin as the patient reports on his inner landscape. Only in this way, only if he allows such an immersion, can the analyst rely on his subjective experiences to tell him something about the mind of the patient.

Even then, I believe, the analyst's subjective experiences cannot be equated in any direct or simple way with those of the patient. When he or she is listening well, the analyst's thoughts and imaginations provide a clue – but only a clue – to the patient's world. As Arlow (1993) has maintained, it is always necessary for the analyst to check his subjective reactions against the data of the hour. Listening for associative links, for the contiguity of the material, for tone, syntax, and phrasing, and for the outcropping of metaphor, the analyst seeks to confirm or reject the hypotheses, that is, the intuitive hunches, that form in his mind partly in response to the subjective experiences that arise as he works.

This view of the analyst's subjectivity – one articulated by Arlow (1993) and that also draws on some of Loewald's (1960) formulations – differs in substantial respects from the idea, not infrequently found in the Kleinian literature, that patients are able to put their thoughts and feelings into the analyst. This notion, central to certain views of projective identification, assumes that there is a kind of pipeline from the unconscious of the patient to that of the analyst. This channel allows for the direct transmission of mental contents from one to the other, so that, in this formulation, certain of the analyst's experiences can be viewed as reproductions of what the patient is experiencing.

Closely examined, this idea contains within it a magical belief in thought transmission concealed within the familiar notion that resonance between the minds of patient and analyst is a regular part of the analytic process.

My own view is that while it is true that when the analyst is listening well such resonance does, in fact, occur, it is also true that resonance is not the same as replication. Given what is known about the complexity of the mind and the multiple interweaving forces that enter into the production of thoughts and affects, it is evident that the patient's perceptions and projections will mix, fuse, and be altered by the analyst's thoughts, memories, and fantasies. The product that results is not a simple or straightforward duplication of the patient's mental state, but a creation formed by the interplay between the minds of patient and analyst. While, clearly, the well-established principle of compromise formation applies equally to the mind of the analyst as it does to that of the patient, in certain formulations this basic fact is ignored or overlooked. The idea, for instance, that the mind of the analyst functions as a transcribing instrument or as a container into which the patient projects mental contents that are held there and "metabolized," but not otherwise transformed by interaction with the analyst's subjective responses to that material, does not do justice to what we know about the nature of the mind and the principle of multiple functioning.

I would like, also, to clarify my views of two concepts about which much has been written in recent years: enactments and countertransference.

From what I understand – at the time I had no idea that this was true – I introduced the term *enactment* into our lexicon in a 1986 paper entitled "On countertransference enactments". In doing so, I had no thought of coining a new term. As far as I was concerned, enactment was a familiar English word that seemed preferable to the term *acting out*, which by then had become threadbare and loaded with pejorative connotations.

Almost immediately after my article appeared, the word *enactment* was taken up by analysts in America and, during the past dozen years, has been so extensively and loosely used that, like other terms so popularized, it has begun to lose meaning and became platitudinous.

What I had in mind when I spoke of enactments was something quite simple. I was referring to behaviour on the part of patient, analyst, or both that arises out of, and is stimulated by, the transference–countertransference interaction taking place at that moment but which is also linked via memory to certain psychological experiences of childhood or adolescence. Thus, for me, enactment always implies re-enactment.

The patient, for instance, who is late for a session because he is ashamed of certain sexual acts that he has performed and expects criticism from his analyst is clearly enacting a superego condemnation projected onto the analyst. This behaviour does not only express a current inner conflict, however. It also relates quite specifically to the patient's behaviour as a teenager, when, having masturbated and fearing his parents' disapproval should they discover this shameful act, he avoided them for several hours after indulging in this secret vice.

Today the term *enactment* is used in several ways, being synonymous for some authors with action of any kind and defined by others as behaviour that always involves both patient and analyst. While there is merit to these views, I have continued to believe that a definition that focuses on the link between past and present and that recognizes that enactments can occur in either or both participants most satisfactorily describes the situations that we encounter in analytic work.

Some analysts (Renik, 1993) hold that enactments on the part of the analyst are not only ubiquitous, but that they cannot be monitored or in any way contained. Inevitably they are lived out in treatment and can only be analysed and understood after the fact.

My view is somewhat different. While I concur that countertransference enactments are an inherent part of the analyst's responses and that, often, they spill over into action before they can be grasped or understood, I do not believe that this is invariably the case. In my view, part of the analyst's effective functioning involves a self-reflective component. I am not referring here to a deliberate effort to focus on oneself, but rather to that aspect of evenly hovering attention that is inner-directed and that, when the analytic instrument is working well, is accompanied by a preconscious process of scanning of one's inner responses. Operating rather like signal anxiety, this function serves to alert the analyst to affects that are impelling to action or are causing a shift in his or her level of attention. When this happens, momentarily the analyst's attention shifts to himself and a checking action ordinarily takes place – one that allows the analyst to grasp what he is experiencing, process it, and, when possible, utilize it to craft an interpretation that draws on his subjective experiences, as well as on the flow of the patient's associations.

It is well to remember, I believe, that not all enactments can be lumped together and thought of in the same way. There are enactments and enactments. While some represent accurate readings of unconscious messages, or function as interpretations in action (Ogden, 1994) that serve to advance the analytic process, others do not. Some enactments are destructive. So hurtful are they to the patient and to the analytic process that they cannot be effectively analysed after the fact. They do permanent and irreparable damage. It is, I believe, the analyst's obligation, as part of his analysing function, to monitor him- or herself for such potentially damaging impulses and, through self-reflection, seek to convert them into useful interventions.

With regard to countertransference, I believe that a similar trend has developed. The positive and useful side of countertransference, its unquestioned value as a pathway to the unconscious of the patient, has been so much emphasized in recent years that there has been a tendency to forget that many of our countertransference responses interfere with our correct understanding of, and responses to, the patient's communications. Especially important in this respect are those countertransference reactions to the analyst that represent ongoing character difficulties; traits of personality that surface time and again in our work and that have a negative, and sometimes disruptive, effect on treatment. In the current analytic climate, which emphasizes the unique and positive value of countertransference, the troubling aspect of the analyst's responses, so important for him to detect and confront in him or herself, has, like those potentially harmful enactments that arise out of unrecognized character problems, been comparatively neglected.

Finally, I wish to comment briefly on the therapeutic relationship and its role in the process of change. For many years, and for many reasons, classical analysts have denigrated the idea that in its own right the relationship between patient and analyst acts as a healing force in analysis. For good reasons, this notion, essentially the idea of a corrective emotional experience, has been rejected as too simplistic, as failing to take into account both the complexity of neurosis and the dense network of protections that keep it in place.

For these and other reasons, including political ones, classical analysis has minimized both the contribution that the relationship between analyst and patient makes to the therapeutic action of analysis and its close connection to insight. Experience both within and outside of analysis has shown that ongoing supportive relationships aid personal growth and change. In recent years, these common sense observations have been verified by the work of Wallerstein (1986), who, in his study of treatment carried out at the Menninger Clinic, demonstrated that for not a few patients supportive psychotherapy carried on over a number of years resulted not only in behavioural but in significant structural change.

While such studies underline the value of the relationship aspect of treatment, analysts are well aware that the so-called new relationship in treatment is, for some time at least, psychologically not new. Because of the power of transference and the distorting lens that is an inherent part of it, patients initially experience the analytic relationship in the light of conflictual ones from the past. As a result, whatever benefits may accrue from a relationship with a new object – that is, the internalization of new perspectives, new identifications, new ways of responding and thinking about old issues and the like – can take place only to a limited extent in the early phases of analysis. Through interpretation of the transference, however, and the gaining of insight into its distorting influence, patients are gradually able to separate old from new objects. Insight and working through, essential elements in analysis, are the chief vehicles through which this separating out process takes place and expansion of the patient's vision of himself and others takes place.

Only gradually, in other words, can the analyst be experienced as a new object and the potential for growth inherent in the internalization of aspects of that relationship be realized. These positive changes add to, and complement, the changes that take place through the gaining of insight into, and the working through of, long-standing conflicts.

Once regarded as odd bedfellows, in other words, insight and experience have, in fact, turned out to be rather good companions. Working together in ways that enhance the therapeutic action of analysis, each contributes to those changes, both in our patient's lives and in their inner worlds, that we call analytic progress.

On Becoming a Psychoanalyst
BARBARA MILROD

Arnold Cooper was my residency training director at the Payne Whitney Clinic and the psychiatric world was different when I was a resident. It was possible for a training director, if he chose, to place tremendous emphasis in terms of time and resource allocation to careful clinical education of psychiatric trainees. Arnie expected his residents to perform clinically at their very best at all times. His psychoanalytic background was at the core of what he communicated as an educator. Working with Arnie, it was difficult to imagine becoming a solid clinician without having the benefit of a psychoanalytic education.

Nonetheless, long before I first met Arnold Cooper, it was inevitable that I would become a psychoanalyst. Both of my parents are psychoanalysts; my father is on the faculty of the New York Psychoanalytic Institute and is a psychoanalytic scholar in superego pathology and depression. My mother is a child analyst. Everything in my home seemed to revolve around psychoanalysis. My parents were excited about psychoanalytic concepts and they viewed so much of the world, from art to people, through an analytic lens. For me, the aura of the field was emotionally charged. The story that I eventually told one of my interviewers when I applied to analytic school was emblematic: my father's office was located in our home, and as a young child I used to sneak out to his waiting room to try to overhear what was happening in his office. I often heard ladies crying. I was dying to know what he was doing in there.

In *Invisible Cities*, Italo Calvino has Marco Polo say to Kublai Khan: "Every time I describe a city I am saying something about Venice.... To distinguish other cities' qualities, I must speak of a first city that remains implicit. For me it is Venice" (1972, p. 86). For me, it is fair to say that everything in my life has, in one way or another, always been about psychoanalysis.

When I was 15 years old I had a huge argument with my father's closest friend, who was also on the faculty of the New York Psychoanalytic Institute: I will call him Dr. T. At that time both Dr. T. and my father were closely involved in running the curriculum and educational wing of the institute. I told Dr. T. (and my father, who was also present) that it seemed to me from what I understood that psychoanalysis could be described as an art form, but that it wasn't a science in any sense of my understanding of it. How was I distinguishing these things, Dr. T. wanted to know. I said that in my view, an art was a honed craft at which one developed an expertise and fluency, that it could be transporting and even explanatory. On the other hand, science seemed to imply the idea of reproducible observations leading to tests of hypotheses. Oddly, Dr. T. became enraged at me and told me that I had no idea what I was talking about. Despite his vehemence, he seemed unable to defend his emphatic position that psychoanalysis was a science. My father took a more rational position in the argument and said that criteria for scientific status were not only to be found in reproducible, empirical studies, as I was implying. He talked to me about clinical medicine, and pointed out that doctors often didn't know why things made people get better. In the end, he admitted that what I had said was in part true. He also highlighted how cumbersome and pointless it would be to turn psychoanalysis into the type of science I was suggesting. At the age of 15, I could only agree with what seemed to be an unarguable point. In many ways, I still agree.

During my psychoanalytic training at the New York Psychoanalytic Institute, the educational experiences that I enjoyed the most and found to be most powerfully compelling were those that encompass the elements of psychoanalysis least easily captured by simple description, hence also the least amenable to anything resembling empirical scientific study. These were: my first truly careful reading of *The Interpretation of Dreams* (1900a) in my first year of psychoanalytic training; my wonderful supervision with my first two psychoanalytic supervisors, who taught me how to navigate transferential phenomena and to understand and interpret the fabric of patients' dreams and fantasies; and my post-graduation colloquium with Jacob Arlow, where I began to understand and focus on the deep, drive-derived meanings behind so many of the almost unnoticeable actions that patients perform with their doctors. In my clinical experience, among the many things that I as a psychoanalyst do for my patients, it is particularly the understanding and unravelling of these fantasies and actions that I believe have led to the greatest degree of therapeutic change for my patients.

Despite the power and richness of psychoanalysis, by the time I received my analytic education, the field was clearly in crisis. Patients who had in the past trudged through years of analysis for their anxious or depressive symptoms were responding rapidly to medication. Also, after years of having been inappropriately touted by analysts and others as a cure-all for everything from stage fright to autism, the popular and professional image of psychoanalysis had considerably weakened. At the time that I embarked on my analytic career, attacking psychoanalysis had already become an easy way to sell popular magazines and books. Friends at Payne Whitney, analysts and non-analysts alike, shook their heads and asked why I was bothering to pursue it. Worse still, psychoanalysts themselves at my own institute and elsewhere seemed unable to agree on what was germane to discuss, making anything resembling an organized response to community misperceptions difficult.

Nevertheless, it was compellingly clear to me from personal experience that psychoanalysis and psychodynamic psychotherapy were both effective therapeutic interventions for emotional problems if wisely and appropriately applied. The focus of my work has become the demonstration of what so many analysts have accepted on a clinical, and hence anecdotal level, but have yet to prove scientifically to others. For me, in part as a result of having gone through the process of acquiring the skills to articulate what has influenced me to be the way I am in my own analysis (something that at the outset I also had the impression wasn't possible), I have come to believe that it is also possible to describe rigorously and accurately what we do clinically as dynamic psychiatrists and to evaluate it with clinical trials.

Much of the public no longer looks to psychodynamic psychiatry as a treatment for specific psychiatric syndromes. Most psychoanalytic literature likewise does not focus on the psychiatric treatment aspect of our craft. Nonetheless, it is in this arena that the field must prove itself if it is to remain within the domain of *medical subspecialty*. We have yet to demonstrate that our treatment is effective. Hence, I have begun the gruelling but essential task of psychodynamic psychotherapy outcome research. I decided to study psychodynamic psychotherapy because it is less complex and multidimensional than psychoanalysis. It can thus be more easily articulated in a manualized, and therefore reliably reproducible form, while allowing for a certain degree of latitude in response to differences between patients, than psychoanalysis can. I chose to focus on outcome of psychodynamic psychotherapy for panic disorder also for personal reasons.

I initially went to see my psychoanalyst in medical school because I had *DSM-III* panic. After seeing him for several weeks, my panic remitted. Although I remained in treatment with him, first in psychotherapy and later in analysis during my analytic training for years, I have never had panic attacks since that time. I have never had other specific, anti-panic treatment. I ended my analysis years ago. As someone who is now experienced in the area of panic symptom monitoring and outcome methodology, I clearly fall into the category of "remission" as a result of my psychotherapy and psychoanalysis. My story is not uncommon, demonstrated in my review of the psychoanalytic literature (Milrod & Shear, 1991). As a psychoanalyst and a former analysand, I am well aware that my panic symptoms were fairly unimportant in the breadth of the focus of my own treatment. Nonetheless, the solid clinical tools that are so carefully acquired at psychoanalytic institutes are also (from a non-empirically demonstrated, clinical perspective) effective treatments for psychiatric symptoms. I believe that this relatively simple, testable point becomes easily ignored in the deluge of theoretical arguments that have dominated the psychoanalytic literature since I joined the field. It is essential that psychoanalysts focus their attention on devising accurate methods to demonstrate this to a community that cannot be expected to understand an unfamiliar and complicated clinical methodology.

Of course, studies of psychodynamic psychotherapy such as my own cannot be directly extrapolated to psychoanalysis. Psychoanalysis is a different methodology, and is obviously employed as a more comprehensive treatment for a broader set of difficulties than any form of simple symptomatic treatment. It is time-consuming and expensive for both analysts and patients. I believe that for some patients, it is lifesaving in a way that no other form of treatment or lifestyle change can be. Two of the overwhelming technical difficulties in designing relevant psychoanalytic outcome research will be to define measurable but realistic desired outcome variables, and to articulate credible control treatments. It will be of tremendous benefit to the fields of both psychoanalysis and general psychiatry when these difficulties are addressed as psychoanalytic outcome is studied.

Nonetheless, there are three crucial reasons for psychoanalysts to study psychodynamic psychotherapy, our less complex treatment: (a) because most psychoanalysts practise as much psychodynamic psychotherapy as psychoanalysis, these studies can provide solid, empirical evidence for the efficacy of some of the things that we routinely do. Although the point has yet to be studied empirically, I am convinced that psychoanalytic education permits psychoanalysts to perform this form of treatment with a higher level of skill than other clinicians; (b) if psychodynamic psychotherapy can be demonstrated to be effective for specific psychiatric syndromes, then the continued importance of maintaining a visible psychodynamic teaching presence within academic departments of psychiatry can be highlighted; and (c) if psychodynamic psychotherapy can be demonstrated to be effective, it will provide support for continued psychoanalytic enrollment, education, and funding at psychoanalytic institutes, particularly in the current cost conscious, data-oriented health care climate.

From Bellowing to Mellowing:
My Changing Views on Psychoanalysis
ALLAN D. ROSENBLATT

I encountered my first psychiatric patient some 50 years ago, as an intern at Los Angeles County Hospital, the first night I was on call on the psychiatric service. I was awakened at 3 A.M. by an ungodly racket, and I rushed from my room onto the ward. There I saw a tiny wizened old lady, with grey straggly hair down to her waist, holding at bay about a half-dozen nurses and attendants. This latter-day witch was spitting at them, wildly brandishing a cane, and screeching epithets and curses in Yiddish, such as "*A choleriyah auf dir!*", meaning, "You should contract cholera", and other more colourful curses, one translated to mean, "You should be like a chandelier – hang by day and burn by night!"

I tried vainly for some time to calm her, but my fledgling professional demeanour eventually crumbled into feelings of helpless frustration. I bellowed at her as loud as she was screaming at me, "*Soll sein shah!*", roughly meaning, "Shut up!" The effect was magical. She became quite still, shuffled over to me and peered into my face for some moments, then asked quietly, "Are you my brother, Sol?" With all of my 22-year-old authority, I said, "Yes, now go to bed." And she quietly complied. Thus was I introduced, two years before starting my analytic training, to the power of transference, though not exactly to its analytic use.

Since that first powerful teaching exposure, much has changed in my views on psychoanalysis, and certainly in my approach to patients. Yet, since my analytic training, there is much that has remained *unchanged*. I still hold to what I believe are the core concepts of psychoanalysis: that all behaviour is determined and motivated, that mentation is predominantly unconscious, that current interactions are greatly influenced by earlier experience, and that anxiety and other stress can provoke defensive responses, as well as regression to earlier modes of behaviour. What has changed, are, with few exceptions, shifts in emphasis not much different from those experienced by other analysts who have benefited from decades of personal experience and the scientific contributions of colleagues.

It's relatively easy to set down what I believe now, although space permits only what I think are my most significant changed views. It's harder to recall what my beliefs were then, uncomfortably recognizing the error of my early ways. It's most difficult, and often impossible to reconstruct the process of change and identify the factors that evoked the changes. In that respect, I suppose, the task is analogous to trying to reconstruct the process of one's own analysis.

As a student and graduate of Columbia Psychoanalytic Center during Sandor Rado's tenure, I was primed to question established orthodoxy, a tendency that resonated with certain personal characteristics. With Rado, however, I learned, as did most of our class, that the liberal innovator could be every bit as authoritarian as the dogmatic conservative. Given my rebellious tendency, this lesson speeded up my personal analysis considerably.

When I graduated, I was thoroughly imbued with Rado's adaptive framework and the disavowal of libido theory, but, I confess, I was given to speaking loosely in terms of structural theory, rather than using Rado's idiosyncratic terminology. In my consulting room, I thought and still think primarily of wishes, fears, conflict, compromise, and how the patient evaluates experience, consciously and unconsciously, rather than in metapsychological terms. But then, I have yet to find an analyst who can give credible examples of using structural theory in the minute-by-minute conduct of an analysis.

With my background in neurophysiology, I was interested in searching for ways to bridge the mind and brain, to develop concepts that at least offered some promise of correlation between the two realms of data. As a first step to articulating the problem, my colleague, James Thickstun, and I co-authored a critique of psychic energy, which led to subsequent collaboration (Rosenblatt & Thickstun, 1970). The outcome that evolved was, we thought, a more adequate framework within which to integrate psychoanalytic theory, utilizing systems and information processing theory and replacing the quantitative role of psychic energy in accounting for intensity of affect or urge with the information processing concept of priority (Rosenblatt & Thickstun, 1977).

We proposed a different structural model, wherein myriad motivational systems are each guided by a single-minded, narrow, affective appraisal of incoming information, from both internal and external sources, as to whether that current environment is favourable or unfavourable to the achievement of the respective system's goals. Their interaction creates a dynamic and shifting motivational fabric. These motivational systems can be grouped into a few functional classes, according to the type of goal (the idea and term later appropriated by Lichtenberg, 1989b), which roughly approximated the three major structures of ego, id, and superego, plus a class of self-systems. Each class has its own characteristically experienced affective evaluations (when conscious), depending on whether the action is appraised as reaching the goal versus being blocked in its attainment. What relationships the individual motivational systems have with each other depend on what subsystems they may share in common.

In retrospect, it seems that our conception represented a way to retain the dynamic and heuristic advantages of structural theory, in its categorization of types of motives and goals, without the untenable energic framework. It is gratifying to see, twenty years later, that our conceptions correlate with recently published concepts of current neuroscience (see Edelman's category valuations, 1989, and Dennett's multiple demons, 1991).

Parallel to my interest in the problems of general theory was my increasing awareness, as my clinical experience accrued, that the then-existing standard theory of technique did not correspond to my effective practice experiences. That model of technique, wherein interpretation alone was idealized as the only route to enduring change, seemed less and less applicable to what I and other competent analysts actually did (sometimes in contrast to what they wrote).

The nature of the analyst–analysand relationship, and its importance in the analytic work, did not seem adequately encompassed by only the sum of the transferences and introjections of the patient, even if the countertransferences of the analyst were added to the mix. Greenson's and Wexler's (1969) explication of "the real relationship" still didn't seem to address the therapeutic effect of the relationship. It certainly seemed to me that some corrective emotional experience was being experienced by my patients through the relationship, and its enduring therapeutic value was not accounted for solely by insight through verbal interpretation.

It seemed that our systems and information processing model could be applied to the therapeutic process, as well. The analyst–analysand relationship could be conceived of as an interacting system, where information was exchanged and reactions occurred in a reciprocal fashion. The relationship, in this view, is something that is generated by the present and past experiences of both analyst and patient that complexly interact.

I now see the relationship, itself, as a source of information *implicitly* communicated. Such information, experienced by the patient, can be schematically represented as, "He/she really likes me and wants to understand me. . . . He/she doesn't think my secret fantasy or impulses are bad and shameful. . . . I am safe here, etc." I think this kind of information is what Strachey believed to be involved in the mutative effect of a transference interpretation, which evoked the modification of the patient's harsh superego by incorporating the perceived benign superego of the analyst. Put propositionally, "My analyst doesn't think what I fantasize/feel is so bad or frightening, so I needn't."

I believe now, with other analysts, that such implicit, experiential (and usually unconscious) information can evoke enduring structural change and that it probably occurs in all analyses, as well as in psychotherapies. Implicit information about the analyst's acceptance is a necessary prerequisite for any explicit verbal interpretation of resistance, transference, etc., to be therapeutically effective.

> The therapeutic effects of such implicit information provided by the analyst may not be immediately apparent. A woman who had been repeatedly denigrated by her mother since early childhood came to analysis with profound feelings of inadequacy. In one session, she related an interaction with her pubescent son, who had been quite distressed by a school incident. It was clear she had dealt with her son in a most empathic and capable way, but she quickly went on to an old-hat refrain about her husband's passivity and disengagement. Rather than directly point out her quite skillful dealing with her son's problem, which she would have rejected out of hand as a repetition of her father's phoney compliments, or offer other possible interventions for a variety of reasons, I commented that her son must have felt comforted and relieved by her handling of the incident. She responded in a noncommittal tone that her son "was a good boy", apparently minimizing the value of her intervention. Many months later, she recalled the incident as a turning point in the analysis, since it was the first time anyone had "told" her that she was a competent mother.

I do not minimize the value of conscious insight. The insight achieved through the use of language is of inestimable value, in that it provides a conscious, cognitive "handle" that enables one to generalize the newly acquired information, to practise its utilization in flexible fashion, and render it less vulnerable to being lost through regression.

I think, now, that the varied sources of change can be better conceptualized within an information processing framework, wherein change is effected by the communication and processing of information, *not* merely intellectual, but also experiential and affective, about the analysand's unconscious ways of appraising and interacting with the world and its people. Most significantly, this information is not dispensed by the analyst alone, but discovered by analyst and analysand in a collaborative search.

Implicitly conveyed information enables the analysand to perceive the analyst as a real person with definable human qualities, a perception that is crucial to the success of any analysis. The effectiveness of any transference interpretation depends on the patient seeing the therapist as a real person who is *different* from the transference object. I don't think the analyst has to dissimulate à la Alexander to display that difference.

As do most analysts with considerable clinical experience, I now regard rules of analytic technique more as guidelines than prescriptions, and ones that vary with changing theoretical positions. The issue of gratification is an example.

After graduation, my peers and I would jokingly boast that we were so analytically correct that we wouldn't give our patients "the time of day". We had been taught the historical basis for withholding gratification from the patient, namely the theoretical belief that the discharge of libido (in Freud's hydrostatic model) lowered the pressure toward making the unconscious conscious and recovering memories. The patient should therefore undergo treatment in a state of abstinence. I recall struggling with what constituted unwarranted gratification and feeling at times awkward and stiff in my anxiety. Should I laugh at a patient's joke, or would that constitute an unacceptable breach of technique? (Not all of my supervisors were "liberated".)

I've come to realize that, in fact, we gratify patients in many ways – by a smile, common courtesy, offering hope of help, understanding, empathy, etc. What we try to avoid is *inappropriate* gratification of *regressed* wishes that would subsequently interfere with further insight and autonomy. With this rationale, the question to me has become what gratifications will impede the analytic process, rather than enhance it. The dynamics of the individual patient then become the guide.

Anonymity is also relative. The patient knows the analyst's gender, appearance, style of dress. The pertinent consideration is *how much* personal disclosure the therapist should engage in. For questions that one would expect in normal social discourse, e.g., "Do you have children?", "Did you see such-and-such movie?", the meagre analytic returns from refusing to answer are usually offset by the patient's sense of being rebuffed and distanced. A more productive technique for me has been to first answer the question, consistent with my sense of privacy, and then explore with the patient the meanings of the question.

A rationale for refusing any disclosure, including any disclosure of the analyst's evoked emotional responses to the patient's communication, has been that it "contaminates the transference". Within Freud's prized metaphor of the surgeon operating in a sterile field, self-disclosure has been viewed as the equivalent of the analyst vomiting into the operative incision. However, I believe our understanding of the analytic process has progressed to where this metaphor is obsolete.

Moreover, the fear that subsequent transference manifestations will be clouded by any self-disclosure and impede their analysis has been unfounded, in my experience. Patients are not likely to be confused by facts – they will still just weave them into interpretable transference attitudes and fantasies, which will surface. Obviously, there are limits to appropriate self-disclosure, just as there are in everyday social interaction, and these limits in treatment must be shaped again by the individual dynamics of the patient.

With regard to rules, I believe that, as experience is accrued, one relies less and less on algorithms and more and more on recognition of patterns. To pursue Freud's analogy to chess, grandmasters think little of the rules of play, but rely mostly on matching the pattern they see on the board with one of the thousands they have encountered and stored, following the line of play they have learned to be the most effective for that pattern.

Similarly, the experienced analyst relies more on intuitive pattern matching from a vast store of complex behavioural and relational patterns that reflect underlying dynamic constellations, rather than on theory-based procedural rules. The intuitive insight is then followed by more conscious, rule-based evaluation (Rosenblatt & Thickstun, 1994). When intuition comes up wanting or in error, I will revert temporarily to rules and theory to try and make sense of the data.

I had earlier mentioned the issue of practising, which has received little, if any, attention in our field. Early in my career, I was satisfied that the concept of *working through*, the repeated analysis of resistances in different situations, adequately explained the necessity to revisit conflicts after the initial interpretations. Yet, time after time, some patients, even though they had emotional insight, would report that they would repeat the same maladaptive behaviour automatically, until they would "catch" themselves (often with the help of the analyst) and substitute a more adaptive approach, each time being able to "do it a little better".

Continued experience has led me to conclude that there is a place for learning theory in understanding the course of some analyses, where practising the insights obtained seems necessary, over and above addressing the resistances to change. In most instances, insight alone is not enough, even when it's generalized; it is necessary to put the insight into action. With most patients this process goes on smoothly and almost silently. However, with some patients, especially those with problems around passivity and magical expectations, it is necessary to address the issue explicitly.

Rather than the reconstructive tours de force that I admiringly read about as a beginner, I have found to be far more frequent the incremental reconstruction of early relationships and the climate so engendered by them, the memories of which have not been so deeply repressed as much as affectively "washed out", isolated, trivialized, or otherwise defensively altered. I think now that a reconstruction that can evoke affectively charged memories can act as an organizing template for the restructuring and resymbolizing of currently maladaptive experience and behaviour. Whether the accumulated reconstructive picture reflects historical or psychic truth perfectly accurately is often moot. I suspect, however, that the closer it conforms to historical truth the better it serves as a template.

I'm certain, although I can't specify just how, that my changing views about psychoanalysis also reflect changes in myself. Being very bright as a youngster and quite precocious, with an overindulgent mother, certainly shaped my narcissistic convictions that I had the right answers, and this was reflected, I'm sure, in my practice (e.g., playing clever detective). Not only as a result of my personal analysis, but also through experience and aging, I've become less concerned about demonstrating how smart I am and more interested in my impact on others.

Concomitantly, I find myself focusing more often on how patients "come across" to others in their habitual modes of relating. Of course, explorations of such attitudes toward the analyst in the transference and their genetic roots are common. Yet I've rarely seen in the literature explicit use of such information to generalize and explore the patient's impact on others in his or her world. Many patients with characterologic problems haven't the slightest clue as to their impact on others and the resultant evoked responses. Tactful explorations, generalizing from transference–countertransference experiences, have been quite helpful to patients.

The change in my views in the 45 years since my graduation from analytic training has been shared, I think, by most analysts who have lived through that period and has paralleled the development of psychoanalytic theory and practice. Perhaps also paralleling societal changes toward more informality, my behaviour with patients has become less formal, less implicitly demanding of conformity to rules (e.g., lying on the couch), and more *related*.

In short, I think I've mellowed – though mellowing does not imply sloppiness. I'm more willing to acknowledge and make use of my less admirable countertransference responses, more willing to juggle a number of competing formulations and tolerate the ambiguity, rather than opt for one theoretical preconception, more willing to actively engage a patient without worrying about being "psychotherapeutic, not analytic", and more willing to acknowledge how much I don't know about a patient, yet feel confident about what I do know. On the whole, I think mellowing is preferable to mere aging – and it's better than bellowing.

Current Views on Psychoanalytic Practice
ALLAN COMPTON

I am a classical psychoanalyst. To me, the statement means that Freud's fundamental hypotheses – a lawful mind in significant degree outside of conscious awareness, mental conflict and clinical phenomena as compromise formations – remain, in my view, the best available set of hypotheses for understanding human mentation and other behaviour. Further, I mean that set of hypotheses continues to guide my clinical work, which consists of understanding and conveying to my patients the roles of wishes (urges, impulses, drive derivatives), unpleasure affects (anxiety and depression), and defensive operations. In my view, the structure of theory and practice provided by so-called classical analysis, as I have just characterized its scientific basis, remains the substructure, at least, of most of the psychoanalysis practised and taught in the world today: it is still the mainstream, even if in some degree subterranean at this point.

The submerging of adherence to Freudian theory seems to me to be primarily a matter of style at this point. It is common in our field that someone with a new idea believes that dissemination of the idea can be achieved only by insisting that Freudian analysis is wrong, not just a part thereof, but ostensibly all of it. Leo Rangell's (1997) argument concerning *pars pro toto* replacement is cogent here: a new and essentially untested theory is offered as a replacement for "classical analysis," while "classical psychoanalysis" is awarded everything the innovator does not like about psychoanalysis. Much of what is apparently repudiated, however, is kept, while the new theoretical approach, which might well fit in with Freudian theory, is held to replace Freudian theory altogether.

Apparently new paradigms of the human condition regularly arise in this way in our field. The introduction of a succession of sweeping changes has had, in my view, a deleterious effect on our science and practice, for the following reason: in order to establish such platforms it is necessary to eschew real scholarship and close scrutiny of existing theory and practice. Lack of attitudes of scrutiny and scholarship, in turn, has made formal scientific research almost impossible. I have asserted (1997) that these trends have resulted in a batch of competing religions – that is, semi-structured assertions that rest upon authority, mysticism and style rather than evidence.

My observation of these trends has fortified my devotion to historically based scrutiny of psychoanalytic ideas; to rigorous logical dissection of theory in the context of contemporaneous theoretical propositions – the scientific context; and finally to the advocacy of major efforts to carry out formal empirical research in our field. Arnold Cooper has set a certain standard in the development of psychoanalytic empirical research, in his role as a leading force in studies presently in progress at Cornell. Those studies, on panic disorder and its treatment, are distinguished, especially, by their thoroughly clinical grounding, orientation, and aim (Milrod, Busch, Cooper, & Shapiro, 1997).

My ideas about psychoanalytic practice have changed in concert with the development of my views of psychoanalytic hypotheses. Psychoanalytic practice – activities carried out in one's consulting room – is not a form of research, nor is it a form of science. This does not differentiate psychoanalytic practice, however, from any other form of practice. A physician practising internal medicine, for example, is not practising science. His or her work is, hopefully, based on the results of scientific research and choices are made according to reason disciplined by scientific training. But the requirements of formal science are hardly met by the daily routines of practice in any field.

Psychoanalytic practitioners are, in fact, at two disadvantages relative to internists. First, we have not achieved, at least in recent years, much, if anything, that can legitimately be designated as "advances in knowledge", meaning clear rejection of certain hypotheses leading to support of other hypotheses. We are lacking the scholarship and the funding necessary to mount even the most essential formal studies. (For example: Does frequency of sessions make a detectable difference in outcome?) As a result, we have developed no methodology for procedures in "the context of justification": "The scientist invents concepts and hypotheses in the context of discovery and tests hypotheses in the context of justification" (Edelson, 1984, p. 21). Psychoanalysts take pride in discovering. We do not, thus far, test in any scientifically meaningful way.

Psychoanalysts have a second disadvantage in relation to other health practitioners. The question of what constitutes adequate training for a psychoanalyst and how much science should be included are more complex than parallel questions in the training of health practitioners in non-mental health fields. One of the solutions we have been adopting in recent years, under a variety of pressures, is to de-emphasize the necessity for scientific training, and even for prior clinical experience. Advocacy of the position that psychoanalysis is not science at all is not infrequently heard and increase of that advocacy may be anticipated.

These trends, and the pressures responsible for them, have the inevitable effect of decreasing the scientific discipline of our practitioners. Decrease in the scientific discipline of practising psychoanalysts makes them more vulnerable to charismatic "new ideas", which then become incorporated into an eclectic puree of clinical interventions and goals. This further accentuates the same directions and tends to make even scientifically based clinical reasoning unacceptable.

There is another side to all this, however. The ability to practise psychoanalysis effectively does not depend *solely* upon education in science and epistemology, nor upon clinical experience in working with ill people. A psychoanalyst also needs knowledge of, and sensibility for, myths, literature, painting, sculpture, architecture, music – all of those bodies of work that have captured essential aspects of human unconscious as well as conscious mentation. We need to be educated in history and the essential theories and findings of anthropology and sociology. We need to bring to our psychoanalytic work a broad education in the arts as well as in science, neuroscience, and technology, accompanied by experience in taking care of other people.

Studies carried out in the fields of linguistics, semiology, social psychology, and many other disciplines are relevant to our work. My objections to the introduction of such ideas and observations for psychoanalytic consideration are stringent but limited. The first objection is the *pars pro toto* replacement, already described. The second is that psychoanalytic application of ideas derived from other disciplines must be scientifically based; as health practitioners and theorists of the causes of illnesses, we have different responsibilities than pure scholars do. Clinical psychoanalysis is a form of treatment for mental illness, one form among many. Symptoms do count. Any treatment that leaves the patient with the same or worse symptoms cannot be regarded as successful. Outcomes matter. Process research not disciplined by outcome measures dangles in the middle of nowhere. To proceed without scientific research altogether is to go nowhere altogether. The substitution of "narrative truth", or its congeners, in place of a quest to know real facts, cannot be ultimately acceptable in a health care field.

I continue to hold that the theory of mental conflict and psychic structure, as developed by Freud and many subsequent contributors, holds the most promise for scientific investigation and, pending the results of such investigation, the most promise for effective clinical work. Classical psychoanalytic theory and technique are not static, but continue to evolve steadily. Brenner, for example, has gradually introduced a series of crucial changes in theory over a period of years, among which one might note the parallel role in conflict for depressive affect and anxiety (1979), and dropping standard terms for superordinate structures (ego, id, and superego) (1994). All of Brenner's innovations have immediate implications for psychoanalytic clinical technique. Another set of technical developments, called *close process attention*, has been pursued by Paul Gray (1994) and explicated by Pray (1996) and others.

My own experience, both personal and professional, has led me to retain the conviction that people with neurotic and character disorders improve through understanding, in a deep emotional sense, of their own roles in producing their own lives. The object of psychoanalytic treatment is to produce particular changes of beneficent kind in the mind of the patient, which means in the brain: mind, as Brenner has said (1982), is a function of brain. Physical changes in the brain as a result of differential experience have been anatomically demonstrated by neuroanatomical researchers.

The vehicle for the production of such change by psychoanalytic treatment, or any other talking treatment, is the relationship that occurs in the psychoanalytic situation. We attempt to contemplate that relationship in the terms *transference* and *countertransference*. The basis of all relationships is, however, the same. There is nothing unique about the psychoanalytic relationship except what we do with its products, as Freud noted in 1912: all human relationships derive from templates of infancy and early childhood, templates that accrue complexity and become modulated as development occurs. "Classical psychoanalytic theory" contains an elaborate (though still incomplete) theory of objects and relationships (Compton, 1985a; 1985b; 1986a; 1986b; 1987; 1995).

The idea that clinical improvement occurs as the result of "non-specific relationship factors" is foreign to me. We might better say that there are elements of the psychoanalytic and other relationships that we have not yet observed and conceptualized clearly. The psychoanalytic relationship is not an end in itself. The goal of treatment is not that the patient should become more intimate with or feel closer to the analyst. Nor is the goal that the patient should feel "safe" with the analyst. The goal is to eliminate the symptoms with which the patient came, and to alter the characterological basis of the formation of those symptoms and other life difficulties.

If, as I believe, the general goal of psychoanalytic treatment is to influence the patient's mind (that is, alter the brain), then it follows that appropriate clinical interventions do not always address "transference", that is, not all interventions ought to be relationship oriented. While Gill (1982) was probably correct in saying that most treatments that fail do so because of inadequate transference interpretation, he was overly emphatic in his insistence on addressing only transference. Treatment strategies that adhere to Gill's maxim may produce sessions that are more alive and interesting for the analyst, especially since attention to a relationship, and to both sides of the relationship, is more narcissistically gratifying than trying to understand the patient. A sitting-up patient, very experienced in psychoanalysis and other psychodynamic treatments as a patient, one day observed: "You look sleepy. I know how to fix that. Say something about the analyst! He sits up, his eyes brighten, his colour improves, his hair turns glossy."

However much strain may be put on the analyst's capacity for concern with others, interventions that address the functioning of the patient's mind are essential in their own right, *even though* there may be transference significance in the background.

> A patient came because her husband of many years suddenly moved out. She was distraught and taking no steps to protect herself financially. After she became less distraught, she still would take no steps in that direction. She said she felt no anger with her estranged husband, who continued to exert iron control over her finances. I tried to approach this by noting evidence of her aggressive feelings toward me. She had none of those either, she assured me.

What she did have was a set of definitions, very carefully worked out in her mind, definitions for anger, hostility, annoyance, irritation, frustration, and several other terms on the same spectrum. Anger occurred only rarely in life, a feeling from deep within that arises only when one is being treated unfairly and unjustly. My uttering any of the words on this spectrum of aggression consistently resulted in her becoming silent and writhing in the chair. Eventually I learned that she was struggling with her set of definitions and could not, ever, find the right word to discuss the experience I was alluding to. This inevitably brought the discussion to a halt or allowed it to continue only on a truly Aristotelean plane. This behaviour was not unique to her time with me; she had struggled with these definitions all of her life and other members of her family had similar concerns. These morally suffused, obsessional/ intellectualizing defences against aggression served to prevent the development of anxiety and depressive affect (in some degree); served to arrange for deprivation (punishment) in her life; and served to express an impulse to control me and the sessions, in the office, and the rest of the people in her life, out of the office. Through some combination of genetic predisposition, familial pressure, identification, and education in religious strictures, her mind had formed in this way. And her mind functioned in this way before me, with me and without me, with other people and by herself. There was simply no way that she could begin to think about her aggression in the analytic session until we had explored the cognitive nature and genetic origins of her patterns of thinking. Her mind existed, and exists, as a function of her brain, with or without another person being involved in actuality. I would agree with what, I think, is the opinion of the majority of analysts: these issues do require resolution in the cauldron of the analytic relationship, eventually.

I have designated some of the trends prominent in psychoanalysis today as matters of style. That is not necessarily a pejorative designation, although it is a concept about which I have always had reservations from a psychoanalytic viewpoint. I think it would be hard to argue convincingly that most analysts today conduct sessions in just the same way as 20 years ago. Someone has said, "There has been a global warming in the offices of psychoanalysts all over the United States." This has certainly been true of our professional organizations. Individually, it does not necessarily constitute an alteration of the fundamentals of analytic technique. Rather, the reverse is true: if we had continued forever in exactly the same style, we would in that way have lost the essence of our technique. The expectations of society have changed in many ways, including a tacit consensus about what constitutes professional behaviour. I have always considered psychoanalytic technique from the viewpoint of social role behaviour – that is, professional behaviour – as well as from many, more inherently psychoanalytic stances. Professional styles have changed in the last 20 years, and in most such periods. The same behaviour now on the part of an analyst that was suitable for Freud in Vienna in 1900 would not carry the same significance for a present-day analyst or patient. In fact, I believe that we lagged far behind usual and necessary changes in style, and are only beginning to catch up. In order to function in a society that has changed its presentations, analysts are appropriately changing as well.

I am more apt to answer *some* questions now, laugh more often in sessions and with less sense of doing something off-beat, and more freely admit errors and doubt about my memory of events. Once or twice I have even sung a line from some song that seemed to catch an essence perfectly. I always, I think, made it clear that my interpretations are hypotheses rather than pronouncements, invitations to open a discussion rather than to close one. That has not changed. I am more likely now to include some description of how I put together the evidence by which I arrived at the interpretation. I say more on the telephone now.

The last item – the telephone – may offer the simplest example of what I mean by style. When I was a small child, my family did not have a telephone. When I came into contact with telephones, they were mysterious and somewhat frightening. Communications technology has changed our styles of doing things. A telephone conversation has now become a relatively intimate form of dealing with someone. Matters that are strictly business are handled by fax and e-mail; what is most formal, and especially what has legal implications, is dealt with by old-fashioned letters. In a world with all this change, one with open and explicit sexuality and violence in books, movies, and television, the reserved professional style of 1930 or 1900 is out of place, and is a disservice to the work to be accomplished.

Respect for the regressive nature of the treatment experience must be conveyed in somewhat different ways. But none of this change in our environment, our culture, and our style has altered, for me, the ideas of unconscious mentation, a lawful mind, and human behaviour as the outcome of conflict and compromise formation.

The Development of My Ideas about Psychoanalysis

ROY SCHAFER

Where to begin? Perhaps with the history of the Jews in Eastern Europe and then my parents' wretched childhoods and emigration to the United States, carrying with them poverty-tainted ideals of learning and little emotional preparation for gratifying family life; this leading to a childhood that featured more than enough bad times emotionally and an adolescence overshadowed by the sense of futility and pessimism engendered in the 1930s by the Great Depression, the rise of fascism, and the massive discrimination against and persecution of Jews – all of which together fostered the deep feelings, "What's wrong with people?" and "What's wrong with me?" Under the influence of these feelings I adopted the role of cautious observer, outsider, and interpreter of what people said and did as well as doubter of the meaning and validity of my own ideas and feelings. It was in this soil that there grew my lifelong interest in interpretation, and it is the intensity of this interest that I consider the red thread running through my personal life, my occupational skills, and the development of my ideas about psychoanalysis.

I was helped to put these predispositions and interests to good use by a number of factors: my good native intelligence and my heightened feeling of integration and morale whenever I plunge myself conscientiously into work that uses my assets; my introduction to psychoanalysis and projective testing by the excellent psychology faculty of the Psychology Department at the City College of New York in the early 1940s; my subsequent employment by David Rapaport, then at the Menninger Clinic, as research assistant in his epoch-making research into, and development of, diagnostic psychological testing, in which capacity I received from Dr. Rapaport many years of instruction in both psychoanalytic ego psychology and careful scholarship; my introduction to psychotherapy, particularly of young borderline patients, at the Austen Riggs Center in Massachusetts, to which I had moved in 1947; my learning these new skills under the brilliant supervision of, among others, Merton Gill, Margaret Brenman, and Erik Erikson; after moving to the Yale University Department of Psychiatry in 1953, my psychoanalytic training at the newly formed and hospitable Western New England Institute for Psychoanalysis, during which time I received further inspiring instruction from Rapaport and Erikson and also from Hans Loewald, among others; my second analysis during those years with William L. Pious, which, unlike my first analysis, was addressed effectively enough to my paranoid/schizoid and depressive tendencies to begin the liberation of significant aspects of my feelings and my creative work; my experiences during these years as Chief Psychologist at the Yale Psychiatric Institute, which helped to further my study of, and psychotherapeutic facility, with borderline and psychotic patients; and then at the Yale University Department of Mental Hygiene, where for 13 years – part-time – I worked psychotherapeutically with gifted late adolescents and young adults.

All in all, it was an extraordinarily rich and fortunate accumulation of opportunities and experiences. It contributed not only to such success I had as a teacher, first of psychological testing and then of psychotherapy and psychoanalysis, but also as the author of comparatively many articles and books in both fields.

For some years I conscientiously followed Rapaport's model as teacher and author. However, first in testing and then in psychoanalytic theory I began to recognize Rapaport's limitations and their inhibiting effects on me. In testing, I moved on from his focus on diagnostics that was to be carried out only through careful assessment of different aspects of ego function, and become absorbed in the use of tests to develop psychological portraits that included but went beyond the formal ego-psychological analyses that Rapaport could appreciate and support (which pained me a great deal). In theory, too, I found it necessary to change, helped along partly by my exposure to Erikson and Loewald and partly by my own teaching of theory in the Western New England Institute for Psychoanalysis. Through that teaching I was constantly exposed to my students' tough questions and also many of my own. Then there was the student protest period of the late 1960s and early 1970s, which fostered my own challenging spirit with respect to all aspects of received wisdom. And I can add to this sequence my increasing experience with hard-to-treat patients in analysis and psychotherapy.

At this point of my account I must bring in another set of powerful influences on the development of my ideas about psychoanalysis. From an early time in my career, my preoccupation with interpretation had led me to develop a keen interest in academic critical theory, first about literature and, later, philosophy: in philosophy, successively, existentialism with its emphasis on action, responsibility, and individuality of experience; then the ordinary language philosophy of Wittgenstein, Austin, Ryle, and others, with its searching way of raising basic questions about hitherto unquestioned assumptions, concepts, and answers in philosophical thought; simultaneously, the philosophy of history, especially its concern with hermeneutics and pluralistic interpretations of the past, both of which inevitably highlight constructivism, the omnipotent influence of personal values, and the idea that we inevitably end up dealing only with versions of the truth; finally, feminism, with its critiques of established modes of thought and language usage that have always drawn freely from all the humanistic disciplines.

These additional influences played into my rethinking the entire edifice of psychoanalytic conceptualization. My moving away from Rapaport's model now included selective doubts about the increasingly dominant ego-psychoanalytic formulations of Hartmann, Kris, and Loewenstein. The change began to take shape in connection with my intensive work on the topic of identification. Preparing to write a paper on identification, I was now ready to realize that I also had to tackle not only introjection, incorporation, and internalization as the rubric for all three processes, but all of ego psychology as the foundation of any Freudian theory of internalization.

This work culminated in my book *Aspects of Internalization* (1968). Especially significant for my development was my learning from my survey of the pertinent literature that, contrary to institutional mythology, Freudian theory was in a very poorly integrated state. Key terms were being used, defined, layered in importance, and selectively emphasized every which way. Even Hartmann, Kris, and Loewenstein, systematic though they were, did not see eye to eye on every topic (for example, *neutralization* as against *sublimation*). My discovering that there was no monolithic theory to draw on, and meanwhile my becoming better acquainted with feminist critiques of Freud, greatly stimulated my already active questioning of the foundational assumptions of Freud's mixture of metapsychology and ego psychology.

After turning out a series of reconceptualizing papers between 1968 and 1974 (on activity and passivity, the mechanisms of defence, the psychoanalytic vision of reality, and problems in Freud's psychology of women), I finally faced the necessity to go beyond critiquing the received theory and begin to explore alternative forms of conceptualization that would still remain true to the clinical operations of psychoanalysis, about which I had developed only increasing conviction. Here my readings in critical theory and philosophy led me toward the concept of *action*. I was encouraged in this direction by my recognizing that effective psychoanalytic interpretation makes patients increasingly conscious of their active, though hitherto unconscious, role in the problems and symptoms they have usually been presenting to the analyst in passive, victimized terms. This being the case, by the end of treatment patients tend to have a far more developed sense of their own agency and responsibility for their lives than they had to begin with, and this change seemed to be central to the benefits of their having been in analysis. In this way, by emphasizing a broad conception of action, I was not devising a new technique – a project in which I have never been interested – but thinking through what was implied, even if not officially conceptualized, in the activity of psychoanalysing people and also in psychoanalysis as a field, insofar as it could be conceptualized operationally.

After 1970 I wrote some papers on action, subsequently pulling them together and developing them further in my next books, *A New Language for Psychoanalysis* (1976) and *Language and Insight* (1978). These works aroused a good deal of interest among analysts, much of it critical. Of the criticism a good deal seemed to centre on the idea that I was recommending a new technique, and, by teaching patients to take responsibility, tossing out the idea of the unconscious. These criticisms seemed to have been stimulated by my providing verbal examples to illustrate the difference between ways patients and analysts can disclaim action and the ways they can affirm it. I presented these examples not prescriptively but to sharpen the reader's sense of what I was talking about. I was also much criticized for developing a system of conceptualization that could not explain everything that psychoanalytic ego psychology, *under the banner of a general psychology*, had tried to explain, such as the development of mentation in early childhood and its changes in dreaming, psychosis, etc. These criticisms mistook me to be trying to develop a new general psychology. I would say that I was trying to *narrow* the ambitious scope that psychoanalysis had taken on under the influence of the great ego psychologists. I was advocating a view of psychoanalysis as a discipline in its own right, one that called for a theory that was tied closely to its operations and to the changes it was able to facilitate in patients' lives when it was working well, and one that was ill-equipped for many aspects of a general psychology.

Additionally, I was criticized for taking the position that psychoanalysis is a hermeneutic discipline. I tried to clarify the hermeneutic aspects of interpretation – the way interpretation develops from part to whole and then back again from whole to part, in which respect much of interpretation is dictated by one's general theory, so that external validation of interpretation loses meaning. In this way I was critiquing the received theory of interpretation as fundamentally stemming from objective naturalistic observation. Whether out of an author's narcissism or sound judgement, I have over the years encountered no sufficient reason to alter my ideas about action.

The philosophy of action emphasizes that action exists always "under a description". This formulation specifies that there is no single, final, definitive account of an action, for the action always reflects the point of view that has been adopted in designating it. Strictly speaking, the same action under a different description is a more or less different action. I realized then that many disputes in psychoanalysis over "the facts of the case" were and still are about differences in recommended perspectives on action. From this clarification I developed, first, an interest in the perspectival basis of schools of psychoanalysis, in other words, the pluralistic universe in which psychoanalysis had developed and continues to develop. Now I could recognize the undecidability of many long-standing controversies in that different theoretical perspectives call for different methods, elicit different phenomena, require different concepts, different use of such general psychoanalytic concepts as transference, different criteria of evidence, and different criteria for assessing therapeutic results. In this way, each school of thought is self-validating and self-sustaining.

My arguing for this view of psychoanalysis drew much criticism. I was seen as advocating a reckless relativism that can only culminate in an "anything goes" attitude. Not at all. I was steadily emphasizing how each perspective that is at all well developed includes more or less well-worked-out criteria for assessing methods and reporting data and conclusions. It is "common ground" that is illusory. The perspectives exist; they have adherents organized in "schools"; advocating them is beside the point.

There is a second aspect of the idea that actions exist only under a description, my recognition of which was stimulated by my readings in critical theory: there is an intrinsic link between action and narration. I began to see that there is a large narrational aspect of the entire psychoanalytic enterprise. Narration is involved in the formulation of theory, in the presentation of case material, in the development of arguments, and in the dialogue of patient and analyst. Interpretation is a narrative enterprise. I have never conceived of narration as being just a matter of the analyst's whipping together a therapeutically helpful or reassuring life history; nor have I felt bound by the narrow conception of narrative as necessarily having a beginning, a middle, and an end. Rather, I have steadily conceived of any and every telling of anything as being an instance of narration. There is always more than one way to tell "it", even though it can be argued that each variation constructs a new "it." This argument has been developed rather far by certain philosophers of history. Accordingly, I began another series of papers about the narrational aspects of psychoanalysis, and I pulled these together and developed them further in my next two books, *The Analytic Attitude* (1983) and *Retelling a Life: Narration and Dialogue in Psychoanalysis* (1992).

Yet another significant influence on the development of my ideas about psychoanalysis had been operating since the 1960s when, as a further manifestation of my developing liberation, I began a less prejudiced study of the Kleinian literature. This I did in connection with my work on internalization, having found in this literature many illuminating ideas on that topic. Although Melanie Klein's claims about the beginning of fantasy life in the first weeks of life, if not before, and about rapid-fire interpretations were not and still are not acceptable to me, I found her interest in transference and object-relational aspects of the analytic situation very stimulating. Equally stimulating was my reading the work of Winnicott, Fairbairn, Guntrip, and others working in that general area. My interest developed further when, around 1970, I was able to offer an elective course at the Western New England Psychoanalytic Institute on the British object-relational thinkers. Things developed still further when I was in London in the mid-70s as the first Sigmund Freud Memorial Professor at University College, London, and struck up an acquaintance with Hanna Segal and Betty Joseph. At that time, I was also a guest at some meetings of the British Psychoanalytic Society; there I heard papers presented by members of the contemporary Freudian group associated with Anna Freud that nevertheless seemed to me to be showing the influence of important aspects of Kleinian thought.

Subsequently, there began to appear a series of papers authored by Betty Joseph. These seemed to me to bring Kleinian work much closer to the best of contemporary ego-psychological work; in particular, they were close to the model that I was trying to follow. Her work featured little attempt to reconstruct early development or to dwell on part-object, organ-centered fantasies; it was much more centred on the here and now in the analytic dialogue while retaining a very strong interest in unconscious fantasy as the shaper of meaning of the therapeutic interaction and of events in the patient's surrounding life. Also, she was making it plain that a much more developed interest in countertransference had become part of the Kleinian analytic technique, the concept of projective identification now playing a prominent part in finding a way to use countertransference reactions as sources of information about the patient's present emotional position in the analysis. My interest in Kleinian analysis grew stronger as the years went by so that by the late 1980s and into the 1990s I was attempting to integrate more and more of the contemporary Kleinian work in London with the way of working I had developed and in which I felt confident. This development culminated in my first writing a paper and then editing a book on their work, *The Contemporary Kleinians of London* (1997a).

I have now reached my present position. I do not see it as fully unified, for the foundational assumptions of ego psychology and contemporary Kleinian theory seem to me to be irreconcilable. This is so even though the Kleinians continue to pay homage to instinct theory in their occasional references to theory, while I meanwhile view "instinctual drives" as an optional narrative of human motivation. Qualitatively and quantitatively, these Kleinian "theoretical" references are overshadowed by attention to clinical presentations used to illustrate specific dealings with problems that stem from primitive levels of organization of the personality, specifically the paranoid/schizoid and the depressive positions and the points of suspension between the two. My development in this direction seems to be matched by changes that are occurring in the outlook and the work of many psychoanalysts; they are finding in object-relational theory, often in the Kleinian version but also in other versions, a boost to their interest, versatility, and understanding in their clinical practices. One finds increasing numbers of object-relational references in all the psychoanalytic journals. In another book, *Tradition and Change in Psychoanalysis* (1997b), I tried to address a number of important issues from a Kleinian point of view but with attention, too, to its parallels and some of its roots in traditional ego psychology. Further work in this area seems to me to be among the most important tasks lying ahead for contemporary psychoanalysts.

The question has been raised whether this turn in my development indicates that I have forsaken my interest in action language and narration and dialogue, and the answer to this question is No. I find in the Kleinian emphasis on unconscious fantasy a world of persons engaged in actions with respect to one another or in isolation from one another as well as the constant necessity to present, in what I regard as narrative form, the essential features of these fantasies both in interpretation and in writing about psychoanalytic work. I am aware that the Kleinians do not conceptualize their work in these terms. For many reasons they seem to prefer to adhere to long-standing traditions of formulation in psychoanalysis. Here, I think that their conceptual model has lagged behind the very high level of effective psychoanalytic work that they have developed and practise.

The Elusive Wisdom of the Analyst
ARNOLD GOLDBERG

INTRODUCTION

Waiting to become wise seemed the only possible course. I came to that decision when, as a young analytic candidate surrounded by a variety of sage elders, there seemed to be no clear unambiguous path to pursue to achieve that sought-for state of serenity, knowledge, and peace: wisdom. Convinced as I was of the possession of that precious condition by most, if not all, of my teachers and supervisors, I could not at first fathom how such a diverse bunch of beings had managed to arrive at the same similar and sought-for spot. They were all wise, of that I had no doubt; but that they seemed to manifest different evidence of that state was a matter of temporary puzzlement. One wise teacher, for example, told me never, under any circumstances, to accept any sort of gift from a patient, while another equally prescient one insisted that this should not be a worry. It may even be a benefit to allow oneself to be so gifted. These supposed contradictions were, however, ultimately not the problem, inasmuch as I could, with some careful consideration, see that wisdom clearly took different forms at different times. My puzzle had to do with the way to wisdom, that is, just what to do to get there. There seemed to be no easy answer. Finally I decided that reading or studying was not the path, nor was it to be attained by an emulation of my elders, nor was striking out on an original course the proper pursuit. I was left with no alternative but to wait until somehow, in some way, I, too, could lay claim to membership in that elusive circle. This now is the story of that essentially passive journey: its course and its resolution. It is a story with no surprises.

THE PATH

I cannot date an onset to my personal interest in the achievement of wisdom, but I remember hearing René Spitz say how astonished he was to read of Heinz Kohut's description of wisdom. Spitz could not understand how one so young as Kohut could manage such a comprehension of a state regularly reserved for the old. Kohut (1971) characterized the evolution of wisdom as proceeding from information through knowledge on to that "cognitive peak of human development." Its attainment included the emotional acceptance of the transience of individual existence, and this was felt to sometimes emerge in the end of an analysis in a "modest and limited form" (p. 328). I myself was willing to settle for such a modest and limited form and was heartened to soon hear a senior analyst report to a group of us as to his own embrace of that state. He told a story of the return of a female patient who had come to see him after many years hiatus. This returnee told the analyst that he was a changed person in comparison to what he had been or had been seen to be in her first, earlier analysis. She noted that the analyst seemed more relaxed, more at ease, more willing to give advice, and especially to reveal his own feelings to the patient. Thus the analyst, in conjunction with this patient, summed up his new demeanour as the attainment of wisdom. I remained sceptical, although encouraged, since these above-noted traits seemed to have ever been present in my teacher. But he seemed secure in his accomplishment and, now, being wise, was no longer to be challenged or doubted. That, of course, was an added benefit of wisdom.

Inasmuch as the particular qualities of wisdom are debated and discussed as they have been through the centuries, I cannot take on that task as well. Suffice it to say that my pocket dictionary's definition of wisdom as "sound judgement" seems both convincing and compelling and can serve as an agreed-upon endpoint to mark one's achievement of the state. This definition also allows one to launch an investigation into a determination of how analysis can be revealing of such sound judgement in each of the participants of that process, that is, how does it emerge in the analysand, when does it become established in the analyst, and is it elusive or perhaps it is a commonplace?

THE PLACE OF WISDOM IN ANALYSIS

I recently read a case report, telling of a patient who brought a basket of oranges to her analyst. He reported that he was a bit startled at the offer but then proceeded to explain to her that it would be importune for him to accept her gift, inasmuch as it would not be in the best interests of her analysis. In a rather laboured effort at the justification of his position, he appeared to be summing up his rejection of the offering as necessitated by the rules of the analysis. I myself read his apologia, his justification, as being foolish rather than sound. What he took as gospel, and presented as an act of wisdom, came across to me as more befitting one of folly. Yet there could be little doubt that this analyst felt that these rules were those of concern for the best interests of the patient, and so he acted accordingly.

After reading this case report, I read a quote attributed to Bion, who said that "it is difficult to stick to the rules. For one thing, I do not know what the rules of psychoanalysis are" (Bion, 1990, p. 139). The quote was reported as a claim to wisdom. However, it clearly could also qualify (at least to me) as downright foolish. Surely psychoanalysis is filled with rules ranging from the requirement for free association to those of various ethical proprieties. How could one not know what they are? Now I found myself trapped between two positions of foolishness parading as wisdom; while it seemed equally clear that my own sense of conviction could and would be seen by these presenters of certainty – my first quoted author and now Bion – as wrongheaded and stupid. Alas, now wisdom was coming perilously close to mere matters of opinion. Whereas one analyst refuses oranges on the basis of a theoretical stance based upon fundamental convictions about drives and drive gratification and so derives a rule, another accepts this offering upon an equally firm conceit involving a necessary alliance with the patient, one equally productive of a rule but of opposite content; a third claims that he is ignorant and innocent of rules of all sorts. Three positions of the wise, barely concealing a percolating kettle of foolishness, could only be resolved on the basis of the coexistence of contradictions. Interestingly, this seemingly unhappy stance was once espoused by Kant, who suggested that the antinomies of life are not to be eliminated but rather should be seen as the limitation of reason (Kant, 1781). Perhaps this was a start, a beginning insight to the achievement of wisdom being based upon a life of contradiction joined with one of certainty.

As I cast about in my mind to settle upon a patient who exemplified wisdom, I came to one who might not ordinarily be thought of as possessing this trait, since she was seen by most as a flighty, society lady who spent lots of time shopping. She had originally been referred for analysis with the clinical tag: "This is the most severe case of hypochondria I have ever seen." Indeed she was someone possessed by bodily fears and preoccupations, but she did well in analysis and over time emerged relatively free of these worries. Not surprisingly, many of her imaginary illnesses led her to talk about aging and dying, and this was sort of a final common pathway for all of her concerns. Death was never absent for very long from her thoughts, and its inevitability seemed to haunt every area of her life. She wrote about death in her poetry, she seemed to know legions of people who were sick and dying, her analytic hours were rarely free of references to either growing old or dying or both. Yet as the analysis proceeded and the transference became focused on issues of separation between me and her, the talk of death receded along with the associated fears of cancer and an assortment of new and strange ailments.

I routinely treated her ailments as metaphoric messages. Together we agreed upon the messages that lay behind these images of disease, and so illness became less and less of an issue in her life. She was, however, quite unable to completely separate from me, and I continued to see her over the years. What slowly seemed to penetrate to my own consciousness was something that could only be properly thought of as a certain detached or philosophic attitude of hers toward illness and death, an attitude that I myself could gradually both appreciate and understand. My patient demonstrated what, for me, became a striking and fundamental feature that now I feel is an essential quality for an analytic experience: she could both look back upon her life in the now popular formation of a narrative or life story, but she also looked forward to its finiteness. The future, one that necessarily meant the end of her life, not only was a point that lay ahead of her, but it was incorporated as an essential part of her. She had a life's trajectory, a picture of continuity, as if she could see herself in two directions. The past, which had been the focus of much of her time in analysis, was not just a storehouse of memories but was now joined in this line with the life ahead. I am afraid that this may sound trite and obvious, and so can only beg the indulgence of the reader to join me in what seemed to be a new vision, one that could contemplate a life of completeness with both a beginning and an end, an act of contemplation that for me seemed to herald the arrival of wisdom. In a way, she ceased looking for answers.

The sense of time or the passage of time surely has a different valence for us as we move from a childhood of the endlessness of time, to adolescence that treats the future with varying degrees of fiction, to the adult who reckons with time's limits, all the while denying the inevitable end of time. The capacity to step outside and see this entire passage is what emerged in my patient, and this I believe also comes to exist in the analyst's achievement of wisdom. Psychoanalysts are, in one sense, stuck in the past. As Proust beautifully said, "Whether it is because the faith which creates has ceased to exist in me, or because reality takes shape in the memory alone, the flowers that people show me nowadays for the first time never seem to me to be true flowers" (Proust, 1913, p. 201), so, too, does psychoanalysis ask for us to seek our reality and truth in the past and to leave the future as an area beyond our concern and beyond our ability to know it, save for a place to wonder and perhaps to worry. It is to this conceptualization of the future that wisdom comes to take place and begin to form. As it does start to take shape it need not qualify for a place of depth of intellect or profundity, but more for what we may call a range of vision. We, too, start to see it all. And this capacity is not necessarily a boon for us.

THE PLACE OF WISDOM IN THE ANALYST

One way to present my thesis about the arrival of wisdom in an analyst is to follow the path of our rescue fantasies that are the absolute necessary ingredients to launch a career of assisting people who wish, with our help, to rearrange their psyches in both form and contents. However, a caution is in order lest one think that the fantasy of saving the neurotically sick must be tamed into a submission of resignation, a recognition of the limitations that frustrate our wishes to heal. Having had an experience of a patient similar, say, to a new patient who is being evaluated, we regularly make a silent comparison and prediction. We begin to know what the future will hold. However, having had an unfortunate or unhappy experience with a like patient, we aim and hope to alter the possibilities of the future. We move back to the uncertainties of what will be. With each of these postures that we have posited, we alter our place as a mover in the particular enterprise of change. We are both a part of the process as well as an observer of it. This is not to say that we merely recognize our limitations and accept them, as much as it is to say that our experiences infect every new moment of our lives. Every patient carries the history of our lives as well as of their lives. Along with the mutual history – what some call an autobiography constructed by two authors – the future impacts on each point of the narrative that we make. As analysts we hope to change the patient, to guess where the patient will end up, and then to assume a position of seeing the entire story. I think that that last step is the entry point to wisdom, and its elusiveness exists because we may remain involved in the niceties of the process. That is not to be seen as bad, since there sometimes needs to be a blindness as to what will unfold. We now see the gains and losses that result from the tension between eagerness and reasonableness. There comes a peculiar conflict in each of us as more of life's puzzles and problems become solved and our inherent restlessness becomes diminished. My anxious patient had no hesitation in exchanging her worries about her body to an almost serene state of mind. There is no doubt that seeing "the big picture" gives one both a chance to relax and to be seen as wise. But we need also to fear as Flaubert (1869) said, "The idleness of the mind and the inertia of the heart" (p. 411). For just as my patient started to "see it all", so, too, may we become infected with the virus of experience and thus robbed of the mystery of the future. This then is the downside of our expanded vision.

DISCUSSION

To bring together the above-mentioned recognition of "the entire story" as a narrative of continuity without a corresponding complement of special perspicacity moves one to a conclusion best summed up in a word: familiarity. As I began to hear certain episodes in a patient's life, certain forms of dreams, certain transference configurations, they took on a sense of recognition. What had at one time seemed foreign and challenging became transformed with experience into the familiar and expected. And through no demand of my own, I, too, surprisingly found myself being treated by others as wise. Certainly without humility and with no more cynicism than was part of my usual demeanor, I was cast into a role by students and colleagues, a role once assigned to my own teachers and supervisors. It seemed that the only step that I had managed to take was that of no longer, or at least very rarely, being surprised. I recalled being offered a book to read by my analyst entitled *Surprise and the Psychoanalyst* (Reik, 1937), but only the title remained, first with meaning and then with regret, in my memory.

With the diminution of one's fantasies of rescuing patients from their turmoils, with the self-assurance of proceeding in a tried and true way, with the certainty of knowing just how and why we can and will be effective, along with the equally solid resoluteness as to what cannot be accomplished, we find ourselves embraced by wisdom. We have a somewhat detached perspective that goes beyond mere information and knowledge. We become tired. We seem to have fewer and fewer questions. More's the pity.

SUMMARY

Ludwig Wittgenstein, a philosopher both entranced by and critical of psychoanalysis, said that Freud was clever but not wise (Wittgenstein, 1958, p. 41). I explained this to myself with the defence that Wittgenstein knew only of Freud as a controversial writer and did not or could not see the entire work of Freud as a whole and in retrospect. Then, I was sure, he would qualify for wisdom. But perhaps Wittgenstein was correct. Perhaps Freud's cleverness was enough. My same pocket dictionary describes that quality as "quickness in learning and understanding things". I do not wish to offer a mere play on words, but perhaps there is something to be said for the essential elusiveness of wisdom. Once it does overtake us – or, in another direction, once we manage to possess it – we reach a state of the expectable and the familiar. One cannot help but wonder if we are apt to associate that with the comfort of knowing things for sure. Such comfort can surely beckon us but can also become a danger. We might do well to worry if wisdom is worth it.

Musings about My Intellectual Development
HERBERT J. SCHLESINGER

In contrast to analysts I have long envied, I didn't read Freud as a boy. We had a good-sized collection of books at home with a fair representation of world literature and leftish political thinking. I knew our well-hidden, brown-paper-wrapped volume of Krafft-Ebing, but we had no Freud. My recollection of first hearing the name is perhaps a screen memory: a radio announcer gravely reported that Freud had died. It was during a broadcast of the New York Philharmonic on a rainy Sunday afternoon. It always rained on Sunday when I was a boy. Freud was described as the author of the recently published *Moses and Monotheism*. At that time, if there was anyone I was less aware of than Freud it was Moses.

My intellectual heroes were Roy Chapman Andrews, who explored for dinosaur fossils in the Gobi Desert, and the naturalists Martin and Osa Johnson. A distant cousin was a bacteriologist, and I loved the word before I had any idea what it was about. I was stunned by her microscope, binocular and with three objectives. My father gave into my entreaties, and I received an antique model and spent many hours putting anything small enough under it, playing with stains and preparing specimens.

I assumed I would major in chemistry at Brooklyn College, but I was waylaid by psychology. Lewinian Field Theory and Gestalt Psychology were taught by professors who had been colleagues and students of Kurt Lewin and Max Wertheimer. My psychological education was totally un-American. To paraphrase a saying from the Reconstructionist South, I didn't realize that "damnedbehaviourist" was two words until graduate school. I loved messing around in laboratories and, while doing some experiments in perception, I became convinced that the individual differences that I had been taught to regard as "measurement error" might be of greater psychological interest than the generalizations that scientists were supposed to be seeking. I recall that I learned nothing about psychoanalysis in college. Freud was an object of derision, featured mainly in the annual department skit. It was not until graduate school that I heard anyone take Freud seriously.

World War II interrupted my intended career in research. After enlisting, I was allowed to finish my senior year. I thought that mental patients might demonstrate individuality in perception and so spent most afternoons hanging around at Kings County Hospital in Brooklyn. Sol and Karen Machover, the psychology staff, provided benevolent oversight. I was deeply impressed by the seriousness with which my mentors arrived at nuanced diagnoses, but I did not gain much respect for the prospects of relating diagnoses to clinical care. All of the clinical dispositions could be handled by a four-fold table: hospitalize or not, and shock or not.

Discharged in 1946, I returned to Kings County Hospital to consult my mentors. I proposed to study clinical psychology in order to gain access to severely disturbed patients whose psychopathology might provide natural experiments in the effects of personality on perception and cognition. Pointing to the two-volume set of *Diagnostic Psychological Testing* by David Rapaport, Roy Schafer, and Merton Gill, which had just come out, they directed me to the Menninger Clinic in Topeka, Kansas, a place I had never heard of.

At the Menninger Clinic, Phil Holzman, my classmate and best friend, and I found George Klein, who was working on perception, cognition, and personality precisely along the lines I had been mulling over. We three hit it off immediately, and put together a research programme that opened the "New Look" movement in psychology. Our programmatic statement was, "Where is the Perceiver in Perceptual Psychology?" (Klein & Schlesinger, 1949). A series of articles spelled out the details. We were a close-working team until George left Topeka. Ultimately, with Bob Holt, he founded the Research Center for Mental Health at NYU.

While engaged half-time in research, and two-thirds time in a four-year clinical internship, I also studied with David Rapaport, Robert Holt, Milton Wexler, Robert Knight, Karl Menninger, Margaret Brenman, Sybille Escalona, Merton Gill, William Pious, Rudolf Ekstein, and others at the Foundation and commuted to the University of Kansas for the rest of the required graduate school curriculum. It all seemed quite "natural"; I had not the slightest awareness that it was only by pure luck that I had fallen into the hands of a stellar faculty the likes of which would probably never be assembled again. And it turned out that the brand of psychology I had absorbed as an undergraduate was ideal preparation for studying Freud with David Rapaport.

Under Rapaport's tutelage, we read Freud closely, the way rabbinical students absorbed the Talmud. We spent most of a year on an exegesis of the seventh chapter of the *Interpretation of Dreams*, but we also pondered why Freud thought and wrote as he did and the scientific and cultural context that shaped his efforts. Rapaport had us replace Brill's version of Freud with his own translation of critical passages. We were impressed with Freud's ability to make bold hypotheses and then to discard them when further observation revealed their inadequacies. In contrast, others among our teachers showed a dismaying ability to shape their observations to fit their preconceptions.

Rapaport's insistence that we think critically and support our opinions with evidence and logical argument was supported by studying the history and philosophy of science, methodology, and systems theory at the University. We read Henri Poincare, Ludwig von Bertallanfy, Moritz Schlick, Herbert Feigl, and Philipp Frank, among others, who examined the nature of theories and concepts and their relationship to data. We learned to separate concepts, which "true" or not might have heuristic utility, from much that seemed to be gratuitous speculation. Unlike my later experience in the Institute, we were learning why Freud went about theorizing as he did rather than being expected to regard his theories as successive approximations to ultimate psychoanalytic truth. Theories in themselves were not meant to become objects of belief.

These distinctions were not always so clear. Rapaport's deep investment in the economic point of view and his wish to demonstrate through research the power of the idea of cathexis for cognitive functioning seemed odd. The idea that "drives" could supply a literal energy to explain emotion and motivation seemed improbable and a naively literal translation of the experience of peremptoriness. I recall that signal theories were just then being proposed to replace the mental hydraulics being taught in the classroom, and, though they were much drier, they seemed likely to ultimately be more useful in explanation.

Also, for all of Karl Menninger's challenging our sloppy thinking and writing, his insistence on the necessity of a death instinct, which he also made a test of personal loyalty, seemed an anomaly. For he was an optimist who stressed the healing power of hope and inveighed against stigmatizing patients through careless use of diagnostic labels. He urged us to look for what makes the patient's life "work", as well as what led him to fail; to look for what the patient's peculiar behaviour does *for* him, not just what it does against him and others. Few of my colleagues took the idea of a death instinct seriously, but no one argued the position publicly. Many of us also came to view Freud's metapsychology as an interesting attempt to build a model of the mind. It had certain formal properties that could be useful in visualizing how the mind in conflict might work, so long as one did not take the model too seriously, that is, take it as the mind itself.

It may be difficult, at the end of the twentieth century, to imagine the state of psychiatric residency training in the immediate post–World War II years. In 1946, I was a member of a class of would-be psychiatrists and clinical psychologists numbering about 110. Many of them had applied for analytic training or for a personal analysis, and there were long waiting lists. Karl Menninger, always the expansionist, used this demand to invite displaced European analysts to resettle in Topeka, resulting in an influx of notable analysts and teachers including Hans Jokl, Jan Frank, Michelina Fabian, Rudolf Ekstein, Ellen Simon, Alfred Gross, Helmuth Kaiser, Nelly Tibout, Herman Van der Waals, Benjamin Rubinstein, and Trygve Braatoy. While Anna Freud made several visits, ultimately she was unwilling to move to Topeka. Later, Ernst Ticho, Gertrud Ticho, and Otto and Paulina Kernberg joined us.

I had no ambition at first to be a working clinician of any kind, let alone an analyst. Only during the clinical assignments of my internship did I find that I enjoyed clinical work and that I was effective at it. Figuring out what made psychotherapy and psychoanalysis "work" then became a preoccupation that continues to this day. But how I ended up in the Institute is an interesting story.

Unbeknownst to me, the senior staff members wanted to open up psychoanalytic training to psychologists. Their hope was that psychologists trained in research as well as in the clinic might enrich the field intellectually. The Institute agreed to ignore the poorly formulated policies of the American Psychoanalytic Association that were intended to bar such independent action. In the summer of 1947, the members of my class "who were interested" were asked to fill out a perfunctory application to the Institute. I was pretty sure I wasn't interested, but I yielded to social pressure to apply anyway. It then turned out that Phil Holzman and I were two of the four who were selected, or rather drafted. Luckily, there were no interviews to inquire into my motivation. I first heard about my fate when, while in New York on vacation, I received a telegram saying that I should come back to Topeka; the time of Rudolf Ekstein, my training analyst-elect, could not be held for more than a week. I immediately sought counsel from my classmates, who responded as if I had won the lottery. I felt I was being urged to elect brain surgery. I left my puzzled parents and the cool forest and streams of the Catskills and returned to Topeka, possibly the most reluctant candidate ever.

My ascent to the couch felt to me something like that of a virgin being urged up on a Mayan altar. While I was shy of manner and sarcastic of tongue, and felt quite lonely, I took it as the way I was supposed to be, not as something needing treatment. It was flattering that the "opportunity" thrust upon me fulfilled a wish of the senior faculty to enrich the field. So if good for me or not, it would be right to jump through the window of ambiguity in the rules of the American Psychoanalytic Association as an act of constructive social rebellion. While I had doubts aplenty, I did not seriously consider declining the honour. I did not want to disappoint my respected teachers, who possibly knew better than I what was good for me. But I also felt a sense of impending adventure. It was something like joining the Army, not something I would have sought under ordinary circumstances, but also not one to avoid when the time came. And while I knew the Institute had its share of teachers-from-the-book, there were also several respectful nonconformists with whom I wanted to study, teachers who valued psychoanalysis more for the deep questions it raised than for the tentative answers. It was highly tempting to think that I might be able to experience psychoanalysis personally and then test the ideas authentically. Once I was in analysis, eagerness replaced reluctance. The reader may understand that when it later fell to me to assess applicants to an institute, I was less impressed than others with the predictive power of conscious motivation.

In the Institute, I discovered that most of what I was to learn about Freudian psychology I had already learned in the two previous years. The didactic programme, other than Karl Menninger's course on technique and Ekstein's on dreams, added little. But these two teachers, and several excellent supervisors, encouraged us to think critically about the psychoanalytic situation, how and why it worked when it did, and what might have interfered way when it didn't. They appreciated observations about a case that the canon would not have predicted, or observations that implied that the canon was able to shed even more light on the case under discussion than had been appreciated. An interest in conceptualizing the process of psychoanalysis, as well as the process of psychoanalytic supervision, has remained with me over the years and has yielded a series of articles (Holzman & Schlesinger, 1972; Klein & Schlesinger, 1949; Schlesinger, 1969; 1970; 1974; 1978; 1981a; 1981b; 1981c; 1981d; 1988a; 1988b; 1990; 1992; 1994a; 1994b; 1995a; 1995b; 1995c; 1996; Schlesinger & Appelbaum, in press; Schlesinger & Holzman, 1970). A central idea is that change occurs immediately following any correct interpretation, but that it is essential that the analyst follow up in terms of the patient's response if the change is ultimately to become "structuralized". Aphoristically, it matters less what the analyst says than what he says next.

I discovered that I enjoyed analyzing, and I was soon regarded as a good analyst. But I regretted that I had abandoned research, my first love. I had begun analytic training while only a year into graduate school, and was graduated from both institutions at about the same time. Absorbed with analysis, I took on a great deal of clinical work. Rewarding opportunities to teach and supervise soon opened up. For over 10 years I was largely out of touch with the research programme that had been my main reason for entering the field. By the time I might have rejoined it, perhaps even better able to tackle some of the problems that had baffled me earlier, it was too late. The paradigm we had developed seemed exhausted, and I had lost my taste for demonstrating in the laboratory matters that now seemed self-evident in the clinic. Phil Holzman was better able than I to remain true to our original commitment to research. He was able to use his analytic training and clinical skills to inform a succession of research investigations toward the genetics of schizophrenia for which he has since achieved international recognition.

I was teaching Institute courses even before I had been graduated. And the Institute also had much need for administrative leadership. In order to build the School of Psychiatry, Karl Menninger had become the Manager of the Veterans Hospital, and had taken control of the Topeka State Hospital, another of our teaching services. The Institute had to get along as best it could. Most of the senior faculty of the Institute were now not native speakers of English, and none had any appreciation for the bureaucratic minuets that dealing with the American Psychoanalytic Association required. While elections were held regularly so that the honorific position of Director could be passed around the group of training analysts, as "Executive Assistant" I became the permanent civil service.

In about 1960, Karl Menninger proposed that Phil Holzman, Ernst Ticho, and I be recognized as Training and Supervising Analysts and asked the American Psychoanalytic Association to waive its usual requirements. After being vetted by site visitors Jack Arlow, Sally Bonnet, Joan Fleming, and Stanley Goodman, the waivers were granted. It was several years, however, before we were considered eligible for membership in the Association.

I had become so enmeshed in teaching, clinical work, and administration that I saw no way to return to research in Topeka. In 1969, I was invited to take the professorship in psychiatry at the University of Colorado that had been vacated by the death of John Benjamin. I accepted with the proviso that I would not do any administration other than to help with building a new psychoanalytic institute. Then, in 1973, when Chairman Herb Gaskill retired, the Dean of the Medical school appointed me Acting Chairman and Superintendent of the Colorado Psychiatric Hospital. Why? He said I was the only non-volunteer in the Department. I was charged to rebuild both the Department and the Hospital. Two years later, with those tasks completed, Herb Pardes came to take the Chair and I had the opportunity, with Emily Mumford, to open a research programme on the effects of outpatient psychotherapy on use of medical-care services.

Emily wanted to return to New York and, since I had been in Denver for 16 years, I too felt it was time to return. I had come to know Arnie Cooper through committee assignments at the American Psychoanalytic Association, and found in him a kindred spirit, knowledgeable about psychoanalysis, a benevolent sceptic with a keen sense of the absurd. We comforted each other though many a dull meeting. I was especially impressed that he too had lived a full analytic life in an academic setting, finding as I did that the two sets of values complemented each other. Arnie urged that I affiliate with the Columbia Psychoanalytic group and I have found this setting to be a most congenial and stimulating one in which to teach and write. Columbia has welcomed the ideas I have been trying to develop about the processes in psychoanalysis and psychotherapy that promote and hinder change. I expect to move no more. And since I finally have aged out of administration, there are only the internal obstacles to putting my ideas into some more systematic form.

A Psychoanalytic Stance
MILTON VIEDERMAN

PSYCHOANALYTIC TRAINING AND EARLY AFTERMATH

The imagined Freud of theory as elaborated in his papers on technique is quite different from the Freud who revealed himself in his clinical work and as revealed by the experience of his analysands. I made first acquaintance with the imagined Freud at the Columbia Psychoanalytic Center where I trained. Its founder, Sandor Rado, had founded the Hungarian Psychoanalytic Society before becoming a major figure in the Berlin Institute. Upon arriving in New York he developed the first curriculum at the New York Psychoanalytic Institute. His repudiation of aspects of classical theory led to controversy and he decided to found a University Institute at Columbia with the idea of bringing psychoanalysis into the mainstream of academia. By the time I began my training his highly authoritarian, anticlassical stance was losing its influence in a faculty that was remarkably eclectic. Yet there was concern about orthodoxy among the candidates. Psychoanalysis was an ideal, an ideal to be achieved through an understanding of theory rooted in Freud's work and an ideal to be practised in analytic work. It had a purity that was not to be defiled. The analytic situation was seen as having an exquisite sensitivity. Inappropriate "nonanalytic behaviour" could have dire consequences and interfere with a true analysis, for indeed there was a true analysis. My response to this was to be extremely cautious analytically, to defend against my inclination toward spontaneity and to be constricted in my analytic role. Skolnikoff echoes the persistence of this theme among analysts in an unpublished paper in which he speaks of the "analytic conscience", the sense deeply imbedded in analytic training and practice, that one must avoid deviation from "the rules". To do so is to deviate from the single prescribed and meaningful analytic stance. The path that I was to take involved an escape from that rigidity to a position of greater freedom with the awareness that appropriate spontaneity not only engages patients who would otherwise not be engaged but generally facilitates the process of analysis.

TRANSITION

It was the experience of working analytically and at the same time applying psychoanalytic principles in an extra-analytic setting that fermented a change in my views. My work directing a psychiatric consultation service in a medical centre and working with the physically ill confronted me with new demands. Although these patients rarely called for psychoanalysis as treatment, psychodynamic thinking as applied to consultation with the physically ill patient offered a rich opportunity for understanding the emotional reactions of such patients and for formulating approaches to the engagement of patients in treatment. Work with people in crisis and particularly those with physical illness imposed a demand for activity and spontaneity, which I had previously denied myself in my analytic work. The often intense and sudden regressive behaviour in such patients called for interventions that involved vigorous emotional responses. There was a latent drama in these situations, a drama that was less apparent in the psychoanalytic situation. Often I was confronted with patients who were manifestly hostile to psychiatrists. The task was to engage them rapidly, to crystallize their attention, and to establish a therapeutic alliance (Viederman, 1984). Frequently these interviews took place in conferences that involved 20 or 30 observers. Here one had to engage the patient in a dialogue that would facilitate the development of a dyadic relationship in the presence of a crowd. Observation, formulation, and hypothesis generation followed by rapid interventions and observation of the response of the patient became a useful framework for a much more active engagement. The interview itself became an experimental procedure (Viederman & Blumberg, 1993). I found myself interacting in different ways with each patient and discovered to my surprise that some could change rapidly in situations of crisis, especially in the context of loss. The idea of psychological crisis as a potential opportunity for change under certain circumstances rather than simply as a threat to psychological organization led to a series of papers on personality change in the context of crisis (Viederman, 1986; Viederman, 1989). I began to formulate ideas about active brief interventions, in particular one that I call the Psychodynamic Life Narrative (Viederman, 1983). The conceptualization of this psychotherapeutic intervention useful in crisis situations came upon me from a clinical experience.

> A 60-year-old woman, a marquise, had been referred for evaluation of depression, having been treated with all categories of antidepressants available at the time and even with electroshock treatment. It became apparent that she had developed a depression after the death of each of her two husbands, reminiscent of her experience of the loss of her father in childhood. The patient was psychologically obtuse though not unintelligent. My frustration during the extended consultation pushed me to offer a narrative to help her understand the logic of her current depression. I began by saying, "Of course you're depressed. Listen to the story you have told me," and then continued. To my surprise the patient appeared improved in the next session and continued to improve until she arrived one day in a floridly manic state, having proposed to the taxi driver who had brought her to me. Hardly a therapeutic success, but could one deny the power of words?

I developed this intervention in a more formal way and discovered that it could relieve anxiety and depression and re-establish a previous homeostasis in people whose lives had been disrupted by crisis. This intervention – the Psychodynamic Life Narrative (Viederman, 1983) – gives meaning to the patient's emotional reaction to the crisis, by demonstrating it to be a logical and "inevitable" product of previous life experience. As such it addresses three characteristics of crisis: (a) psychic disequilibrium; (b) regression with intense transference wishes for a benevolent protector; and (c) a re-examination and reconstitution of a disrupted life trajectory. It has much of the quality of a transference cure. A relatively simple framework guided my intervention in work with these patients. The task was to understand the meaning of the patient's experience (the illness or its treatment for example) and to see this meaning as an intervening variable between the stimulus and the patient's painful dysphoric reaction. The appropriate communication of these meanings to the patient was highly supportive and often alleviated distress. These interventions were ego syntonic and of the order of clarifications rather than interpretations of unconscious material. However, intense positive transferences were generated that I came to see as representations of fantasised and wishful ideal benevolent parents of childhood. These transferences had power in sustaining these patients as they negotiated difficult reality situations. I realized that this extra-analytic experience was influencing my view of the psychoanalytic situation. I discovered that a greater presence, a theme that I will elaborate below, could facilitate the process of psychoanalysis. Gradually this led to a changed stance in my psychoanalytic behaviour. For some time I had been concerned that my responsiveness in analysis was psychotherapeutic rather than psychoanalytic. It became apparent to me that to conceptualize the work in this dichotomous way raised a false question, although there are differences between psychotherapy and psychoanalysis. They lie in quantity rather than quality and in particular the degree to which interpretation rather than support plays a role in the interaction, as well as the handling of the transference. The unique characteristics of each psychoanalytic or psychotherapeutic relationship is such that a rigid dichotomization is not meaningful. Furthermore, it became apparent that even elements of what had been viewed as the formal structure of psychoanalysis, such as frequency or the use of the couch, were not absolute criteria of what should be called psychoanalysis. It is the nature of the process that defines the type of treatment rather than the formal elements. Here much depends on the patient's talent for self-examination and his capacity to attach meaning to internal psychic processes.

It was in this context that I began to reconceptualize my view of the psychoanalytic situation. The confrontation with patients in crisis involves intensity and drama. There are dangers as well as possibilities for change. In examining this situation one can observe in fast motion therapeutic interventions and responsive change that in the psychoanalytic situation take place over a longer period of time, thus blurring some of the influences and elements of change. It is not unlike the difficulty in conceptualizing organ function from data generated by microscopic examination of the cell. I became more and more impressed by the uniqueness of each relationship with a patient, the special qualities that evolved in each relationship. Greater spontaneity and self-disclosure within bounds seemed to facilitate the process of change.

MY CURRENT PSYCHOANALYTIC VIEW

In retrospect, my first analytic paper in 1976 touched on the influence of the real person of the analyst on change (Viederman, 1976). A patient identified with her fantasy of my wife, based upon her perception of me in the psychoanalytic situation. This identification consolidated her sense of femininity. It was years before these ideas crystallized into a more general view of the nature of the psychoanalytic situation that has a personal slant.

It became evident that an important feature of change in psychoanalysis involved a corrective emotional experience, not in Alexander's sense of a contrived acting out by the analyst to counter the impact of pathogenic developmental experience, but rather as an authentic experience occurring at a moment of emotional receptivity. It is this that modifies configurations in the representational world. It became apparent that the analyst's emotional availability determines the climate of analysis and that the real person of the analyst, his responsivity at particular times, his spontaneity, humour, the nature of his language (and of the language developed by both parties in the dyad), his attitude toward positive action by the patient, and progressive change in the patient affect the therapeutic process and lead to change (Viederman, 1991). These elements, combined with traditional interpretive interventions, engender an ideal transference. Here I distinguish the ideal transference from the idealized one. The ideal transference reflects the good, perfect, gratifying, and wished-for good parent of childhood, and the idealized transference represents a primarily defensive attitude against forbidden wishes, often aggression, though neither exist in pure culture. It is the *presence* of the analyst that crystallizes an enactment of the ideal parental transference, this contributing to the corrective emotional experience and change. This is complementary to the usual analytic work of interpreting transference and reconstructing the genetic roots of conflict.

These ideas led to a more formal description of what I call *presence*, a term hard to define precisely but one that encompasses the view that the analyst is, and is experienced by the patient, not only as a real person in his life but as the ideal parent he never had. The wishful, ideal parental transference is an attempt to find a state of peace and a state of understanding that decreases the sense of isolation that neurotic symptoms and their distortions engender. The full and rich affective re-enactment of the discovery of the wished for ideal parent is operative to a greater or lesser extent in a wide range of therapeutic situations, including psychoanalysis. What is curative in analysis is not only repetition and analysis of transference distortions but in addition a new experience that includes the ideal parent.

By *presence* I do not mean a uniform or standard response to the patient. Here the uniqueness of every relationship, whether in life or in analysis, comes into play. Particular qualities in the patient evoke a special type of responsiveness in the analyst. We develop personal languages in our dialogues with patients: modes of speaking, of delivery, special ways of communicating whether by humour, idiosyncratic vocabularies, use of metaphor, or tones of interactions that are unique to the particular dyad. This is enriched progressively by the shared experience in the treatment, in the common language that develops between the two participants. The analyst's responsiveness and spontaneity in this regard is often automatic, intuitive, without conscious awareness, particularly initially, though it is experiential and hence can be understood. It is what makes him a person in the analytic situation. Though difficult to define, what I call presence exists, although unfortunately it may be limited by the repertoire of personal responses available to an analyst in his response to the patient. Constricted analysts may offer less presence, though patients are variable in their individual requirements in this respect. In some situations distance is required to maintain a proper climate in the analysis, one in which the patient can best function. Analysts have different aptitudes and inclinations that affect their ability to respond to different patients. What I am describing is an experiential phenomenon and hence available for interpretation. To interpret, however, is not to undo. This conceptualization relates to the influence of the analyst on the thrust for change, which continues throughout the life cycle.

This concept may be extended to the power of genetic reconstruction, the unique experience of the patient as he re-examines his past (Viederman, 1994).

> This became apparent in particular with one analytic patient for whom an important part of change involved a changed representation of himself as child, a child worthy of love in the new situation. His worthiness was now validated by a new object, myself, who was experienced by him as a benevolent witness to the past and as a benevolent presence in the past now re-experienced in the present. It was this that consolidated change and influenced the patient's self-representation. Although he had described feelings of personal unworthiness related to poor parenting, he developed a sense of himself as worthy of receiving and capable of giving in analysis. He decided to have a child, an inhibition that had been one of his motivations to begin analysis. He now recognized that he could parent as he had not been parented. In the context of this new experience the patient spoke of listening to himself with compassion, being tolerant and empathetic for the child he had been and being listened to by me in the same way. One year after the end of the analysis he sent me a photograph of himself with his

infant son. Included in the envelope was a button that said "It's never too late to have a happy childhood".

My views of the analytic situation have changed considerably over the years. I recognize, however, that it was not for naught that psychoanalysis has been "called the impossible profession". Each analysis stands as a structure in its own right, and there is difficulty in comparing one analysis with another. In a successful analysis there are fundamental changes in well-ingrained patterns of behaviour that reflect a new attitude toward the self and toward the world (changes in the representational world). In this respect analysis is its own control. However, there can be no testing of one interpretation or another or one interpretive stance or another or one person of the analyst with another. Consequently what would happen under alternate circumstances is not easy to determine. Although re-analysis, after impasse in a previous analysis, may be informative, the second analysis takes place under different circumstances.

The uncertainties of interpretation (both *establishing* and *communicating* meaning) are themselves open to question. This was forcibly brought to my attention when Good discussed a paper I had written that described an analysis in great detail (Good, 1998; Viederman, 1995). He offered many alternate interpretations, each intelligent and reasonable. However, many of them seemed to be emotionally removed from what I experienced during the analysis, admittedly now many years in the past. My most powerful argument for the validity of the establishment of meanings was that I was there and I was in the flux of the emotional interaction. The responses of the patient both affectively and in her associations were determinants of whether they were meaningful to her. I could imagine other meanings and other interventions. Clearly these would have influenced process and the evolution of the analysis. That the analysis had a successful outcome did not of necessity confirm the validity of the particular interpretative thrust. Elements of suggestion cannot be denied and have been generally accepted as influencing outcome. Good also pointed out that our (the patient and my) reconstruction might be considered a screen reconstruction, a reconstruction that in itself defended against other fantasies and/or memories. This may be the case. One might say that the unconscious has unfathomable depths. But at some point one must stop (Viederman, 1998).

The time and nature of the analyst's interventions pose another problem. One is caught always in a delicate balance between interventions that lead to closure, and silence that permits the further evolution of trains of thought. Where does one draw the line and how is the line consistently modified between the analyst's participation, his presence, and the establishment of a space that facilitates the patient's freedom of expression and self-discovery? At one point the analyst intervenes, interprets, and thus influences the field – what is to follow. There is no perfect interpretation or moment of intervention. This is not to speak from a relativistic point of view but to recognize the problems implicit in the analytic situation.

The view that I have described is neither radical nor discordant with changes that are occurring in psychoanalysis. However I believe that the idea of presence and enactment of the wish for the ideal good parent is a vehicle for change. This position, with its benevolent implications (comic in the literary sense, suggesting that all is well in the best of all possible worlds), seemed to contradict the tragic view of life so persuasively insisted upon by Freud. Yet I have come to believe that the special qualities of the dyadic relationship, including the responsiveness of the analyst, have an important role in the outcome of analysis. The individuality and idiosyncratic nature of each analytic situation makes for difficulty in defining proper technique and evaluating subtle influences on process and outcome. In the final analysis, this is simply a comment on the richness and diversity of human experience and the pleasure in novelty that can pervade analytic work.

Psychoanalytic Curriculum: A Study in Change and "The Anxiety of Influence"[1]

ELIZABETH L. AUCHINCLOSS

INTRODUCTION

In 1996, in a panel discussion on psychoanalytic education, I was asked the question: "Should we change our curriculum?" I was delighted with the question because it had become a favourite of mine, having been the first I had asked myself when I became the chairman of the curriculum committee at the Columbia Center for Psychoanalytic Training and Research in 1991. Back in 1991, I found the question to be an exciting one, alive with possibility and opportunity. Gradually it became a preoccupation, evolved into a rumination, and finally developed the haunting quality of a reproach with suggestions of problems overlooked, rigidities, hidden orthodoxies, or just plain laziness. It was not until I was asked the question again, in the panel discussion of 1996, that I was able to organize my thinking and clear up my symptoms.

Ultimately, I came to understand this change in my experience as reflecting a successful if painful transition from an eager new administrator to a member of the establishment. When I began my psychoanalytic education at the Columbia Center in 1980, I was a member of the last class that studied a curriculum designed by Dr. Arnold M. Cooper (1971–1977). For me, therefore, the contemplation of change always begins from the

---

1. Versions of this paper were presented at: the William Alanson White Institute (November 1996), the Association for Psychoanalytic Medicine (November 1997), and the Massachusetts Institute for Psychoanalysis (November 1997).

starting place of "the Cooper curriculum"; I have no thoughts about psychoanalytic education that do not bear the mark of his influence. In fact, the most powerful forces for change in curriculum, at least as I have experienced them, have emerged from the struggle to work through what Cooper himself (1997), citing Harold Bloom (1973), has called the "anxiety of influence". In this chapter, I will discuss aspects of this struggle as well as other forces for change in psychoanalytic curriculum.

NOTES FROM THE CURRICULUM COMMITTEE: 1991–1997

My attempt to identify the pressures to which our committee felt a need to respond in the years between 1991 and 1997 has been a helpful way for me to organize my thoughts about change. First of all, our committee felt a need to respond to new knowledge about psychoanalytic theory and technique. We also felt a need to respond to new knowledge from related but non-psychoanalytic disciplines as well as to changes in the structure of our field including patterns of practice, our relationship to academic psychology and psychiatry, and our place in the larger intellectual world. Finally, we felt pressure to make changes simply because we were bored. In short, we wanted to do things our own way.

CHANGE IN RESPONSE TO NEW IDEAS ABOUT PSYCHOANALYSIS

Among the changes in curriculum that are easiest to chart are those that occur in response to new knowledge about psychoanalysis. Our curriculum is structured, as are many, with a track for psychoanalytic theory of the mind and a track for psychoanalytic theory of technique; each track includes an introductory course in the first year and advanced courses in the later years. Not too surprisingly, the rate of change of the reading list is slowest in the first-year Freud course and most rapid in the later courses.

Both the third-year course in "Advanced Theory and Concepts" and the third-year course on "Advanced Theory of Technique" have led to the development of new courses as growing segments split off from the parent course. The course on "Advanced Theory and Concepts" led to a course on "Psychoanalysis and the Cognitive Sciences". The course on "Advanced

Theory of Technique" spawned new courses on "'Parameters and Modifications in Psychoanalytic Technique", "Psychoanalysis and Medication", and "Converting Psychotherapy to Psychoanalysis", all developed in response to changes in practice patterns (Donovan & Roose, 1995).

Changes in my own teaching include the fact that when I first started in the "Psychopathology" course several years ago, we assigned the case studies of Freud, as well as the work of Freud revisionists such as Kanzer and Glenn (1995). In the last few years, we have dropped this "revisionist literature" after observing that critiquing Freud no longer seems revolutionary. In a similar vein, in our course on "Parameters and Modifications in Psychoanalytic Technique" (co-taught with Arnold Cooper), we observed that Eissler's concept of the "parameter" (1953) no longer dominates and/ or terrorizes the work experience of our candidates as it had in the past (Cooper, 1992); many candidates enter the course having never heard the term. We concluded that while the problem of defining the boundaries of psychoanalysis remains, liberation from excessive dominance by a single concept may have been achieved.

CHANGE IN RESPONSE TO NEW KNOWLEDGE FROM RELATED DISCIPLINES

We have been intrigued by the question of how to respond to new knowledge from related disciplines outside of psychoanalysis, including neuroscience, cognitive science, the philosophy of science, the social sciences, and literature. Among the loudest voices of concern has been that of a large group of faculty and candidates who feel that psychoanalysis will become extinct if we continue to isolate ourselves from important scientific advances in other fields (Cooper, 1997; Cooper, Kernberg, Schafer, & Viederman, 1991; Michels, 1994; Olds & Cooper, 1997).

In the last five years, we introduced a course on "Psychoanalysis and the Philosophy of Science". Our new course, "Psychoanalysis and the Cognitive Sciences", includes topics such as semiotics, connectionism, computer models of the mind, and evolutionary psychology. We have made forays into the neurobiology of dreams, studies of gender and sexuality, memory research, and affect theory. One of the most interesting areas of change, cutting across our entire educational effort, has been in our approach to understanding those patients with homosexual orientation. Changes here have occurred in response to complex forces, including input from gay candidates who have only recently felt free to be open about their sexual orientation (Ellis, 1994).

CONTROVERSY AND DEBATE

Change, however, can never occur without controversy. Our Center has been the forum for several ongoing debates. First of all, in contrast to those who raise concerns that we do not keep sufficiently in touch with other disciplines, are those who are concerned that attempts to conform to quantitative and, at worst, reductionistic scientific methods will endanger the psychoanalytic process. This group reminds us that the data that are unique to psychoanalysis emerge from the clinical situation and that we must maintain the conditions under which this data can be generated and experienced anew by each generation of students through deep and prolonged "immersion" in clinical experience. Challenges to immersion include not only the intellectual seductions of non-psychoanalytic models of the mind but also the changing realities of contemporary professional life.

A related controversy surrounds the place of psychoanalytic research in our curriculum. Our faculty has spent many hours in debate on this issue, much of it quite heated, expressing a wide range of opinion from the feeling that psychoanalytic research holds the key to our survival (Michels, 1994) to the feeling that it holds the seeds of our destruction.

THE ANXIETY OF INFLUENCE

Debates about the theory curriculum are those that have most clearly reflected the struggle among generations. These debates have centred around two issues. The first is whether we should have an historically based or a conceptually based curriculum. The second is whether we should have an integrated curriculum or a curriculum taught from multiple points of view.

Our committee structured the theory track around a philosophy that concepts can best be understood if they are explored from an historical point of view. We have felt that students capable of scholarship and research must be taught to examine the development of schools of thought and to explore the assumptions of each about epistemology, the nature of data collection, the basic categories into which phenomena are divided, and the conceptual parameters along which phenomena are approached.

Let me quote from an unpublished memo written by Dr. Lucy LaFarge to the curriculum committee of the Center in 1995:

> A more historical approach would ... emphasize branching points within the development of theory. An advantage of this approach might be that it emphasizes the problems within theory which have led to the development of new theories; it might also emphasize more the areas of uncertainty and the unknown. Objections to the historical approach have included the possibility that it confuses candidates who need the certainty of a single integrative point of view.... However, as analytic thought becomes more pluralistic, a historical approach might help candidates to develop their own perspective on new knowledge.

However, while our present curriculum is based on the convictions of its designers, it has also been built in the context of our history within the Columbia Center. In other words, our present historically based curriculum has its own history.

Here is my version of Columbia's curriculum history. Let me begin with "ancient", the story of events that occurred before I joined the Center, which form the foundation for my experience yet which are known to me only through archive and legend. The Columbia Center for Psychoanalytic Training and Research was founded when the maverick Hungarian Sandor Rado led a splinter group away from the New York Psychoanalytic Institute in the 1940s. For many years it was an educational goal at Columbia to preserve the work and teachings of Rado and other members of the original group (Roazen & Swerdloff, 1995). In the early 1970s, new leadership at Columbia initiated efforts to redefine our identity within mainstream psychoanalysis while maintaining our commitment to provide a home for thinkers from many schools of thought. Although we no longer teach the ideas of Rado (Cooper, Kravis, Tomlinson, & Makari, 1995), the fact that he established our Center within a university with a strong research mission has exerted a lasting force on curriculum planning. In all institutes, the legacies of the founders provide the backdrop against which the struggles of later generations take place.

For me, "modern history" begins in 1971 with the development of what I referred to earlier as the "Cooper curriculum", which dominated our training between 1971 and 1981. The philosophy of education that we named the *basic concepts approach* lay at the heart of this curriculum, which was built around a set of core concepts presented from the point of view of a contemporary critique. Although from time to time, we read papers by Freud, there was no introductory course on his work. We read some papers by the followers of Freud, but we made no systematic attempt to understand the development of their ideas. Instead, we read contemporary critiques of metapsychology and contemporary papers on object relations theory by Kernberg and Sandler; we did not read the work of Melanie Klein.

From 1981–1991, the curriculum committee was chaired by Dr. Helen Meyers. "The Meyers curriculum" reintroduced a strong historical element with a full-length Freud course in the first year. It also replaced the framework of basic concepts with the framework of models of the mind, organized in the second-year theory course where competing models of the mind were presented within the integrating framework of ego psychology. The basic concepts approach was preserved in efforts to trace an array of core concepts within the various models of the mind (Meyers, 1990). As described above, between 1991 and 1997 our curriculum became increasingly historical. Junior instructors in the second-year theory course refused to participate in an integrated format, objecting both to its intellectual premises and to its authoritarian structure. This group mounted a successful rebellion against the organizing framework of ego psychology, insisting that multiple schools of thought be taught, each with its own history and each from its own point of view. Controversy going back to the early dissidents has been emphasized rather than integration. As we now teach many papers by Melanie Klein and even some by Rank, Jung, and Adler, the mean year of publication of papers taught is perhaps the earliest it has been in 25 years. We are in the interesting situation where many of our most senior faculty members feel that our reading lists are seriously outdated.

At the same time, whereas many senior faculty have favoured the shortening of the Freud course and the elimination of Freud's case histories (Arlow, 1991; Cooper et al., 1991), the junior faculty has been almost unanimous in defending the concept of a year-long Freud course. There has been no support for the idea of abandoning the case histories (Mahony, 1993). In short, there seems to be a "generation gap" with regard to the teaching of Freud. I understand this phenomenon to reflect the fact that our senior faculty were educated in an era of Freudian orthodoxy during which Freud's metapsychology was presented as dogma. Many of them worked hard to demystify the work of Freud and to challenge the religious approach to teaching Freudian theory. It is our feeling that this battle against Freudian orthodoxy has been more successful and more completely internalized by the next generation than our senior faculty seemed to be aware of in as much as it would not occur to the "younger generation" to read Freud for "the last word".

Our newly designed course on Freud approaches his work with the usual focus on the development of his model of the mind. However, in addition, it focuses on basic observable phenomena such as states of consciousness, motivation, affect, memory, representation, fantasy, and mental processes such as defence, around which Freud first developed psychoanalytic models of the mind. This list of phenomena represents the remnants of the basic concepts approach to teaching theory. The course introduces students to linking points between Freud's observations about these phenomena and efforts in the field of neuropsychology to understand similar phenomena. When students are invited to compare psychoanalytic ideas with non-psychoanalytic ideas about the same phenomena, they are in a better position to appreciate the concept of "psychoanalytic" than were this adjective presented to them with the implied meaning of "pure" or "unassailable" (E. Peyser, unpublished communication to the curriculum committee, 1991).

In any case, when younger faculty members educated under the basic concepts curriculum flocked to join study groups reading *The Collected Works of Sigmund Freud*, some senior faculty members found in this behaviour evidence of disturbing neo-orthodoxy or alarming atavism. What these young Freud readers sought, however, was not religious enlightenment but a grounding in the fundamentals that would allow for intellectual emancipation.

What our senior faculty failed to understand is that their efforts to conceptualize psychoanalytic ideas from a "contemporary point of view", presented in various integrated formats to the students of the next generation, were inevitably experienced by us as a new orthodoxy. Whether it was the exploration of basic psychoanalytic concepts presented from a contemporary point of view ("the Cooper curriculum"), the integration of diverse models of the mind within the framework of ego psychology ("the Meyers curriculum"), or a unified theory of technique organized by the principles of object relations theory (O. Kernberg, unpublished communication, 1996), we rebelled. While we recognized that these integrating schema represent the fruits of arduous and perilous struggles waged by a parental generation against the crushing orthodoxies of their youth, our educator/parents had in turn to understand that these fruits were experienced by us not as forbidden but enticing apples from the tree of knowledge, but as the leftovers of someone else's totem dinner. Each generation must mount its own rebellion. We found the tools for ours in the historical curriculum.

In his wonderful paper, "Psychoanalytic Education: Past, Present and Future", Cooper (1997) writes, ". . . we should look . . . more deeply into the forces that . . . impeded the rise of psychoanalytic diversity. The most powerful deterrent to our intellectual liberation has been our reluctance to commit the murder of the Father that is necessary for new ideas. It is only now, half a century after Freud's death, that we feel somewhat freer in contradicting or even ignoring him." He adds that, "Harold Bloom in *The Anxiety of Influence* (1973), has written of strong and weak poets – the strong are those who are able to overcome oedipal guilt and outdo/demolish[2] the fathers who are their models" (p. 4). When I first read these remarks, I was immediately struck by their undeniable phallocentricity. "Why must we demolish our father?" I wondered. "Why should we not sleep with them and make babies?" While this reverie served to correct the offensive bias of the Cooper/Bloom theory, it did nothing for my symptoms. As Cooper turned to the authority of Harold Bloom, I turned to the strong poet himself for help. Goethe writes, "What thou hast inherited from thy father, acquire it to make it thine" (*Faust*, Part 1, Scene 1); Freud quotes these lines in a discussion of internalization and structure formation (1940a). Loewald (1980) quotes both Goethe and Freud in his exploration of successful internalization in which he distinguishes "emancipation, as process of separation from external objects," from rebellion which "maintains the external relationship" with the object (p. 263). Loewald writes, "the (successful) process of internalization . . . involves a change in the internal organization of the elements. . . . The more clearly the aspects of an object relationship, for instance between father and son are internalized, become part of the son's inner world, the more they lose their object relation character. . . . In insufficient or in pathological distorted . . . development, the sexual-aggressive character of the internalized element is usually pronounced" (p. 51). Optimally, the ego's organizing activity allows for the re-creation of something old into something new. "In such recreation, the old is mastered . . . (;) mastery does not mean elimination of it, but dissolution, and reconstruction out of the elements of destruction" (p. 90). Loewald is speaking here of the destruction of the oedipal object tie, not the destruction of the representation of the object itself.

---

2. See an earlier version of the same paper (Cooper, 1996)

We can only hope that our rebellion has evolved into some measure of intellectual freedom. We sought neither to demolish nor to outdo our fathers but to do for ourselves, or, more simply, to do our own thing. As Cooper (1997) has written, "... our curriculum ... ought to be a clear reflection of our conception of the psychoanalytic enterprise" (p. 12). What I add here is that in our conception of this enterprise, we must understand that conflict among generations is, in itself, a creative developmental process. Even as I write, I expect that the design of our current curriculum is being challenged, indeed overthrown, by those who follow.

Part II

The Changing Ideas in Psychoanalysis

Change Moments in Therapy
ETHEL SPECTOR PERSON

Thirty years ago, most American analysts adhered to the drive-conflict model of pathogenesis and believed that change occurred primarily through interpretation, insight, and conflict resolution. They distinguished between facilitative changes – establishment of the therapeutic alliance, intensification of transference through transference interpretation – and definitive changes – identification and internalization, increased awareness of psychic continuity, utilization of insight, and renunciation of infantile wishes.

By the 1970s, a second major psychoanalytic paradigm emerged that encompassed overlapping theories of object relations, self psychology, intersubjectivity, and relational psychoanalysis. It replaced the earlier one-person model with a two-person model, using interactional, interpersonal, and subjectivist paradigms. All emphasize the therapeutic or working alliance as distinct from transference, the emotionally charged therapeutic relationship as a coequal one.

Conflict and deficit are universal and mutually interact in the course of development. To the degree that one sees one or the other as critical in pathology, one will favour particular technical prescriptions. Whatever theory one subscribes to, conventional wisdom holds that psychotherapeutic change occurs in gradual cumulative ways.

Yet change need not be gradual. Change moments are moments when the patient's perceptual, cognitive, or emotional world is experienced as suddenly significantly altered. They are experienced as discontinuous and seem to interrupt the therapy, to speed, alter, or torpedo its course, often to the surprise of both patient and therapist.

Such moments may be classified as turning points or transformations. Striking as these two classes are, little attention has been paid to their role in the therapeutic situation (exceptions are Böhm, 1992; Chused, 1996; Rothstein, 1997), possibly because they have a formal similarity to a now discredited model of change, based on a naive theory of turning points – the idea that a key interpretation might "turn on the light". While the notion of the pivotal interpretation has given way to a model stressing continuing and multiple acts of interpretation and working through, the importance of the sudden revelation remains pertinent to the recovery of traumatic memories. But like the working through of an interpretation, the recovery of traumatic memories must be assimilated.

Turning points occur in therapy with some frequency; transformations, to a lesser extent. To some degree, therapy may work *because* it makes use of our intrinsic capacity for change moments – for reconfigurations, for discontinuity. I will describe some change moments as they appear in life, literature, and therapy.

TURNING POINTS: EMOTIONAL/COGNITIVE RECONFIGURATIONS

Turning points encompass a subjective sense of a moment in time when one's world feels significantly altered to a greater or lesser degree as a result of changed perception, cognition, emotional set, or sense of the self-in-the-world. They are moments of re-visioning that alter perceptions of external or internal reality, of the past or the present, of the authorship of one's fate, or of the sense of the self in relation to the other. Turning points may be experienced as positive or negative and sometimes herald the sudden end of a relationship. Although it feels emergent, the turning point has often been prepared for by a long pre-history, in a process similar to that by which a creative insight appears as a sudden gift, even though it is the end product of the preconscious process of working through an idea or a hunch (Cannon, 1976, pp. 63–69).

Ibsen's play *A Doll's House* (1879) turns on an emotional-cognitive insight, through which Nora reorders her understanding of her past life in a way that dramatically impacts on her future. Nora is a women burdened by fear. Early in their marriage, Torvald becomes seriously ill. In order to take him to Italy where she hopes the sun might cure him, she forges the signature of her recently deceased father in order to borrow money. Repaying the loan ever since, she is terrified of being found out. Nils Krogstad, an employee in her husband's bank, learns that he may lose his job to Nora's friend Mrs. Linde. He threatens Nora that if he does, he will reveal the fact of her forgery. The play hinges on the problem of what will happen if Krogstad tells Torvald of Nora's secret. Krogstad places the dreaded letter in their letter-box. After reading Krogstad's letter, Torvald scolds his wife for disregarding decency and honesty and creating a major threat to his status. He won't divorce her, but will limit her exposure to their children. Nora becomes suicidal. Krogstad sends a second letter saying that, in remorse, he is destroying the forged bond.

When Torvald fears a public scandal, he violently attacks Nora; with the threat withdrawn he forgives her. Nora is not so much offended by Torvald's initial rejection as she is by his reversal. Far from seeing him as noble, she now sees him as merely self-interested and conventional. Nora understands that "for eight years" she has been living "with a complete stranger." She leaves, and slamming the door behind her, sets off reverberations not only in the theatre world but in a whole social movement to come.

Nora's re-visioning is a fictional example related to the idea of *nachträglichkeit*. For Laplanche and Pontalis, it is not lived experience in general that undergoes a deferred revision but, specifically, "whatever it has been impossible in the first instance to incorporate fully into a meaningful context. The traumatic event is the epitome of such unassimilated experience. . . . Deferred revision is occasioned by events and situations, or by an organic maturation, which allows the subject to gain access to a new level of meaning and to rework his earlier experiences" (Laplanche & Pontalis, 1973, p. 111). Although they see the traumatic situation as consisting of early sexual events, I use the concept of *nachträglichkeit* in a broader sense.

It's no accident that *A Doll's House*, a play about a woman whose sudden insight into the nature of her self-demeaning relationship to her husband (the "traumatic" situation) led to repudiation of her doll-like status and independent action, has become a literary touchstone of the Women's Movement. On the social level, the woman's movement provides the impetus for mass *nachträglichkeit*, a turning point for multitudes of women.

A turning point based on a rewritten narrative – an emotional-cognitive reinterpretation of past events – is a staple in psychotherapy. In an unpublished case presentation (1968) by Aaron Karush of the analysis of a black man, a turning point was pivotal. The patient criticized himself for what he thought was his paranoid distortion of an incident in which he was verbally attacked; first, he interpreted the exchange as racist, but quickly dismissed his perception as a distortion. He castigated himself for his skewed perception and self-pity. When Karush suggested that he *had* experienced prejudice directed against him, he was stunned, but relieved. In bringing in external reality, Karush addressed his patient's need to deny prejudice, relating it to his internalized self-hatred. His intervention focused on the patient's need to deny and opened his eyes, enabling him to re-vision the world and himself in it.

A woman friend described the turning point in her treatment as her analyst's statement that her mother appeared to have suffered from a psychotic depression. Now, rather than viewing herself as the irritant who undid her mother, she could dispense with her guilt and self-blame and begin to see the impact of her mother's depression on her.

Nora, the black patient, and my friend were all able to re-vision the world because of an incident or confrontation/interpretation that forced them to confront their denial, to acknowledge the injuries inflicted on them, and to work through their resulting internalized self-blame, guilt and shame.

Other perceptual-cognitive reconfigurations have more to do with new *self*-knowledge and the act of perceiving shortcomings or conflicts as *one's own*. Such self-knowledge can take the form of a sudden, almost blinding realization. One medical student entered treatment for depression, but a far more serious problem centred around some paranoid traits. He complained bitterly during almost every session of his difficulty in getting to my office by subway. He resisted any suggestion that his complaints were motivated by anything other than real-life difficulties. After some months, and with some exasperation, I commented that I knew his complaints to be motivated by resistance because no other patient travelling the same route – and he knew I was treating several people from the same hospital – had so persistently expressed annoyance. He was stunned and became willing for the first time to consider the meaning of his interminable complaints. He began to grasp that part of his suffering and sense of being burdened was self-induced, that it served some function in his psychic life. Just as interesting is the way it stayed in his mind. Years later, we met by chance, and he told me that he vividly remembered the subway session as the turning point in his analysis. It had revealed to him a dramatically new way of looking at his experience, one that he could consciously exercise thereafter in his subsequent forays into his own psyche.

Self-perceptions and insights such as these often occur in the context of transference. Addressing the question of what initiates the process of self-discovery in analysis, Chused (1996) suggests that for a patient to be able to utilize an analyst's words, something must happen that allows the patient to hear and perceive differently. She labels such change moments *informative experiences*: "[They] arise out of those analyst–patient interactions in which the anticipated, the consciously or unconsciously desired or provoked reaction, does not occur and what does occur is so jarring and discordant with expectations that action and thoughts are derailed, and expectations become suspect. . . . [They] create the emotional dissonance between expectation and experience needed for a shift in perceptual frame, so that what was once denied or ignored is now seen" (p. 1051).

Chused's patient, Alice, was a young girl who had been told that you could always get your analyst to talk by threatening to quit treatment. At a time when Chused felt she and Alice were enmeshed in a sticky transference–countertransference, Alice announced that she was going to quit. She followed this up with the question of whether it would be all right if they stopped the day before Thanksgiving. Chused responded, "Do you want my permission?" The response was unexpected, being both non-interpretive and non-accusatory. In Chused's juxtaposition of the threat of quitting and simultaneously "wanting permission", Alice got into touch with her fear of losing Chused (pp.1059–1060).

The analyst's abstinence may also trigger dissonance. Chused describes how a 33-year-old single doctor, feeling great shame over his "dependency longings," tried to appear detached. He denied any feelings for her and insisted he was in treatment only for his training. Chused remained quiet. After persistently criticizing her and asking why she didn't defend herself, he finally asked what the point of attack was if he couldn't entice her to an interesting discussion. Still she refused to engage. After some days, the patient lamented that nothing he said touched her. With those words, both he and Chused became aware that he *wanted* to "touch" her, but was using a maladaptive mode to try to do so. Earlier in the analysis when she rose to the bait and interpreted his defences, the "fight" between them satisfied his longing for connection, and he had no motivation for self-observation. Only when she removed herself from the interaction was he able to see his disappointment in *not* getting to her (pp. 1052–1053).

Chused sums up informative experiences as experiences that take the patient by surprise and "by creating disarray, chaos where once there was order . . . initiate a mini-'scientific revolution' within the mind of the patient, leading to a reorganization of mental representations of past experiences and perceptions" (p. 1060–1061).

The therapist's acknowledgment of a countertransference error also can be a change moment. One of the strengths of such a moment is that the patient understands the analyst's sincere – and not just token – belief that there is more than one unconscious mind in the room. These moments, too, depend upon an element of surprise. Here, the model of a two-person psychology is particularly relevant.

Thus far I have suggested that turning points have permanent effects in their own right and that they may serve as catalysts in the interpretive process. They also appear to serve an important function in memory. Many analysts concur that their patients, even those with good therapeutic outcomes, remember much of analysis as a blur, without clearly demarcated phases or any overarching, organizing insight. Kris (1956) observes "that insight in some individuals remains only a transient experience, one to be obliterated again in the course of life by one of the defences they are wont to use. And it is not my impression that these individuals are more predisposed to future illness than others" (p. 270). Neubauer (1979) calls it "striking that after analysis insight may not be maintained, particularly if we mean by it the memories of conscious retention of events, ideas and affects which entered awareness during the course of the analysis" (p. 34). Yet change persists nonetheless.

What *do* patients remember? There are no systematic studies. I believe that the most vivid memories of therapy comprise four kinds of events: (a) experiences that first demonstrate the existence of unconscious mental life; (b) dramatic cognitive-emotional insights that follow "confrontation" in the therapy; (c) analyst–patient interactions that alter either the patient's self-understanding or perception of the therapist; (d) emotional catharsis often connected with a specific and painful insight and/or some of the feeling tone of the therapy. Turning points, heavily represented in the first three categories, often serve as the memory beads through which the narrative thread of a therapy are strung.

TRANSFORMATIONS

Transformations are more global, more in the service of a reconfiguration of one's self-identity. Compared to turning points, transformations are relatively rare in the therapy situation. They are more like epiphanic reconfigurations, akin to the dramatic experiences of religious conversion or falling in love (Person, 1988).

In everyday life, transformation probably takes place most frequently through the act of falling in love. The feelings of newness and change that lovers experience is often so dramatic that it seems inconceivable to them that falling in love is an internal process. Rather, lovers experience love as a force that strikes them from the outside world – a thunderbolt, Cupid's arrow, a love potion, or, less fantastically, the inevitable impact of the beloved's irresistible charms.

The actual dynamics of love run counter to our subjective experience. Love arises from within lovers as an imaginative act, a creative synthesis, that aims to fulfill their deepest longing and their oldest dreams, that allows them both to renew and transform themselves. Such transformation depends on the way self, object, and self-object representations are transmuted. Our choice of lover, largely determined by internal need and preconscious pre-existing fantasies, determines the direction of internal change.

All transformations depend on what we might call transference relationships, whether to a god, the beloved, or a hero. Although some clinicians use the term *transference* only as it applies to the treatment situation, a number of analysts and social scientists are aware that the concept of transference, broadly understood, is useful in understanding a number of disparate phenomena that take place outside the treatment situation, not just in romantic love but in the propensity of so many people to attach themselves with extreme tenacity to causes as well as to people.

According to Freud, the emotional content of transference – whether toward a parent figure or toward God – is the child's longing for a powerful parent or surrogate who can serve "as protection against strange superior powers" (Freud, 1924, p. 24). First for the child, then for the adult, transference is invoked by the "need for protection against the consequences of his human weakness" (p. 24). We seek union with some representation of parental potency, not only out of erotic (libidinal) desire but also out of weakness and fear. Transference is a natural outgrowth of the terrors of the human condition – a means of "taming terror" (Becker, 1973, p. 145).

While transference plays a role in any broad-based theory of transformation, transformations in therapy itself are relatively few. But positive transference alone sometimes does catalyze radical change in patients, hence the term *transference cure*. While analysts argue that such change is superficial and that the symptoms may well reappear, this is not always the case.

Many patients use their short-term gains to consolidate a different (and better) self-perception and integration over the long term.

Transference love comprises a special case. Transference love is far easier to predict than romantic love, and is such a regular feature of so many analyses, regardless of the obvious incongruities between patient and therapist, that it almost appears to be random or promiscuous, whereas love in "real" life is much more selective.

Why does love take place so frequently within the therapeutic context? The patient comes to analysis only when he or she experiences some psychological disturbance or discontent, and hence wishes for change. Whatever its cause, the fact of the patient's own psychological insufficiency or discomfort is a narcissistic blow. S(he) is on the lookout for an external remedy. Thus, there is a clear prior tendency that would facilitate the patient's "falling in love" with the therapist (Person, 1988). Prospective patients sometimes have fantasies and dreams about the analyst even *before* analysis has begun. This is a preformed transference, needing only the blank screen of the actual analyst onto which to project itself. The analyst is the perfect foil for such fantasies because s(he) is, by and large, esteemed, respected. Need, imagination, and a blank screen on which the imagination can go to work sometimes seem sufficient to galvanize transference love into being, and that love may be sufficient to catalyze major, global change. Here, too, the experience of transformation is experienced as discontinuous, although continuity may be discerned in the preconscious.

When the patient does not fall in love with the therapist, what he or she sometimes does instead is to fall into identification. How else can we understand the ever expanding recruitment to the cadre of therapists of those individuals whose career paths were decided only in the course of their own therapies?

DISCUSSION

Psychoanalytic research has yet to devise a research methodology to correlate change with a particular therapeutic action, thus constituting a problem in privileging one psychoanalytic theory and its corollary theory of change over another. Short of being able to demonstrate the superiority of any one theory and its associated techniques, we have begun to historicize ourselves. We locate the sequences of re-theorizations not in a line of progressive scientific research, but in the relationship of psychoanalysis to the cultural *zeitgeist*.

Arnold Cooper (1987a) writes brilliantly of "the increasing influence of the modernist version of transference and interpretation [that] represents an adaptation to several long-term philosophical, scientific, and cultural shifts." This adaptation is in response to the "philosophical debate concerning the nature of history, veridicality, and narrative. . . . The analytic task [becomes] interpretation, *with* the patient, of the events of the analytic situation, usually broadly labelled transference – with a construction rather than a reconstruction of the past" (p. 83).

Peter Buckley (1997) notes that commentators, including Cooper, have placed the "revolutionary movement within psychoanalytic theory and practice within the framework of contemporary cultural currents such as post-modernism, the philosophical ascendency of synchrony . . . and hermeneutics." Instead, he suggests that we are "witnessing a late flowering of the romantic movement in which the new theoretical stance emphasizes individual subjectivity, the centrality of the emotional experience" (p. 577).

For me, the cultural change that plays the critical role in the increasing emphasis on intersubjectivity is the shift from a culture of authoritarianism to one the privileges individual autonomy. The erosion of a mutually agreed-upon power differential or agreed-upon hierarchical structure is the end product of the revision of previously shared fantasies about the ideal distribution of power (Person, 1995).

While we await the design and execution of such research projects as might address the mechanisms and efficacy of different therapeutic interventions, we must attempt to observe and describe in as much detail as possible the sequence of events that leads to change. Both turning points and transformations, which are experienced as abrupt changes at the conscious level, have yet to be systematically studied within the therapeutic situation to the same extent as insight and conflict resolution. Yet they are critically important not only in psychoanalysis and psychotherapy but in the course of life as well.

Normal and Pathological Narcissism in Women

EVA P. LESTER

Since Freud's 1914 original essay "On Narcissism: An Introduction", narcissistic issues, narcissistic love and object choice, narcissistic pathology, and, ultimately, the very essence of narcissism have been the subject of extensive writings in the psychoanalytic and the psychiatric literature. Furthermore, the terms *narcissism* and *narcissistic* have invaded everyday language. By becoming such an over-inclusive concept, narcissism is in danger of losing its theoretical and clinical specificity (Taylor, 1992).

This brief essay will examine the question of normal and pathological female narcissism, as well as the differences between the type of object choice among men and women as proposed by Freud in view of subsequent developments on gender and on the earliest stages of object relations. Freud himself was aware of the many unanswered questions his monograph raised. As quoted by Jones (see the Editor's Notes for Freud, 1914c), Freud wrote to Abraham, "The Narcissism had a difficult labour and bears all the marks of a corresponding deformation" (p. 70).

THE CONCEPT OF PRIMARY NARCISSISM

Long before infant observations had established that the human infant is equipped from birth to enter the world of human objects and to interact with such a world, M. Klein (1946a) was observing: "The analysis of very young children has taught me that there is no instinctual urge, no anxiety situation, no mental process which does not involve objects, external or internal; in other words, object relations are the centre of emotional life. Furthermore, love and hatred, fantasies, anxieties and defences are ab initio invisibly linked with object relations" (p. 52–53).

In recent decades, and on the strength of accumulating evidence from infant observations, Freud's original postulates of primary narcissism, autoerotism, and primary undifferentiation have drawn critical comments from several quarters. It is tempting to speculate that Freud's theory of primary undifferentiation in neonatal life was partly related to his relative lack of interest in, and opportunity for, controlled observation of infants and infant–mother interactions in infancy and early childhood. Thus, when Freud (1914c) remarked, "The highest phase of development of which libido is capable is seen in the state of being in love, when the subject seems to give up his own personality in favour of an object cathexis" (p. 76), he neglected to mention the other "highest phase", that is, the investing of the infant with object love by the mother in the average, "good enough", infant–mother dyad.

Infant observations in the last few decades have established that infants are equipped with a perceptual apparatus functioning ahead of the infant's motor development (Meltzoff & Moore, 1992). The young infant's large repertoire of behaviours points to the existence of a type of non-representational, evocative memory. The infant's considerable capacity for intermodal exchanges at birth, long before mental representations are established, allows for a complex interaction with the object from the beginning of postnatal life. What is internalized in postnatal life is not action itself but *interaction*. Stern's (1985) interiorized interaction patterns, RIGs, ("Representations of Interaction that have been Generalized", p. 97) include actions, perceptions, cognition, affect, and proprioceptive experience.

As the concept of primary narcissism elaborated by Freud is being questioned by developmentalists, the content, validity, and relevance of the term itself are equally questioned. Kernberg (1991) states, "In other words, I regard as highly questionable both the concept of autoerotism and that of a self and ego predating the psychic experience of the actual relation of the infant with the primary object" (p. 133).

Within this developmental frame of reference we may postulate that narcissistic libido, the self love of the mother, becomes object libido as it is invested in the infant. The foetus during pregnancy (Lester & Notman, 1988) and, later, the infant itself, through its needs and helplessness, arouses in the mother a strong empathic potential and the urge to protect and nurture. Mother's narcissistic libido, that is, her own investment in herself, diminishes as libido is being invested in the growing child. Such affective investment in the child by the parent allows the development of the child's grandiose self; eventually, and under normal circumstances, this grandiose self will be transformed into the child's Ego Ideal. Parts of the original affective investment, from mother to child, returns to the object as object cathexis of the mother – the first love object of the infant during the period of attachment (Bowlby, 1969). Primary narcissism can thus be seen as the earliest affective investment of the emerging self of the infant by the mother. Object love, in turn, represents not only mother's affective investment in the child, but also the child's love for the maternal object, first observed during the attachment period.

NARCISSISM AND OBJECT CHOICE

Reading the chapter on object choice in the 1914 monograph more than three quarters of a century later, one cannot but notice how historical, intellectual, and cultural positions are clearly reflected in Freud's propositions. Makari (1991) points out that Freud's views on women were strongly influenced by post-Kantian German subjective epistemologists, particularly by Schopenhauer and Nietzsche. He quotes Rieff (1959): "In the nineteenth century, strong links, the forging of which have not yet been closely studied, existed between irrationalism, philosophy and misogyny. Freud's views echo those of Schopenhauer and Nietzsche. . . . To varying degrees, Schopenhauer, Nietzsche and Freud, employed an idea of 'woman' that they equated with human sexuality and irrational truth" (p. 187). Although to some extent an empiricist, Freud went along with Schopenhauer's beliefs of woman dominated by irrational and sexual beliefs. As Makari points out, Freud's later writings on women were seriously hampered by his realization of how his own precarious and subjective position as a man trying to know woman, that is, his unresolved countertransference, was interfering with his understanding of women.

Freud's statement that "Complete object-love of the attachment type is, properly speaking, characteristic of the male" (p. 88) further suggests his middle-class, mid-European, nineteenth-century social environment with its strict ethical code and chivalrous overtones (Mill, 1869). The young woman's "narcissistic self absorption" leading to a narcissistic-anaclitic object choice, represented a historically and culturally determined behaviour of a certain group of women whose overriding preoccupation would be their attachment to a male. Freud's fascination with this particular female personality, generalized to include almost all females, is clearly seen in the following sentence: "Nor does their need lie in the direction of loving, but of being loved: and the man who fulfils this condition is the one who finds favour with them. The importance of this type of woman for the erotic life of mankind is to be rated very high. . . . For it seems very evident that another person's narcissism has a great attraction for those who have renounced part of their own narcissism and are in search of a love object" (p. 89). Reading the following paragraph, one wonders whether Freud was aware of the unfounded generalizations implied in his statements: "Perhaps it is not out of place here to give assurance that this description of the feminine form of erotic life is not due to any tendentious desire on my part to depreciate women" (p. 89).

GENDER AND NARCISSISTIC PATHOLOGY

It is being firmly established that gender represents an important variable in the development and treatment of psychological pathology. As Russo (1991) observed, "Gender differences in the rate and patterns of diagnosis are so dramatic that a basic test of any theory purporting to explain the aetiology of mental disorders must be the ability to account for these differences" (p. 44).

Although narcissistic traits are readily observed during analysis, structured narcissistic pathology of the Narcissistic Personality Disorder (NPD) type presents problems of categorization and differentiation. Kernberg (1988) points out that the presence of a variety of clinical pictures, overlapping, blending into each other, and usually lacking firm features to support definite categorization, make nosological classification difficult. Plakun (1989) maintains that, although the phenomenology of Borderline Personality Disorder (BPD) has more or less been studied and established, there are few available empirical data for NPD. Furthermore, the relationship of BPD to NPD remains unclear. Whether BPD represents the basic broad cluster of character pathology, the NPD being a subtype, or whether narcissistic personality pathology represents a completely separate diagnostic entity, is being debated. Kernberg (1988), among others, sees narcissism at the clinical level as referring "to the normal or pathological regulation of self-esteem or self-regard. Such regulation of self-esteem depends on the strictness and pressure of internalized norms and the internalization of positively invested objects" (ch. 18, p. 7).

Based on a well-designed study, Gunderson and Ronningstam (1991) conclude that ". . . it is possible to reliably identify patients with NPD and discriminate them with high accuracy from a mixed group of patients with related personality disorders and other psychiatric disturbances" (p. 116). Furthermore, ". . . grandiose self-experience, i.e., an unrealistic overvaluation of their own talents, invulnerability, uniqueness and superiority" (p. 117) were found to be the most pathognomonic characteristic of patients with NPD.

Although reliable epidemiological studies concerning the gender specificity of BPD and NPD are lacking, several authors have commented on such specificity. Thus Stone (1986; 1993) echoes several clinicians when he observes that BPD is, predominantly, seen in women. In their overview on NPD, Akhtar and Thompson (1982) state, "One of our observations, not in the literature, is that most of the patients who have been reported on are men" (p. 19). The authors question whether this is an accident of reporting, a diagnostic bias resulting from the "ambivalently special" attitude towards male children that places them at particular risk, or whether "the predominance of men [is] evidence that the development of the narcissistic personality is somewhat intertwined with male psychosexual development" (p. 19).

Discussing gender differences in narcissistic pathology, I will touch briefly on an issue that extends beyond psychosocial research. Ethnologists, according to Bach (1977a), have described a particular type of fantasy, the *narcissistic fantasy*, common to humans through the ages and across cultures. It is the fantasy of "exceptionality", which, because of its very nature, "assume[s] protean forms" (p. 288). Fantasies such as those of Godhead, of reincarnation, the Peter Pan fantasy, vampire and hermaphroditic fantasies, all contain the realization of the wish for extraordinariness. The various forms of the fantasy of exceptionality seem to refer, above all, to the wish for some unification of opposing states or concepts, a *coincidentia oppositorum*. "The *wise baby*, for example, joins 'young and unenlightened' with 'old and wise'; the *double, companion* or *androgyne* joins 'self' with 'other' and 'male' with 'female'; whereas *death of the self* and *rope to heaven* join 'life' with 'death' and 'earth' with 'heaven'" (p. 291, italics in original). Bach quotes Eliade (1965): ". . . many beliefs implying the coincidentia oppositorum reveal a nostalgia for a lost Paradise, a nostalgia for a paradoxical state in which the contraries exist side by side without conflict, and the multiplications form aspects of a *mysterious Unity*" (p. 291, italics added).

Bach notes that the "bipolar conceptual grouping" (p. 291), characteristic of these narcissistic fantasies, first appears in infancy and early childhood, before concrete separation into opposites (self–other, young–old, etc.) forces such a unification wish into the realm of unconscious fantasy. "It may be that the 'unification of opposites' bespeaks either a developmental defect in the self-definitional framework, or a defensive or creative regression involving a dedifferentiation of the self and the surrender of the hard-won achievement for defining, limiting and objectivizing that self within the context of our cultural 'reality'" (p. 291–292).

It is here proposed that pregnancy and early infant care may represent a biologically determined and socially sanctioned partial gratification of the wish for the *mysterious unity* that lies at the basis of many narcissistic fantasies. Winnicott's aphorism that there is not such a thing as a baby, there is only a baby and mother; the myths and tales of child helplessness and maternal fortitude; and, in our own analytic experience, the ambivalent wish for separateness and fusion played out in the maternal transference during analysis, all point to the biological basis of the female's preparedness to enter into a specific form of relationship with the object. Such a relationship could be seen as the very prototype of the mysterious unity at the basis of all narcissistic wishes. It could be proposed that such preparedness and specificity of behaviours in the female may represent a measure of protection against the development of the grandiose self. In the male, on the other hand, the presence of the grandiose self can be seen as a *defensive overcompensation* of deficient parenting in early life (Kernberg, 1988).

Richman and Flaherty (1988), specifically addressing gender differences in the expression of narcissistic personality traits among a sample of first-year medical students, found evidence to support the hypothesis that males, "protecting a core of grandiose self-corrections" related to their early attempts to separate from the powerful primary object, show unusual sensitivity to criticism; females, on the other hand, react dysphorically to what they perceive as indifference, which, the authors believe, may symbolize the rejection of the female's basic need for merger with the powerful primary object. The authors state: "The sex differences involving the greater male prevalence of grandiosity, fantasies of unlimited success and lack of empathy, in contrast to the greater female experience of distress in response to the indifference of others, could be interpreted as consistent with the thesis that early object relations patterns give rise to exaggerated male needs for differentiation . . . and female needs for merger with objects" (p. 375–376).

The above confirms other research findings (Gilligan, 1982; Le Vine, 1991; Stoller, 1976; 1985) pointing to the female's greater need to maintain connection and communication within the existing object relations network, in contrast to the male's need for separation from the primary object, exploration of the material world, and, often, a tendency to establish dominance within the relational network.

Infant research based on direct observations seems to confirm gender-related difference in interpersonal relations. Notman and Nadelson (1991) state: "In sum, two different patterns emerge for girls and boys. Female neonates with their more stable state system, increased awareness of the outside world, and greater involvement in gazing and vocalization, show an increased potential for greater connectedness to the caregiver" (p. 32). Differences are also observed with regard to bonding and attachment, universal developmental steps in all infants. Thus, "The male's greater irritability and lessened responsiveness to calming and soothing make over stimulation a greater concern for the male neonate. The mother's animated face and her gazing, given the male's less stable state system, may be experienced as too arousing. An increase in fussiness, crying, or gaze aversion may follow from this arousal" (p. 32).

CONCLUSIONS

Rapidly accumulating data from infant developmental studies force us to reconsider earlier positions on primary and secondary narcissism, narcissistic object choice, and gender-related differences in these areas. Well-designed clinical studies provide the necessary empirical data for the description, categorization, and classification of NPD as a discrete clinical entity, the central dynamic feature of which appears to be the grandiose experience within the self-system.

Although narcissistic manifestations are not uncommon in women, the well-articulated NPD is, it seems likely, a male personality disorder. It is proposed that the interplay between biological and sociocultural factors may "protect" the female against the development of this personality disorder. Thus, the pregnancy itself, but mostly infant and child care, universally and through the ages entrusted to women, may represent a defensive compensation against "narcissistic self-absorption" as well as against the fantasy of the neglected baby.

"Mourning and Melancholia" Eighty Years Later

OTTO F. KERNBERG

"Mourning and Melancholia" is Freud's (1917e) first and fundamental contribution to the psychoanalytic understanding of normal and pathological mourning, the psychopathology of major affective disorders, and the psychodynamic determinants of depression. At the same time, it also marks major developments in psychoanalytic theory at large, particularly the early formulations of the concept of the superego, the fundamental nature of identification processes, and the role of aggression in psychopathology. There are several strikingly original and fundamental propositions in the theory of the psychopathology of depression put forth in "Mourning and Melancholia". These include the central importance of aggression turned against the self when intensely ambivalent object investments are lost; the role of the superego in this self-directed aggression; the split in the self revealed in the superego's attack on the ego; and the fusion of another part of the self with an internalized object as the victim of that attack.

In what follows, I shall attempt to provide an overview of the development of Freud's ground-breaking discoveries regarding depression and identification in "Mourning and Melancholia", and how these ideas are reflected in our current psychoanalytic understanding of depression and of identification and its central role in the build-up of psychic structures.

First, regarding the contemporary theory of depression, I believe that the contributions of Karl Abraham (1924), Melanie Klein (1940), Edward Bibring (1953), and Edith Jacobson (1971) permit us to formulate a contemporary psychoanalytic theory of depression. Melanie Klein, in her description of the depressive position, pointed to the splitting, in the mind of the infant, of idealized relations with mother from persecutory ones, and to the generation of guilt and depression when integration of these mutually split segments of the ego or self and of the corresponding internal objects would bring about the infant's awareness of his own aggression against the ideal mother. Klein pointed to the normal consolidation of the good internal object and the ego when aggression was not excessive, and how conditions promoting marked dominance of aggressive over libidinal investments prevent such a normal integration, with the resulting intolerance of ambivalence and lack of assurance of one's own goodness creating the predisposition to pathological mourning and melancholia. In contrast to Freud, she felt that in normal mourning there was an unconscious process of reinstating the early good internal object, and that ambivalence characterized normality as well as pathology.

Edward Bibring's (1953) description of depression as the result of the acknowledgment of the loss of an ideal state of self in the context of a severe discrepancy between the ideal self and the real self pointed to the affect of depression as an ego potential predating the differentiation of the superego from the ego. In my view, the potential for the affective reaction of depression to loss of an ideal ego or self state is compatible with Melanie Klein's (1946b) description of the depressive position, when the aggression stemming from the self can be acknowledged as part of the tolerance of ambivalence, and when the implicit comparison between a past illusory, split-off, idealized self and the realistic, integrated, present one signals the loss of that ideal self state.

Edith Jacobson's (1971) analysis of normal, neurotic, borderline, and psychotic depression mapped out a comprehensive psychoanalytic theory of the psychopathology of depression. Jacobson described the originally fused or undifferentiated units of self and object representations in both the libidinal and aggressive domains of experience, and the defensive re-fusion of libidinal self and object representations under conditions of psychotic regression. In psychotic depression, this regressive re-fusion would also affect the aggressively invested self and object representations in the ego, and would involve as well a re-fusion of the earliest aggressive superego precursors with the later idealized ones. It is the regressive fusion of persecutory and idealized object representations in the superego that brings about the sadistic demand for perfection and the typical cruelty of the superego in melancholia. The attacks of this sadistic superego are directed towards the units of fused aggressive self and object representations in the ego. In the process, the frail remnant of the idealized segment of the self that was overwhelmed in the total re-fusion process occurring in the ego succumbs to the generalized activation of guilt, despair, and self-accusation, and as a consequence evolve the nihilistic, hypochondriacal, and self-devaluing delusions of psychotic depression.

Jacobson proposed that in borderline conditions the boundaries between self and object representations in both the libidinal and the aggressive segment of internalized object relations persist, facilitating the defensive processes of dissociation, depersonalization, and projection that help these patients avoid the sadistic superego attacks characteristic of depression. In neurotic depression, a sufficiently well-integrated self relating to integrated representations of significant others still experiences the attacks of the superego in the form of exaggerated, pathological guilt and self-devaluation. But such a well-integrated self suffers neither the fusion processes that, in melancholia, transform guilt into a total, delusional devaluation of the self identified with the object, nor the primitive defences characteristic of borderline conditions.

In all these psychoanalytic theories of depression, depressive affect emerges as the link between the basic experience of loss of an ideal state of self as the result of the loss of an object, with the loss of the object itself assumed to be caused by one's own aggression. John Bowlby's (1969) and his followers' empirical research on normal attachment and its pathology, and the description of the stages of protest, despair, and detachment as a result of catastrophically prolonged separation of the infant from mother, provided a fundamental link between the psychoanalytic theory of depression, on one hand, and the reaction to early separation, on the other. Early separation from mother, if excessive or traumatic, triggers depressive affect as a basic psychophysiological reaction, and depressive affect is similarly triggered by an internal sense of loss of the relation between the self and the good internal object derived from the superego's attack on the self. Early separations trigger depressive affects, a chain reaction of rage, despair, and despondency and their corresponding neuro-hormonal correlates, as we now know, in humans as well as other primates (Suomi, 1995). This link between felt emotion and neurochemical response begins to connect the psychoanalytic theory of internalized object relations with biological research into the genetic and neurobiological determinants of aggressive and depressive affect. Depressive affect is the basis response to the loss of external and internal good objects and the related loss of an ideal state of self.

Freud had speculated on the organic determinants of the circadian nature of melancholic illness. Contemporary research on the genetic disposition to major affective illness, its potential relation to abnormality in the adrenergic, noradrenergic, dopaminergic, and serotinergic systems regulating depressive affect, and on the hyperactivity of the hypothalamic-pituitary-adrenal systems in depression and under conditions of stress, has opened the field for the study of the biological determinants of affect, and of depressive affect as the bridge between biological and psychodynamic determinants of depression as a clinical phenomenon (Nemeroff, 1996).

At this time psychoanalysis and neurobiology are still too far apart in their focus and methodology to permit any satisfactory integration. I believe, however, that it is now reasonable to assume that the psychopathology of depression may be determined by a complementary set of aetiological factors. These include, on the biological side, an abnormal, genetically determined, and neurochemically controlled activation of the affect of depression under conditions of early separation and object loss and, on the psychological side, the development of pathological ego and superego structures under conditions of severe, constitutionally determined, or environmentally caused activation of aggressive affect, with the consequent threat to the normal dominance of libidinally invested internalized object relations in ego and superego over those invested with aggression.

The work of Melanie Klein and Edith Jacobson has enriched the analysis of normal and pathological depressive reactions through delineation of the role of the primitive defensive operations of splitting, idealization, projection and introjection, projective identification, denial, omnipotence, and devaluation. A central dynamic described by both authors is that of a vicious cycle of early aggressive response to frustration, the infant's tendency to project his own aggression onto the frustrating object, and the re-internalization of that aggressively perceived object into the basic layer of the early superego in the form of persecutory internalized object representations.

These vicissitudes of early aggression complement the vicissitudes of normal and pathological withdrawal of libidinal investment spelled out by Freud in "Mourning and Melancholia". While Freud pointed to the crucial function of aggression toward the object in melancholia, his dual drive theory had not yet been formulated. By the same token, of course, the theory of the superego had only emerged very recently at the time of this paper. Both the structural development of the superego so brilliantly described by Edith Jacobson, and the vicissitudes of the aggressive drive spelled out later by Melanie Klein and Freud himself, were important components of the evolving theory of depression.

Perhaps the major theoretical formulation initiated in "Mourning and Melancholia", transcending the subject of depression, was the concept of identification, our next subject. Here, I believe, the work of Ronald Fairbairn (1952a) and Edith Jacobson (1964), who arrived independently at remarkably similar conclusions regarding this essential mechanism, provides major contributions to Freud's original observations in "Mourning and Melancholia" (1917e), "Group Psychology and the Analysis of the Ego" (1921c), and "The Ego and the Id" (1923b). Summarizing in the briefest possible way how I conceptualize the contemporary view of identification, I would stress as a central concept the definition of *identification* as an internalization of a significant object relationship: in other words, the internalization of a representation of the object interacting with a representation of the self under the impact of an intense affect. The more intense the affect, the more significant the object relation, and the more significant the object relation, the more intense the affect state. Here this theory of identification overlaps with the theory of the centrality of depressive affect in normal and pathological mourning: the more intense the predisposition to react with depressive affect to separation or loss, the more severe the identification with an abandoned object and with an abandoning self. The more severe the experience of rejection or loss of a good external or internal object, the more severe the potential for depression.

Whether one accepts Edith Jacobson's proposal that libido and aggression always enter psychic structures as libidinal or aggressive affects linking self with object representations, or whether one accepts Fairbairn's proposal that libidinal investments of internalized object relations (in the form of libidinal self and object representations) constitute the basic human response, with aggressive investments of internalized object relations developing only in response to a frustration of basic libidinal needs, or whether one accepts my theoretical formulation (1992) that conceives of libidinal and aggressive drives as the hierarchically supraordinate integration of corresponding, basic libidinal and aggressive affects, the concept of identification as the internalization of a significant object relationship (the identification being with the interaction of self and object and not only with the object or the self in that interaction) constitutes a common ground.

This concept of identification permits us to conceive of the development of ego and superego structures as resulting from a progressive integration of dyadic units of self representation-object representation-affect state with each other. Ego structures would thus include an integrated concept of the self and integrated concepts of significant others with whom the self is in internalized interaction. Superego structures would include integrated layers of persecutory, idealized, and realistic internalized object relations. There would be a buildup of idealized object representations in both ego and superego, the idealized representations of self and objects in the superego jointly constituting the ego ideal, and such idealized representations in the ego representing desired or aspired to aspects of self and of relations with significant others. The most intense, intolerable aggressive and sexualized dyadic units would be repressed and constitute the id. In short, the dyadic units of internalized object relations constitute the building blocks of ego, superego, and id.

This concept of identification explains the typical enactment, by borderline patients, at different times, of an identification with the self representation while the corresponding object representation is projected onto the therapist, or with the object representation while projecting the self representation onto him, and the corresponding mechanisms of identification with the aggressor, the transformation of passive into active, and the dynamics of omnipotent control and projective identification in the transference. Identification with the relationship between self and object also explains the consistent loss of a state of ideal self with the loss of an ideal, good object.

Returning once more to the determinants of normal and pathological depression, we can now conceive of a genetic disposition to pathological activation of aggressive affects that will be integrated into the aggressive drive, in the form of a structured sense of self or object as victim or persecutor, self and object bound by affects of fear, rage, etc. The result is proneness to the excessive activation of rage, anxiety, and despair under conditions of frustration and object loss. Temperament as a genetically determined, constitutionally given disposition to a certain intensity, rhythm, and threshold of affect activation would link the innate disposition to aggression with the traumatic effects of early separation, trauma, and frustration in the internalization of object relations. By far the most important determinant of the internalized object relations expressed in the tripartite psychic structure will be the earliest mother–infant interaction. This early interaction, however, may not necessarily be "pregenital" and include early development of eroticism and sadomasochism in the context of an archaic Oedipus complex (Chasseguet-Smirgel, 1986).

Severe frustration and trauma in this early interaction, with consequent excessive activation of aggressive and depressive affect, would then give rise to the structural consolidation of a psychic apparatus with a "hypertrophic" superego, and the predisposition to depressive reactions with relatively minor triggering factors from the environment. Extremely severe inborn disposition to depressive affect would exacerbate the development of such pathological structures, while, on the other extreme, even without any genetic disposition, the structural consequences of severe frustration and trauma, with a consequent activation of excessive aggression, would contribute to the build-up of a severely pathological, though well-integrated, superego structure predisposing to depression in later life.

A depressive-masochistic personality structure predisposes to characterological depression and to a superego determined loss of normal self-esteem under conditions of multiple sources of unconscious guilt, the counterpart to the activation of anxiety as a non-specific manifestation of danger derived from unconscious intrapsychic conflict (Kernberg, 1992). Anxiety, in fact, also may be functioning as a precursor of impending danger of unconscious guilt and object loss leading to depression.

"Mourning and Melancholia" points to the central importance of pathologically intense ambivalence, self-directed aggression, severe pathology of internalized object relations, and a constitutional disposition to the activation of depressive affect. It is remarkable how these basic components of Freud's contribution continue at the very centre of our contemporary psychoanalytic theory of depressive pathology. Edith Jacobson's (1971) definition of *moods* as generalized affects that, for a period of time, affect the entire world of internalized object relations points to the mutual reinforcement of the two major aetiological factors in depression: the intensity of depressive affect and the pathology of internalized object relations.

Insofar as the pathology of internalized object relations and of depressive affect both relate to the psychopathology of aggression, a major and controversial issue in contemporary psychoanalytic thinking is the relationship between aggressive drive, affects, and object relations. The sharp division between psychoanalytic object relations theories that reject the concept of drives and those other psychoanalytic object relations theories that affirm the central motivational nature of drives constitutes a major focus of contemporary psychoanalytic theory development. I have stressed, throughout my work in this area, that I see an eminent compatibility and complementarity of the dual drive theory with the theory of structure formation by internalized object relations. The concept of the relationship between affects as instinctive components and drives as hierarchically supraordinate motivational systems permits us, I believe, to do justice to the unconscious motivational forces described by Freud while beginning to integrate psychoanalysis and neurobiology by means of the analysis of the determinants and vicissitudes of affects.

The Role of Curiosity in Psychoanalysis: Changes in My Technique in the Past Fifteen Years

EDWARD NERSESSIAN

Some 15 years ago I was confronted for the first time with a patient who, while perfectly willing to say what came to his mind, did not want to think about the meaning of his associations. Whenever I asked him about an aspect of his thoughts, he was in the habit of answering that he was there to tell me everything and it was my job to figure out what it meant. An intensely exhibitionistic and voyeuristic man, he showed no curiosity vis-à-vis his own associations nor vis-à-vis a whole array of symptomatic behaviour. In a certain way, he was pointing out the inadequacy of the so-called "basic rule". Other patients, when encouraged to say what came to their mind, had spontaneously reflected about it and, therefore, had not provided the opportunity to observe a situation where self-reflection was missing. This patient offered just such an opportunity and this experience was instrumental in my becoming aware of the role of curiosity in psychoanalytic treatment, which resulted in a paper entitled: "Some Reflections on Curiosity and Psychoanalytic Technique" (Nersessian, 1995). Since that time, I have continued to be affected in my analytic work by the attention that I pay to this function and, while it is impossible to hold any one factor as central in one's clinical development, I think my technique has been strongly affected by this focus.

In the paper mentioned above, my interest was more focused on the analyst and therefore I discussed curiosity under the broader subject of analytic listening. For a long time, the analysand's free association has had its counterpart in the analyst's free-floating attention. While agreeing that such a mental attitude is indeed useful, I have argued for a greater recognition of a need for a more active stance, one directed by curiosity. Guided by his or her curiosity, the analyst listens and intervenes in a variety of ways, including asking questions, delineating the patient's problems, illustrating conflicts, and, as part of this process, the analyst gains insights that are then communicated to the analysand. This more active stance on the part of the analyst can best be maintained when the analyst's curiosity is freed from its conflictual offspring of voyeurism. Over time, the analysand too becomes freer in exercising his or her curiosity through an analysis of conflicts, particularly around voyeuristic issues, and also, and I consider this crucial, by identifying with the analyst and developing the same posture of inquiry vis-à-vis his thoughts, defences, fantasies, actions, and memories. Some, especially those in the French school and particularly those following the ideas of Lacan, will look at this proposal with disdain, since any identification with the analyst is considered as too closely related to suggestion and of no value (some would say deleterious) to the exploration of the unconscious. I, however, think quite the opposite, namely that identifying with the analyst's curiosity is of major assistance to analytic work and of value to the patient. In fact, my attention has increasingly focused on the vicissitudes of curiosity in the analysand, and I have come to think that the monitoring of this function can provide us with useful information not only with regard to the underlying conflicts but also in terms of the more subtle and prevalent shifts in resistance.

I distinguish curiosity from attention; the analyst pays attention to all aspects of the analysand's associations, feelings, and behaviour, but is curious only about some of them. Assuming that the analyst's curiosity is not overly burdened by conflict, what determines its direction? First and foremost the curiosity of a psychoanalyst is an educated curiosity, by which I mean it is specific to the psychoanalytic situation, influenced by his education as a psychoanalyst. This education includes his or her personal analysis, theoretical and clinical teachings, supervision, study groups with other colleagues, experience with other patients, adherence to certain schools, and interest in certain areas of theory. In addition to this education the curiosity of a psychoanalyst is also influenced by the analyst's personal experiences, current life circumstances, current interests, his or her predominant mood of the moment, and other matters that impinge on his or her mind with or without conscious awareness. This educated curiosity is then brought to bear on the material presented by the patient.

By observing the curiosity of analysands towards their thoughts, feelings, and fantasies I have come to pay close attention to ego functions that are closely allied to the attribute of curiosity. These functions have to do with looking at oneself and have been described in the literature by Freud (1933), Sterba (1934), Gray (1986), and Busch (1995), though, as the following discussion and the clinical example will demonstrate, there are differences between my conceptualization and theirs.

First Freud and later Sterba recognized the capacity of the ego to observe itself, with Sterba putting a special emphasis on the role and fate of this function in psychoanalysis. I find it useful for psychoanalytic work to distinguish conscious self-monitoring of thought from self-reflection. For example, when someone speaks, there is an ongoing check of a variety of things that take place simultaneously: how to say what one is trying to say, how to form the sentences in a grammatically correct way, when to express an affect and when not to, an assessment of the possible reactions of the other person, what to say and what not to say, and so on. It is aspects of self-monitoring that we ask patients to observe and to report on, in addition to reporting their thoughts. Freud increasingly connected self-observation to what came to be the superego. I think it is clinically useful to view it that way since it underscores the usefulness of early interpretations of superego resistances. As this is done, however, the analysand – pushed in part by his curiosity and in part through identification with the analyst's curiosity – begins to reflect upon his thoughts, fantasies, emotions, and behaviour. Self-reflection, therefore, involves an attempt at making sense of one's associations and paves the way towards self-inquiry, which is already about discovering motivation and in particular unconscious motivation. Stated in a schematic way: a patient reports that on his way to the office he thought of smashing the window of a taxi-cab. He adds that he was debating whether he should tell this to the analyst (self-observation), and then wonders why he was thinking this and recalls the analyst had told him about a week's break (self-reflection). The patient asks himself why he should be upset about the break and this question results in a series of associations and a search for reasons (self-inquiry). Whereas self-observation is related to the workings of the superego, self-reflection and self-inquiry fall more within the realm of the ego.

There are two issues that I would like to take up here with regard to self-reflection and self-inquiry. First, Why are they important? and second, How can they be promoted?

These functions are important in analysis because they are the psychoanalyst's helpers. They help enlarge the analyst's field of vision into the patient's mind, and help decrease the number of educated guesses that one has to occasionally make. They also contribute to the working partnership of analysand and analyst, a partnership that the patient mentioned earlier was opposed to. His interest was in defeating the analyst rather than helping him.

What I specifically attempt to achieve is to have the analysand become curious about his or her thoughts, fantasies, memories, and acts, as well as the inevitable accompanying defences. While self-observation does not require curiosity, I believe genuine self-inquiry cannot happen without it.

The role of curiosity and its related functions in my day-to-day clinical work can best be illustrated by clinical examples, with an elucidation of my thinking processes as the material unfolds.

> Mr. O. began his Monday session with the following words: " For the last few days or maybe a week now, I have reached a plateau in terms of my thoughts. . . . I have no new material."
>
> After a moment's silence, during which I was weighing in my mind various ways to respond or not to respond to this introduction to the hour, I said: "Your recognizing this and bringing it up here is new material".
>
> Mr. O.: "Ha, I did not look at it that way, I did not look at the process, I just looked at the substance. . . ."
>
> After a brief moment, Mr. O. began to describe how during the weekend he was aware of thoughts and then would quickly try not to grasp them. He saw it as almost flirting with his thoughts: "What is this thought, is it serious, is it to be laughed at, is it just fantastic." He had a dream but now did not know what it was about; it seemed like a recurring dream. It made him think of dreams he had in college about having an examination and not being ready for it. He was with his brother over the weekend and, looking at his brother's 2½-year-old son, he was thinking about whether the way they related to the child could affect the child. "It had never occurred to me in a tangible way. I couldn't help feeling that this little person is being formed."
>
> The next day Mr. O. described how, since the session, he had noticed himself observing the fragments of thoughts that went through his mind. He could see the pieces and then they would disappear but keep impinging on his mind, and along with this he would feel a bit of anxiety. Following this, for the first time he reported his daydreams involving rescuing people in difficulty. Sometimes it would be a policeman being attacked; he would be passing by and would wrestle with the assailant and save the policeman.

To those trained in classical technique, the shift in the type of intervention must be clear. Even though my attention was drawn to the announcement by the patient that he was encountering resistance, I chose not to interfere in ways I would have done some years ago. Previously, if I had any idea about what was involved, I might have interpreted it; or I might have simply told the patient that he must be about to have some thoughts he would rather not have; or I might have focused my attention on the use of the word "plateau" and inquired about that; or I might just have waited. In the intervention I actually offered, what I was doing was to sharpen the patient's self-reflective capacity. It was an intervention directed not at bringing to the patient's attention the ego's defensive manoeuvre, but a direct approach encouraging the patient to look inwards. I emphasized the patient's recognition that he was in fact observing himself within the framework of psychoanalysis, and he was recognizing something about what was going on. Hence he was already inadvertently shifting the balance away from the need to defend against certain thoughts (and daydreams) that he was uncomfortable with, and instead was leaning more towards self-observation. The fact that there appeared to be some prohibition and criticism in regard to his observation and daydreams – he was, in my terminology, not self-reflecting but observing – indicated there was still too large a contribution from the superego, and underscored the need to be attentive to this aspect of his mental functioning and give it the necessary weight in interpretations.

The material that follows shows the patient's ability to observe himself and, on occasion, to reflect on his thoughts. The session, I believe, demonstrates the effect of my approach. Over the six months of the analysis, I had interpreted the various impediments to his looking at himself, in particular the various contributions of the superego. In focusing on this aspect of the material, it is important not to lose sight of the various levels of content. Just as the patient's curiosity is directed towards his thoughts, the analyst's curiosity is also directed at the material and the various latent meanings:

> Mr. O.: "Over the last few days I have realized to what degree I stop myself from divulging my thoughts. Sometimes I don't divulge them to myself. Fear plays a role in that: fear of criticism, of appropriateness. In some way it connects also to self-worth, in the sense that it takes guts just to put your thoughts out there, which is at the centre of what this is all about. That's what comes to my mind; I should recognize and speak it out, and then I can sort out the garbage, although it will probably all be relevant. This is all in an area of sexual thoughts. It is like I once mentioned trauma in adolescence contributed to feeling squashed. In 7th to 8th grade with puberty I felt like I hit a wall. Some-

how, the depth of what happened at that age was sufficiently traumatic that it continues to repress my thoughts, particularly sexual thoughts but other thoughts also. One of the things that was stirred up over the weekend was sexual thoughts and feelings about old girlfriends, a couple in particular. In the book I'm reading, there are descriptions of heterosexual and homosexual acts and thoughts, if you will. Everything from affection to anger is what resonated with me, thinking of my own experiences. Two women in particular, Carrie and Emma. What stimulated the connection was the unbounded types of sex we had, specially with Carrie. She was very unbounded, in terms of what we experimented with, anal sex, different positions, no physical constraints about what we would do to each other and with each other. There was tremendous sexual energy and also the breadth of emotion that we kind of afforded one another. If she was in a more active mood or passive mood, or aggressive and hostile mood, it was all allowed to go on. It created a lot of intensity. But something traumatic happened at the end of the relationship, and I'm sure a lot more went on that I've repressed. In addition to some realistic concerns of mine, what happened was more than that. She didn't want it to end and I just withdrew. I wasn't very loving and thoughtful about her feelings and as a result our whole relationship broke. As things got very intense with Carrie I avoided intensity, I withdrew into a state which is like fugue described in the book. I avoided revealing myself."

Choosing to interpret at the level I have indicated in this material does not mean that at other times the interpretation may not be aimed more directly at the content. In the above material, there were a number of issues that drew my attention but that I refrained from interpreting immediately. I wondered what connection there might have been between the revelation and content of the rescue fantasies and the material cited above. Furthermore, I found myself curious about his attention being so strongly drawn by the notion of fugue. I also noticed his mentioning homosexuality, as he had done a number of times in the past, and asked myself if there was something he was having difficulty bringing up in his analysis. On a more speculative level, I wondered about his comment that he could see the fragments of thought that would disappear from his mind and then keep impinging, accompanied by uneasiness. It brought to my mind the report by Lewin (1973) about the two tumblers that rolled away and disappeared, which supported his notion of the dream screen. I thought about the patient's relationship to his mother and the possibility of an underlying depression. Naturally, as always I kept an eye on the transference, which for the time being was one where I was a mentor.

The modification in my technique as a result of my interest in the vicissitudes of curiosity has also been useful in the analysis of patients who are very familiar and knowledgeable about psychoanalytic theory. In a number of such cases the analysand's response to interpretations is to offer associations that confirm the interpretation but do not open the door to further material. In such situations the analysands behave similarly in their self-analysis, explaining their reactions and fantasies in a somewhat theoretical way. In my experience, they are not curious, but have answers. While, in some of these cases, the training situation itself reinforces the defences against curiosity because of the relatively easy accessibility of information about the analyst, nevertheless this form of resistance (only partially iatrogenic) to analytic exploration can best be recognized, in my view, when the analyst focuses on evaluating the curiosity of the analysand. It then becomes essential to analyse the obstacles to curiosity before embarking on other interpretations.

Curiosity and the related ability to tolerate uncertainty are, I believe, essential attributes in both parties in an analysis, and any impediment to them needs to be the subject of analytic scrutiny.

The Shy Narcissist[1]

SALMAN AKHTAR

Ever since the *DSM-III* recognized Narcissistic Personality Disorder as a distinct entity, attempts have been made to refine its phenomenological portrait. An important aspect of these efforts (Akhtar, 1989; Akhtar & Thomson, 1982; Cooper, 1989a; Horowitz, 1989; Kernberg, 1989; Ronningstam, 1988; Ronningstam & Gunderson, 1989) has been to note that the characteristic manifestations of this disorder – grandiosity, exhibitionism, envy, ambition – are sometimes hidden underneath a superficial facade of modesty and shyness. A detailed clinical description of this variant of narcissistic personality disorder, and of its distinctions from the usual flamboyant type, have not yet been provided.

In this paper, I will attempt to delineate the profile of such a "shy narcissist". I will do so by combining the insights gleaned from (1) revisiting the pertinent material covered in my two earlier reviews (Akhtar, 1989; Akhtar & Thomson, 1982) of the literature on narcissistic personality; (2) relevant publications by others since my last review of the topic; and (3) my own experience of treating narcissistic patients. I will also highlight the similarities and differences the shy narcissistic personality has with the usual narcissistic personality and certain other personality disorders. I will conclude by commenting upon the implications of recognizing this syndrome.

---

1. Presented at the Annual Meetings of the American Psychiatric Association in San Diego, California, May 18, 1997. The author wishes to thank the discussants Drs. Arnold Cooper and Otto Kernberg for their valuable comments on this paper.

SURVEY OF THE LITERATURE

Freud introduced the term *narcissism* into psychiatric literature (Freud, 1905d) and delineated its role in object choices and ego-ideal formation (Freud, 1914c). Later, he described the "narcissistic character type" (Freud, 1931a) and noted its impressive, assertive, and power-seeking attributes. Freud's pioneering description, however, offered little clue regarding the existence of a shy or covert type of narcissistic personality.

The first such hint is found in a paper by Jones (1964), written 18 years before Freud's 1931 description of the narcissistic character. While the term *narcissistic personality* does not appear in Jones's paper, the "God complex" it described is perhaps the first portrayal of the condition. Jones eloquently described the narcissist's grandiosity, exaggerated need for praise, search for glory, and love of language. More significantly, he noted that narcissistic grandiosity is often masked by an "unusually strong series" of opposing tendencies. Prominent among these were undue humility, social reserve, and pretended contempt for money in real life. Unlike the flamboyant, openly acquisitive, and assertive type of narcissistic personality, such individuals are:

> characterized by a desire for aloofness, inaccessibility, and mysteriousness, often also by a modesty and self-effacement. They are happiest in their own home, in privacy and seclusion, and like to withdraw to a distance. They surround themselves and their opinions with a cloud of mystery, exert only an indirect influence on external affairs, never join in any common action, and are generally unsocial. They take great interest in psychology . . . phantasies of power are common, especially the idea of possessing great wealth. They believe themselves to be omniscient, and tend to reject all new knowledge. [p. 262]

Following Jones, Reich (1933) also noted that narcissistic personalities either acquire fame and social power or tend toward daydreaming and addiction. Tartakoff's (1966) later distinction between the active fantasy of being the "powerful one" (destined to perform outstanding deeds) and the passive fantasy of being the "special one" (chosen by virtue of inherent uniqueness to receive windfalls) also hinted at two types of narcissistic organizations. Bach (1977b) more directly addressed this issue. He noted that narcissistic patients have a divided self in which the hidden part of themselves shows a "mirror complementarity" with their conscious complaints. To the now well-recognized phenomenon of a grandiose individual being secretly afraid of his timidity, Bach added that those who feel weak and powerless on the surface often harbour a dangerously powerful split-off self image.

Kernberg's (1970; 1975; 1980; 1984; 1989) extensive writings on narcissism largely dealt with the more overt type of narcissistic personality. However, he too noted that "some patients with narcissistic personalities present strong conscious feelings of insecurity and inferiority" (Kernberg, 1975, p. 229). Their unconscious fantasies of grandiosity and omnipotence emerge only after a sustained contact has been established with them. Unlike the usual narcissistic individuals who are often sexually promiscuous, such persons show much restraint in their erotic lives. With the onset of middle age and its threatening reminders of life's limitations, however, the two types of narcissistic personalities tend to switch places. According to Kernberg (1980):

> the sexually more inhibited narcissistic character of early adulthood may now initiate the road to sexual promiscuity and various sexual deviations which other narcissistic patients are already abandoning in middle age because of their accumulated experience of dissatisfaction with the scant narcissistic gratification in sexual encounters. [p. 145]

Kohut (1971; 1977) too mentioned the less colourful and socially hesitant type of narcissistic personality. Such individuals have a "horizontal split" in the psyche, which keeps their grandiosity repressed and, consequently, their reality ego depleted of confidence. They present with symptoms of narcissistic deficiency including low self-esteem, diminished zest for work, and lack of initiative. They also display hypochondriacal preoccupations and a marked propensity towards shame. They feel intense discomfort about their need to display themselves and often suffer from severe stage fright (Kohut & Wolf, 1978). Not surprisingly, such individuals keep their distance from others from whom they desire narcissistic sustenance and feel painfully embarrassed upon the exposure of such needs. Alongside this prevailing symptomatology of narcissistic depletion, there are spasmodic breakthroughs of anxious hypomanic-like excitement, which give vent to their suppressed grandiosity.

The tense and conflicted existence of such narcissistic patients also drew Cooper's (1981a; 1984a; 1989a) attention. He noted that the surface manifestations of narcissistic personality might be charm, ambition, and accomplishment or these might include depression, invitations to humiliation, and feelings of failure. Cooper emphasized that narcissistic and masochistic tendencies frequently co-exist. Indeed, narcissistic tendencies might become unconscious vehicles for attaining masochistic disappointments, and masochistic injuries an affirmation of distorted narcissistic fantasies. More pointedly, Cooper and Ronningstam (1992) described narcissistic patients whose overt presentation is the mirror image of the usual description and who are "too inhibited to expose their fantasies to public view" (p. 94).

In my own two earlier reviews of the literature on narcissistic personality (Akhtar, 1989; Akhtar & Thomson, 1982), the manifestations of the disorder were divided into *overt* and *covert* categories. These designations did not necessarily imply conscious or unconscious occurrence, although such topographical distribution could certainly exist. The overt features included grandiosity, compulsive socialization, intense ambition, uneven morality, uninhibited sexuality, caricatured modesty, and an impressively articulate manner of speech. The covert features included morose self-doubts, envy, chronic boredom, materialistic lifestyle, inability to remain in love, and inattentiveness to details. While it was observed that some narcissistic patients initially display the usually covert features while the usually overt ones remain hidden in the first few interviews, the existence of two subtypes of narcissistic personality was not explicitly noted. The current contribution is thus an extension of my earlier work in this area.

Thinking along the same lines, Gabbard (1989b) observed that the "official" diagnostic criteria for narcissistic personality characterize only the arrogant and boastful individual who constantly demands attention, and fail to identify "the shy, quietly grandiose, narcissistic individual whose extreme sensitivity to slights leads to an assiduous avoidance of the spotlight" (p. 527). Gabbard named the two types as the *oblivious* and the *hypervigilant* narcissistic personalities. The former was characterized by persistent attention seeking, lack of empathy for others, and arrogance. The latter was characterized by hypersensitivity to others' reactions and a self-effacing attitude that hid their "secret wish to exhibit themselves in a grandiose manner" (p. 529).

Masterson (1993) too delineated roughly similar subtypes of narcissistic personality. His *exhibitionistic* type subsumed individuals who flaunt their grandiosity to valued others and his *closet* type subsumed individuals who submit to idealized others and vicariously live out their own grandiose fantasies via such association.

While not mentioning such subtypes, *DSM-IV* (1994) did note that some narcissistic patients give "an appearance of humility that may mask and protect grandiosity" (p. 659). They might drift towards low social functioning in order to avoid the risk of defeat in competitive situations. The combination of such social retreat and defensive humility stands in sharp contrast to the usually assertive, attention-seeking, and entitled picture of narcissistic individuals.

Finally, Hunt (1995) described the *diffident narcissist* whose grandiosity is hidden and who feels enormous shame at revealing it. His omnipotent strivings are not ego syntonic and he professes to be egalitarian. Unlike the overt narcissist who frequently throws temper tantrums, the diffident narcissist shows lofty indifference to realistic setbacks. Unaffected by the present hardships, he lives in the future, continually relying on unrealistic hope (Akhtar, 1996; Mehler & Argentieri, 1989), and waiting for a transforming event without taking much action to achieve it. Hunt further stated that:

> Castration anxiety in men, and in women, fear of loss, or loss of love, are prominent. At least in men, there is in both types a sense of a special relationship with the mother, based on her idolisation of him. The overt narcissist feels that he has won the oedipal conflict. The diffident narcissist may feel the same way, but in him this only increases the fear of the jealous, still dangerous, father. [p. 1260]

The inclusion of such "higher level" (Kernberg, 1975) conflicts, usually ignored in the descriptions of narcissistic personality, was a superior feature of Hunt's description. However, he made little effort to relate the profile of his diffident narcissist to the existing but scattered literature on this topic and to distinguish the syndrome from the phenomenologically akin obsessional and schizoid personality disorders. These deficiencies are rectified in this current paper.

CLINICAL PROFILE

Synthesizing this literature in the light of related observations made in my psychotherapeutic and psychoanalytic practice (Akhtar, 1991; 1992; 1994; 1996; 1999) yields the following composite profile of the shy narcissist.

Like the ordinary narcissist, the shy narcissist is ambitious, omnipotence-seeking, involved with fantasies of glory and fame, lacking in empathy for others, and defective in his capacity for deep object relationships. He also yearns for acceptance by everyone, praise, and widespread recognition. Like his better known counterpart, the shy narcissist too believes that he or she is unique and can only be understood by other special or high status people. Unlike the usual narcissist, however, the shy narcissist keeps his grandiose beliefs and aspirations tightly under cover. He appears modest and uninterested in social success. Indeed, he might display overt disdain for money and material acquisitions.

The shy narcissist also possesses a conscience stricter than that of the ordinary narcissist. He holds high moral standards and is less vulnerable to ethical lapses. More than his flamboyant phenomenological sibling, he feels gnawing, dark remorse at his oedipal transgressions as well as at his incapacity to empathize with others. While unable to feel genuine concern for others, he is forever helpful to them. Unlike the ordinary narcissist, who discards others after having used them for his purposes, the shy narcissist is capable of feeling grateful and offering reparation to others. The strict conscience responsible for this also pushes his grandiosity and ambition into hiding. Unlike the usual narcissist, who feels humiliated upon the exposure of his blemishes, the shy narcissist experiences shame upon the unmasking of his ambition and grandiosity. Indeed, he might live out his own ambition vicariously by playing "second fiddle" to someone whose success he has himself silently engineered.

Keeping a tight rein on his wishes to be noticed, the shy narcissist feels especially uncomfortable upon being photographed; the attention of a camera suddenly floods his ego with primitive exhibitionism and causes him much anxiety. Though yearning to be recognized, he "prefers" to be left alone in social get-togethers. Such reticence gives the shy narcissist yet another quality. His impaired capacity for deep relationships does not become readily visible to others. The difficulties of his sexual and marital life, resulting largely from chronic self-absorption as well as from clandestine and barely disguised transgressions of the incest barrier, also go unnoticed for long periods of time.

Cognitively, the ordinary narcissist comes across as impressively knowledgeable, decisive, and opinionated. The shy narcissist, in contrast, appears dreamy, forgetful, a bit absent-minded, and unable to carry on a sustained intellectual debate with another individual. However, in a circle of close associates, where the availability of soothing admiration is assured, the shy narcissist can shed his reserve and allow his suppressed raconteur self to emerge. Often this requires the help of alcohol. Indeed, the shy narcissist, more than his assertive counterpart, is vulnerable to such dependence. The apparent inconsistency between pervasive reticence on the one hand, and talkativeness with a select few of similar persuasion on the other, is due to the underlying mechanism of splitting, which keeps the two aspects of his personality apart.

DIFFERENTIAL DIAGNOSIS

The particular variety of narcissistic personality disorder described here also needs to be distinguished from obsessional and schizoid personality disorders. Both narcissistic and obsessional personalities display high ego ideals, perfectionism, and great need for control (Akhtar, 1989; Akhtar & Thomson, 1982; Kernberg, 1975). Like the obsessional, the shy narcissist appears modest, careful, emotionally restricted, and interpersonally reticent. Unlike the obsessional, such an individual shows hidden grandiosity, limited empathy with others, an impractical lifestyle, disdain for details, and vulnerability to daydreaming.

Both the narcissistic and schizoid individuals prefer ideas over people and lack wholesome rootedness in their bodily existence (Akhtar, 1989; Bach, 1977b; Kernberg, 1975). Like the schizoid individual, the shy narcissist is self-absorbed, timid, socially hesitant, lacking in spontaneity, and driven by his secret, innermost plans. Unlike the schizoid individual, however, the shy narcissist is ambitious, covertly optimistic, and given to an increase in his hidden grandiosity under stress, not withdrawal into objectless states of psychic emptiness. Facing disappointments in others and/or injuries to self esteem, the shy narcissist resorts to "transitional fantasies" (Volkan, 1973), that is, imaginary and rather banal tales of personal glory mentally evoked for the purpose of self-soothing. Schizoid individuals typically lack the ability to soothe themselves under such circumstances.

COMMENT

While the foregoing demonstrates the existence of the shy narcissist syndrome, little seems to be known about its actual prevalence. The use of masculine pronouns throughout this paper is only for literary ease and not meant to suggest that all shy narcissists are men. Indeed, I have encountered the syndrome in both male and female patients; Hunt (1995) has also mentioned such patients of both sexes. Also, while the syndrome can be more readily discerned in the setting of intense psychotherapeutic contact, it is not restricted to individuals undergoing such treatment. Shy narcissists might present with dysthymic complaints, vague inhibitions, and hypochondria to general psychiatrists and might, at times, be brought to clinical attention by their frustrated spouses. Another aspect of the syndrome's epidemiology pertains to culture. Since child rearing patterns play a crucial role in the manifestation or suppression of an individual's ambitiousness, it is possible that cultures that place a great emphasis upon modesty might have a greater prevalence of the shy type rather than the boastful type of narcissistic personality. My earlier observation that *narcissistic asceticism* (Akhtar, 1992, p. 63) might be a more frequent presentation of narcissistic personality in Oriental cultures is pertinent in this context.

Delineating the syndrome of the shy narcissist serves to underscore the centrality of splitting mechanisms in narcissistic personalities (Akhtar & Thomson, 1982; Bach, 1977b; Cooper, 1989a; Cooper & Ronningstam, 1992; Kernberg, 1970; 1975; Volkan, 1982) and to highlight their divided self. It also brings to attention the fact that diagnostic criteria relying exclusively on manifest symptomatology fail to diagnose narcissistic grandiosity when only the defences against it are clinically apparent. In contrast, the description of the shy narcissist offered here is based upon the inclusion of both the manifest symptomatology and deeper, sub-surface constructs. With this broadened vantage point, multiple and even contradictory psychic phenomena can be accommodated in a clinical profile that is closer to human complexity than the grasp offered by behavioral check lists; it is only with such a perspective that one can understand the occasional occurrence of a hysterical overlay on a schizoid core (Fairbairn, 1952b) and the co-existence of expedient mendacity (Tobak, 1989) with moralistic self-righteousness in paranoid individuals. This not only gives sounder theoretical underpinnings to the disorder's phenomenology but also prepares the clinician for the "mirror complementarity" of the self that Bach (1977b) has noted. The therapist's awareness of the essentially dichotomous self in such individuals will encourage further inquiry and prevent misdiagnosis.

The clinician also will benefit from the awareness that psychological weakness, hypochondria, undue stoicism, chronic waiting for magical events (Akhtar, 1996; Angel, 1934; Mehler & Argentieri, 1989; Potamianou, 1992), and exaggerated humility often mask grandiosity, omnipotence, and masochism. Knowledge of such a defensive constellation will enhance his or her empathy with the patient's underlying, if conflict-ridden, agenda. Interpretive efforts, at first directed at the anxious need for such defence, and later at the covert narcissistic and masochistic fantasies, can then be made.

Finally, the recognition that some narcissistic patients are painfully shy opens up challenging aetiological realms for investigation. For instance, does the conflict between exhibitionistic desires and their inhibition emanate from an upbringing in which fame was upheld as desirable and modesty as virtue? Or does this tension emanate from a battle between a constitutionally given, "hard-wired" propensity towards shyness (Kagan, 1984; Thomas & Chess, 1977) on the one hand and an environmentally acquired pressure for outstanding recognition on the other hand? Or does some combination of the two hypotheses, or even explanations hitherto not adequately considered (e.g., involving cultural factors), apply here?

While answers to such questions await further research, it seems that recognizing the syndrome of the shy narcissist does have implications for aetiological, diagnostic, and therapeutic realms alike.

On Abstinence

DANIEL WIDLÖCHER

The principle of abstinence was considered very early by Freud as a basic requirement of the psychoanalytical technique. In "Observations on Transference Love" (1915a) he wrote, "The treatment must be carried out in abstinence" (p. 165) and added, "It [is] a fundamental principle that the patient's needs and longing should be allowed to persist in her, in order that they may serve as forces impelling her to do work and to make changes. . . ." (p. 165).

But it is not very clear whether the principle concerns mainly the doctor or the patient. For many years, attention has been paid mainly to the former case, abstinence from the psychoanalyst's point of view. There is heated debate between "deprivers" and "gratifiers", the question dealing with "the balance of gratifications and deprivations" that "have to be purposefully employed in the conduct of a psychoanalysis" (Fox, 1984, p. 228). So the question of abstinence is closely related with neutrality (Schachter, 1984) and the debate seems particularly relevant to Freud's initial concern about the love demands of his women patients (1919a, pp. 159–168).

But the question seems to have shifted from the psychoanalyst to the patient, from neutrality to the place of the treatment in the everyday life of the patients. This shift is related to the transference neurosis theory as it was described in the twenty-eighth lecture of the "Introductory Lectures on Psychoanalysis" (Freud, 1916–1917). Transference not only links the patient to the treatment, and facilitates knowledge of the childhood conflicts that recur in the treatment; it also brings out the compulsive fixations and the intra-psychic conflicts that were frozen in the patient's neurotic structure and that were at the origin of symptoms, by shifting them to the patient–psychoanalyst relationship.

The two basic phases of the process are outlined: the shift of clinical neurosis towards transference neurosis, and the therapeutic resolution of this new form of neurosis. Freud successively considered two situations. The first one had to do with the abstinence rule. For transference to exert all of its shifting power, the patient has to be placed "into the situation most favourable to the solution of the conflict which is our aim" (1919a, p. 162). The patient must be forced to seek gratifications in transference, which otherwise fuel the neurosis: "Analytic treatment should be carried through, as far as possible, under privation – in a state of abstinence" (p. 162). In "Observations on Transference Love" (Freud, 1915a, p. 165), he had used the example of the dog race that a joker disrupts by throwing a sausage on to the middle of the track. In psychoanalysis, it is necessary to make the patient renounce substitute gratifications in life that may deprive transference from a part of his/her libidinal investments. In 1919, he writes, the patient "makes use of the enormous capacity for displacement possessed by the now partly liberated libido, in order to cathect with libido and promote to the position of substitute satisfactions the most diverse kind of activities, preferences and habits, not excluding some that have been his already. He continually finds new distractions of this kind, into which the energy necessary to carrying on the treatment escapes, and he knows how to keep them secret for a time. It is the analyst's task to detect these divergent paths and to require him every time to abandon them, however harmless the activity which leads to satisfaction may be in itself' " (1919a, p. 163). In short, to Freud, the desirable activity consists in forbidding such substitute satisfactions; it "must take the form of energetic opposition to premature substitutive satisfactions" (p. 164).

If one considers the problems of current psychoanalysis in relation to these "new lines of advance" of seventy-five years ago, the two situations we have just considered are particularly acute and up to date. The first issue, the supposedly necessary active technique with regard to transference dynamics, poses the still very present problem of the abstinence principle. The second issue, the supposed necessity to use active technique to correct symptoms, poses another very current problem, that is, that of psychoanalytical psychotherapy. I would like to elaborate on the second one first.

Freud's address to the Fifth International Psychoanalysis Conference raised, for the first time, an issue that is still relevant: the similarities and differences between psychoanalytical treatment proper and psychotherapies derived from it or inspired by it. There is no need to remind the reader of the profuse literature that has since tackled this issue. It is quite impossible to mention all the criteria developed in attempts to clarify the issue. I would merely like to emphasize one point that underlies any reflection on active technique: analytical psychotherapy does not fall short of psychoanalysis, but rather adds to it. To Freud, the idea was to alloy the copper of suggestion to the gold of psychoanalysis.

The idea of defining psychotherapy by what it adds to psychoanalysis certainly is not new or devoid of technical contributions, including very recent ones. But one has to admit that in practice, it meets fierce resistances for which I would like to give two reasons. The first, and probably the most important, is the fear of altering the purity of the psychoanalytical technique with processes extraneous to its spirit. Is it not the mark of beginners or incompetent psychoanalyst to bolster the psychoanalytical process with a little back-up advice, command, or interdict? In that respect, Freud's alloy may be related not to a therapeutic practice applied to the masses, but to all the deviations and so-called softeners promoted by the dissident schools.

The second source of resistance is linked, in my view, to the fact that if one is attached to preserving, one way or another, the predominance of psychoanalysis, one has problems defining in positive terms the psychotherapies that derive from it. Whatever the quality of gold–copper alloy, gold remains on the side of the psychoanalyst, and copper on the side of suggestion. No reflection on the theoretical and technical bases of psychoanalytically inspired psychotherapies can escape this hierarchy. But in daily practice, and I emphasize that I am here referring to what psychoanalysts do, not to what experts say, these psychotherapies will usually be defined by what they lack compared with psychoanalysis proper, rather than by what they add to it.

But what they lack is the force of transferential investment and the conditions required to induce this investment. How do we define psychotherapy? By the smaller number of sessions, by the face-to-face relationship. In short, psychotherapy too often looks like a "light" psychoanalysis, akin to "Diet Coke", that is, a psychoanalysis in which the pressure required to sustain transferential dynamics has been reduced. Freud's question therefore has to be reworded as follows: if the benefits of psychoanalysis are applied to a larger number of patients, under which conditions is that possible? But let us be clear, these conditions are neither financial nor time-related. It is not a matter of shortening treatments to meet increased demand, nor shortening sessions to reduce their cost. It is a matter of motivation. If the poor have so little to expect from life, what can curing their neurosis bring them?

Such a view is not entirely unjustified. In many countries, the biological life expectancy makes even short-term application of psychoanalytical benefits unrealistic. But things are different in industrialised countries, where social and economic decisions have led to a caring system that is equally accessible to all. The question, therefore, that concerns us all, at least in the short term, and that answers Freud's question, is indeed that of applying psychoanalysis within public health social policy. It is within such a policy that authorities, patients, and psychotherapists have always been keen to reduce the cost of psychoanalytic treatment. Psychoanalysts made the error of letting people believe that they could achieve good results at low cost. By implying that psychoanalytically orientated psychotherapies were "light" psychoanalyses, they let people believe that just as much effect could be obtained at lower cost.

An example of this debate is the weekly number of sessions. It is often said that psychoanalysis can only be considered at a rate of 4 sessions per week, and that below that frequency it can only be psychotherapy. We shall come back to the session frequency issue, but let us discuss the idea that psychotherapy is linked to a slackening of the psychoanalytical constraints. What is the point of saying that psychotherapy implies fewer weekly sessions, if other differences in the content of the sessions are not also described? If the expected process is the same, and the intervention technique is identical, why make a distinction between the two? Does it amount to admitting that psychoanalysis is too demanding? This is the conclusion drawn by health authorities in many European countries. Why pay for more sessions if the results are the same? Or should it be concluded that different things are achieved in three sessions than in four, which indeed means that psychoanalytically inspired psychotherapy has to be defined by what it adds to psychoanalysis. The active technique proposed by Freud and Ferenczi (Ferenczi, 1922) was an attempt to meet the objective. By tackling the symptoms earlier, the active technique proposed to complement the benefits expected of the psychoanalytical process proper.

It seems to me that psychoanalysts should recognise what remains of these active techniques in the psychotherapies they practice, and that they should not be reluctant to continue the reflection initiated by Freud and Ferenczi. Again, the point is not to add a dose of behaviourism or so-called cognitive therapy to the psychoanalytic technique, but to introduce the effects of a suggested change in the patient's attitude to the psychodynamic investigation.

Now, let us go back to the first issue: the use of the active technique, not for acting on the symptoms but to bolster transference. Here, the active technique is on the side of abstinence. Freud remained rather discreet in explaining how an active technique can reinforce abstinence. He merely said that the psychoanalyst should ensure that psychoanalysis unfolds in the context of privations, so that libidinal investments are shifted to fuel transference. Ferenczi went much further in actively mobilizing these libidinal investments, and that probably was the most hazardous of his innovative techniques. But let us stay with the problems that gave rise to the technique, rather than with the adventurous sides of it.

If the abstinence rule appeals less to psychoanalysts today, is it because the transference neurosis model no longer is the kingpin of the therapeutic process. Who still dares to say that the shift of libidinal investments from the frozen state of clinical neurosis to the transference dialectics constitutes the decisive step of the therapeutic process? Or has it been debated recently on the very model of transference neurosis, as a part of the knowledge of changing processes in psychoanalytic treatment? Such relative discrediting of transference neurosis is in my view wrongly linked to the extension of indications for psychoanalytic treatment. The psychoanalytic model of neurosis does not necessarily coincide with what former or recent nosologies consider as clinical neuroses. Clinical neurosis and the psychoanalytical model of neurosis should not be mistaken.

If, as I believe, the model of transference neurosis remains our paradigm, the issue of handling abstinence obviously arises. How can one make sure, for each patient, that this privation climate prescribed by Freud is maintained? The problem lies in that we have to *customize* our approach. The point is not to set sexual interdicts, nor financial requirements applicable to all, but to try and set, for each particular case, the fields within which pathological libidinal investments are fixed and will thus not shift into transference. This motion, specific to each individual case, can be detected at the preliminary interviews. This even constitutes one of the most interesting features of these interviews, that is, to be able to detect in which field and in which particular situation the patient expects to preserve some secret investment. Here can be quoted Stephen Dom's Vienna tale, where Freud, as all Viennese, was convinced that all robbers were, since that location guaranteed them impunity. To test the field where an investment is emerging as an area of resistance to transference does not mean that some rule has to be immediately set up to state which deprivation should be created, but that this domain will be subject to the psychoanalyst's special attention during treatment.

It is just as difficult to identify these substitute investments, as early as possible, as to lead the patient to forget them. Of course, the ideal situation would be that interpretation would be sufficient and that the mere awareness of the substitute character of the symptomatic act would entail its disappearance. But here we are confronted with two problems. The first is that the link between external investments and transference does not make much sense to the patient. This equivalence is economic, in terms of relief, and it is not easy to make a patient understand that what unfolds in his professional or private life hampers transferential investment, that is, repetition of the past, especially since what Freud called privation is not always a consciously felt pleasure deprivation but the privation from acting out, from the fulfilment (*Erfüllung*) of an unconscious fantasy. How can the patient realize that what is a fulfilment in work or love has to be placed in a transference-linked fantasy? In another words, one can but demand abstinence, for any sense to be realized later.

One has to know how to *suggest* such a privation, which will remove a decisive part of libidinal life from life outside the sessions, in order to bolster transference. The difficulty here is linked to the degree of conviction of the psychoanalyst: not only the conviction that such or such a privation is really necessary, but that the psychoanalyst has a right to demand it, inasmuch as he believes in the value of his prescription. This is not a case of overall confidence in psychoanalysis, but rather the reasoned confidence that one has that, by proposing psychoanalytic treatment to that precise patient, the psychoanalyst pledges to personally bring about, in all probability, the benefit mentioned in the preliminary interviews. The psychoanalyst's faith in his/her own treatment for this given patient is therefore not blindness or narcissistic self-awareness, but a commitment for which the analyst shall be accountable to the patient. It is in the name of this conviction, of this common commitment, that the psychoanalyst will be able to suggest the necessary adjustments.

But the difficulty in establishing this climate of abstinence does not depend only on the psychoanalyst and patient. It has also to do with the standing of psychoanalysis amongst the social and therapeutic practices, at least in our societies. Here we come back to the final reflections of the 1918 address: the rich could afford the trip to Vienna or Budapest to commit themselves fully to psychoanalytical treatment for a few months. By vulgarizing psychoanalysis, not to the poor but for ordinary people who had to go on making a living in the professional rat race, psychoanalysis was able to become a form of psychotherapy recognized by the authorities, to become commonplace. The patient comes to the session, between his working hours and his private life. As far as possible, psychoanalytic sessions are fitted in to a network of activities and investments, just as a yoga lesson or a physiotherapy session. How then can abstinence be envisaged? It is no longer a question of the regulation of money or private life alone. Psychoanalysis has to fit in with modern life. It is then that the number-of-sessions issue comes up. In my view, there is no doubt that the best way to maintain the abstinence principle is to restore the place that psychoanalysis has to occupy for a time in the patient's life, namely the first place. The best way for it to take that place is through frequent sessions. I think that there is a direct link between the abstinence principle and the number of weekly sessions.

To conclude, Freud's question on the lines of advance required by applying psychoanalysis to the general population are still up to date. Indeed, the issue is not, as envisaged by Freud, to distribute the benefits of psychoanalysis to the starving poor. The problem we are facing is to practice psychoanalysis in countries where the principle of equal access to care has been increasingly recognized. The technical difficulties described by Freud, justifying his interest in active techniques, are equally encountered in today's practical problems. The psychoanalysis–suggestion alloy is undoubtedly necessary in psychotherapies derived from or inspired by psychoanalysis. The relevance of the abstinence rule should be underlined to prevent psychoanalytical treatment from becoming too mundane or commonplace. Before being a treatment, psychoanalysis is a human experience that requires deep commitment, both by the patient and the analyst.

Coming of Age
KATHERINE DALSIMER

The theme of this volume honouring Arnold Cooper brought to mind a remarkable article by the poet Kenneth Koch (1971).[1] It was about teaching children to write poetry. The poet described his experience in a public school in New York City, working with children from first to sixth grades. To begin, he found that it was important to remove obstacles like rhyme and metre, which impede the free flow of feelings and associations. And in an atmosphere that encouraged the young writers to take chances, Koch gave them wonderful subjects to write about: write about your wishes, he told them, write poems that are lies, write about your dreams. But the poems that most delighted me – and that have remained so vivid in my mind all these years – were the poems whose alternate lines began "I used to . . . / But now . . .":

> I used to drive trucks, but now I drive racing cars.
> I used to be in first grade
> But now I'm in second grade.
>
> I used to have an apple dress
> But now it doesn't fit me.

---

1. The article, "Wishes, Lies, and Dreams: Teaching Children to Write Poetry," was first published in the *New York Review of Books* (April 9, 1970) and subsequently as a chapter in Koch's book of the same title.

> I used to be a baby saying Coo Coo
> But now I say "Hello"
> I used to be a goldfish
> But now I am a girl.
>
> I used to be as silly as David
> But now I am sillier than David.

These children, invited to think about the contrast between the past and the present, felt themselves to be growing better – to be getting bigger, and faster, and funnier. I expect that adults invited to write such poems would find the contrast between past and present less advantageous: we might well allude to sadness, or some sense of loss, and the tempering of expectations. But the editors of this *Festschrift* have kindly invited us to write about that aspect of getting older in which we believe ourselves, at any rate, to be getting better – they have asked us to write about the development of our ideas. The theme of this volume pays tribute to Dr. Cooper's own lifelong contribution, both in his writing and in his teaching, to the intellectual vitality of psychoanalysis.

I'd like to reflect on the development of my views about adolescence. I've spent a good deal of my professional life working with college students – doing clinical work and supervision at the Columbia University Mental Health Service, and teaching about adolescent development at Columbia. I've written a book, *Female Adolescence: Psychoanalytic Reflections on Literature* (1986), in which I considered literary texts about adolescent girls in the light of a psychoanalytic understanding of development. Currently I am working on a book about Virginia Woolf, examining her inner life as she was becoming a writer through a close reading of the diaries and letters, essays, and fiction of her adolescence and young womanhood.

So the period of adolescence has long interested me, and I find that over time my thoughts about adolescence have changed. Why? Postmodernly, I must begin with the eye of the beholder – with myself. I'm older now than I used to be. I'm further from my own adolescence, and I am a mother now, as well as a daughter. My own world has changed, and the larger world has changed: the period of history that we have lived through over the past decades has radically altered the social context of adolescence. At the same time, changes in the structure of the family – the variability of what we mean by the word *family* – have transformed the context in which adolescents come of age. Both in my office and outside my office, what I have observed has changed the way I think about adolescence. And I find, when I return to those classic psychoanalytic papers that were so important in shaping my own thinking about adolescence, that I see these writings, too, in a different light.

Above all, what strikes me from my present vantage point is the enormous sympathy these writers had for the *sturm und drang* of adolescence. It is no accident that it is a German phrase that we have incorporated into our vocabulary to describe the high drama of adolescence, for I think that the first, European generation of analysts was half in love with the very excesses of adolescence. They described it beautifully, even stirringly. The mood swings, the passion, the idealism, the arrogance, even the narcissism of adolescence are lingered over in their descriptions, and savoured. Here, for example, is a favourite passage of mine from Anna Freud's classic paper, "Adolescence":

> I take it that it is normal for an adolescent to behave for a considerable length of time in an inconsistent and unpredictable manner; to fight his impulses and to accept them; to ward them off successfully and to be overrun by them; to love his parents and to hate them; to revolt against them and to be dependent on them; to be deeply ashamed to acknowledge his mother before others and, unexpectedly, to desire heart-to-heart talks with her; to thrive on imitation of and identification with others while searching unceasingly for his own identity; to be more idealistic, artistic, generous, and unselfish than he will ever be again, but also the opposite: self-centered, egoistic, calculating. Such fluctuations between extreme opposites would be deemed highly abnormal at any other time of life. At this time they may signify no more than that an adult structure of personality takes a long time to emerge, that the ego of the individual in question does not cease to experiment and is in no hurry to close down on possibilities. [Freud, 1958, pp. 275–276]

I quoted this passage in the introduction to my book on female adolescence; I have used it many times in teaching, and returning to it now I am freshly beguiled. I think it is a wonderfully textured description. But it is more than a description. Listen to the rhythm of the prose: as the rhetorical cadence suggests, this is not only a description, it is a manifesto.

In trying, unsuccessfully, to condense the passage I have quoted, I found that there was nothing I could omit: every clause, in its sense and in its rhythm, contributes to building the rhetorical effect of the passage. This is a statement not only of what adolescence is, but of what it *should* be.

Indeed, the point is made explicitly in this paper: to the question of whether the upheaval of adolescence is inevitable, the answer is clear. "On this point, psychoanalytic opinion is decisive and unanimous.... We know that the character structure of a child at the end of the latency period represents the outcome of long drawn-out conflicts between id and ego forces. The inner balance achieved ... is preliminary only and precarious.... It has to be abandoned to allow adult sexuality to be integrated into the individual's personality. The so-called adolescent upheavals are no more than the external indications that such internal adjustments are in progress" (p. 264). Indeed, if adolescents at 14, 15, or 16 show no such outer evidence of inner unrest, it is "a sign to be taken seriously.... They are, perhaps more than any others, in need of therapeutic help to remove the inner restrictions and clear the path for normal development, however 'upsetting' the latter may prove to be" (p. 265).

Returning to these writings now, in the light of my own experience over the years, I find the descriptions still enormously appealing. What I can no longer agree with, though, is the prescriptive character of the statements. The onset of puberty is of course momentous, and brings in its wake changes in the inner life of the adolescent, in relationships within the family and with the larger world beyond. But I am no longer persuaded that healthy adolescence must of necessity be a time of turmoil, or that the absence of high drama during adolescence is to be regarded with suspicion.

I now believe that there is a wide range of healthy ways to traverse adolescence, a wider range than the classic psychoanalytic literature on adolescence recognizes. The language of these papers insists on a sharp and deep withdrawal from the parents who have been beloved in childhood. The vocabulary is dramatic and extreme in describing even the normal course of adolescent development. Blos (1962), for example, wrote of "the *bizarreness* and regressive character of adolescent behaviour": this is an expression of the struggle to regain an equilibrium that has been "*jolted* by the *crisis* of puberty" (p. 11). "The adolescent *breaks away for good* from infantile love objects. The *finality of this inner break with the past* shakes the adolescent's emotional life to its center...." (p. 88, emphases mine). Adolescence was characterized by "the withdrawal of cathexis from the parents, or rather from their object representations in the ego...." (p. 89). Similarly Anna Freud wrote of "detachment from the past" (p. 270), of "breaking the tie to the mother" (p. 266).

Experience has taught me otherwise: ties are not broken, nor is cathexis withdrawn, nor do adolescents make a final inner break with the past.

Relationships with the parents change over the course of adolescence, and most significantly, internal relationships are altered, but the language of decathexis and detachment is inadequate to describe these processes. The terms are unidimensional, and cannot encompass the richness and complexity of the ongoing internal relationships – cannot encompass conflict and contradiction. I think that it is more useful, and more accurate, to speak of the *modulation* of the adolescent's inner relationship with the parents. This modulation is a process that continues over the course of the son's and daughter's lifetime – continues, indeed, beyond the death of the parents.[2]

This brings me to a related issue, that of mourning. The idea that adolescents are in mourning for the love objects of the past was introduced by Anna Freud, who wrote of the difficulty of engaging adolescents in the analytic process. She likened this to the difficulty of engaging those who are in love, or those who are in mourning, and observed that adolescence has much in common with both of these states. The emotional struggle of the adolescent, she wrote, "is one of extreme urgency and immediacy. His libido is on the point of detaching itself from the parents and of cathecting new objects. Some mourning for the objects of the past is inevitable" (pp. 262–263). The comparison has been widely adopted. Again to quote Blos: "The adolescent incurs a real loss in the renunciation of his oedipal parents; and he experiences the inner emptiness, grief, and sadness which is part of all mourning" (p. 100).

The link between adolescence and mourning was developed most fully by Martha Wolfenstein in her paper, "How is Mourning Possible?" (1969), in which she argued that adolescence not only resembles mourning, but developmentally is a precondition for being later able to mourn. "The painful and gradual decathexis of the beloved parents which the adolescent is forced to perform serves as an initiation into how to mourn" (p. 113). Adolescence is a trial mourning in which "there is a gradual decathexis of the first love objects, accompanied by sad and painful feelings, with reality testing of memories confirming the irrevocability of the childhood past" (p. 122). Unlike the mourner, however, "the adolescent does not know why

---

2. In a paper called "The Vicissitudes of Mourning" (1994) I explored Virginia Woolf's evolving relationship, as an adult, with the mother who had died when she was 13. I examined this relationship through a reading of Woolf's autobiographical novel *To the Lighthouse*, and her diaries and letters, and a memoir, written toward the end of her life, in which she reflected upon the writing of that novel, and its effect on her own inner life.

he is sad or depressed and does not attribute these feelings to the loss of his capacity to feel love for his parents" (p. 116).

Do adolescents lose the capacity to feel love for their parents? I think not. Over the course of adolescence, parents become less idealized, they lose the burnish that oedipal love bestows – but this is not the same as losing the capacity to feel love for them. On the contrary: it is loving them in a different way, a less childish way. The emphasis upon mourning implies a break, a discontinuity, a real loss. This is not the subjective experience of all adolescents; it is not even, I now think, the experience of most adolescents – and it should not be the experience that we insist upon as a necessary condition for psychological health. Many adolescents continue to feel close to their parents even as they negotiate the challenges of adolescence, and I believe our theory should make room for them as well as those for whom it is a more stormy passage.

Moreover, whether we are speaking of adolescence or of mourning, in the inner world there is no such thing as "breaking off" or "dissolving" object relations. Even in the face of death, our internal relationships with those we have lost – or with those we no longer love in the same old ways – are relationships that endure, and continue to be modulated throughout our lives. As Freud wrote in "The Ego and the Id" (1923b), "the character of the ego is a precipitate of abandoned object-cathexes and . . . contains the history of those object-choices" (p. 29). To speak of the finality of the break with the past during adolescence is closer to the conscious experience of an adolescent in the heat of the moment, than to the wisdom of this passage.

* * * * *

In his *Memoirs*, the writer Sherwood Anderson (1942) describes his boyhood in a small town not unlike Winesburg, Ohio. As a boy, he says, he wanted his father to be something he was not, and could not be. He wanted a father who was a proud and dignified man, but instead his father was something of a buffoon, he thought, always showing off. If there was a show, his father was bound to get the main comic part, and make a fool of himself. Or if there was a parade, he'd be right in the front of it, and fall off his horse and make everyone hoot with laughter. And he was always entertaining people with stories – stories that his son knew were lies. How could it be that even respectable people in the town seemed to enjoy spending time with him – the superintendent of schools, or the quiet man who ran the hardware store in town. Listening from his room upstairs to the goings-on on the porch, the son was mortified. How could these men tolerate being with his father? Didn't they realize the stories he told were lies? How could his mother stand him?

And then the young Sherwood Anderson has one of those experiences that in literature are condensed to a single event, a screen memory. The particulars need not concern us here: the compressing of a process that in life takes place over months or years into a single event is like the turning of the hands of a clock in a movie, or the flipping of the pages of a calendar, to stand for the passing of time. In this memoir, the "event" was a silent swim with his father on a rainy night, across a pond. The outcome, momentous for the young writer, was a realization about his father, and about himself: "He was a storyteller, as I was to be."

The very qualities that had most shamed and humiliated him, became the kernel of his identification with his father. In my clinical experience, the discovery of such continuities is liberating and richly sustaining to a young person. In spite of Tolstoy's dictum, happy families are surely not all alike, but in my experience they do share this: each generation has the sense of receiving from the previous generation something that is profoundly valued. And in thinking about adolescence, I would now place the emphasis here: on the importance of a felt continuity with the past – a continuity that is nurturing and sustaining even through the momentous changes of adolescence.

the Changing World
The Changing World Outside Psychoanalysis

Are the Freuds' Ego Psychology, Klein's Object Relations, Kohut's Self Psychology, and Beck's Cognitive Psychology All Alive and Well and Living in the Same Brain?[1]

GEORGE E. VAILLANT

Arnold Cooper has been a life-long synthesizer. In an effort to celebrate his contributions, this essay reflects a homespun effort at synthesis between drive psychology, self psychology, object relations, and cognitive science by an author who is master of none. Nevertheless, this paper will look at Anna Freud's ego mechanisms of defence from these four vantage points.

In his brief history of the cognitive revolution, Howard Gardner (1985) wrote that a crucial "feature of cognitive science is the deliberate decision to de-emphasize certain factors which may be important for cognitive functioning but whose inclusion at this point would unnecessarily complicate the cognitive-scientific enterprise. These factors include the influence of affective factors and emotions, the contribution of historical and cultural factors and the role of the background context in which particular actions or thoughts occur" (p. 6). In sharp contrast to cognitive science, the Freuds' ego psychology is principally concerned with Gardner's three "complicating factors:" emotions, culture, and context. To de-emphasize these factors is to throw the baby out with the bathwater.

Similarly, self psychology and many advocates of object relations currently dismiss the drives, once so precious to psychoanalysis and still

---

[1]. This work is from the Division of Psychiatry, Department of Medicine, Brigham and Women's Hospital, and the Study of Adult Development, Harvard University Health Services. It was supported by a research grant MH-42248 from the National Institute of Mental Health.

to ego psychology, as not just "complicating factors" but downright old-fashioned. Such dismissal is another example of a baby sacrificed in the interests of ridding psychology of superfluous bathwater. No facet of the brain operates in isolation; no facet can be dismissed as old fashioned.

If cognitive psychologists and psychoanalysts as a group fight over whether the cortex or the limbic system is more important, Kohutians, Kleinians, and Anna Freud's disciples fight over whether memories of self-object experience or getting the unruly "drives" to behave are the more important regulatory tasks. How can we get Melanie Klein, Anna Freud, Heinz Kohut, and Aaron Beck to become bedfellows?

Certainly, any discussion of how ego psychology relates to self psychology runs the risk of being a contradiction in terms. The creation of self involves a process of *assimilation,* of taking facets of experience and of other people into the self, metabolizing them, and allowing them to be part of one's identity forever.

In contrast, the deployment of ego mechanisms of defence reflects efforts of the organism to defend against – or to adapt to – those aspects of the world that it cannot assimilate internally or externally. We might call such a process of adaptation *accommodation.* If self psychology is concerned with identity and if object relations psychology is concerned with real object constancy, then ego psychology is concerned with drive regulation and ersatz object constancy, (i.e., fantasy and projection).

The defence mechanisms of ego psychology, those involuntary modes of psychic homeostasis, are summarily dismissed by some cognitive scientists as mere "self-deception". And the "image distorting defences" (Bond & Vaillant, 1986) proposed by Melanie Klein and popularized by Otto Kernberg to understand the vicissitudes of relationships are rarely used in the same breath with the drive-based defences popularized by Anna Freud (Freud, 1936) to understand character disorder. Finally, in *The Restoration of the Self*, the only time that Kohut (1977) mentions defences is to say that "defensive structures play a comparatively minor role" (p. 50). In developmental terms, the Kohutian universe focuses on identity formation to the exclusion of drive regulation and Kleinian object relations. Again, the baby is thrown out with the bathwater.

How can I hope to discuss the role of ego defences in protecting the Kohutian self against loss of coherence, in preserving Aaron Beck's mind from cognitive dissonance, and of guarding the Kernbergian borderline from loss of object constancy? Let me offer a cognitive schema by which to organize the semantic and conceptual differences that may separate a drive psychologist's view of defences from those of Kernbergians and cognitive scientists.

The semantic problems that arise in synthesizing the terms of self *and* drive *and* object psychology are formidable. It is noteworthy, at least to me, that Melanie Klein and Anna Freud, on the one hand, could live nearby each other in London, possess identical professions as child analysts, serve as co-training directors at the same psychoanalytic institute, and have the same man as their ego ideal and, on the other hand, that they could use a completely different terminology to discuss rather similar processes. Equally extraordinary is that in the sixty years that have elapsed since Anna Freud came to London from Vienna, few students have made any effort to translate one woman's terms into the other's. To avoid Kohutian fragmentation (i.e., Freudian anxiety), my own defences for years had allowed Kleinian defences no place in my neuronal networks nor in my writing (Vaillant, 1977). After years of cognitive desensitization I began to believe that Anna Freud's terms for defence (e.g., turning against the self, fantasy, undoing, and projection) could serve to reduce cognitive dissonance about inconstant objects in the same manner as Melanie Klein's terms for virtually the same mental mechanisms (splitting, devaluation/idealization, and projection identification). Michael Bond and colleagues (1983) have used the term *image-distorting defences* to encompass Klein's mechanisms, and Christopher Perry (1986) has made them a separate category in his hierarchy of defences.

One problem is that there is no commonly accepted nomenclature for the defences. For example, within 50 miles of Golden Gate Bridge there were, until recently, five competing, non-overlapping classifications of unconscious control processes (defences) used by five highly respected investigators of stress and coping (Block & Block, 1980; Folkman & Lazarus, 1980; Haan, 1977; Horowitz, 1988; Moos & Billings, 1982). Thus, if we are to avoid the fate of the residents of Babel, we must abandon linguistic quibbles; we must, like the ethologists and the physiologists, cling only to phenomena.

Freud was content to focus on defences that manage affects and drives. Defences against object anxiety were almost an afterthought. Before the undermodulated borderline Anna Freud's ego psychology must, alas, lay down its arms. But in saying this I do not wish to suggest that grief, longing, and rage are any less important to conflict than Kernbergian *objects,* the Kohutian *self,* or the Beckian *attributions* to which affects become attached. It is only that Melanie Klein (and Kernberg, Bond, and Perry) were and are trying to accomplish a more complex task. They correctly conceptualized *defence* as a control process for managing affect laden person schemas *and* the more difficult to articulate self schemas as well as the drives.

The Freuds' emphasis on defence mechanisms can be conceptualized as identifying a creativity that we do not usually associate with intelligent machines or even with Beckian cognition. The Freuds' psychodynamic theories of defences and Kernberg's (1975) hypothesis of metabolized person schemas posit that limbic moods override, and serve to organize, our cortical computer-like logic. Defences are truly creative, and they put into the mind what was not there before. I believe our differences arise when we try to use words (be they Kohutian *fragmentation*, Anna Freud's *ego mechanisms of defence*, or Mardi Horowitz's *person schemas*) to encompass complex brain "processes" that we do not fully understand.

Certainly, defences – so carefully deleted from the indices of Kohut's monographs – must operate in a self psychology universe as well as in the universe of object relations, drive derivatives, and cognitive dissonance.

Let me continue this process of translation by superimposing Kohut's terms of "fragmentation" and "loss of coherence of self" with Erikson's concept, "identity diffusion," and with Anna Freud's less well articulated concept of an adolescent ego overwhelmed by unfamiliar drive states and by the secondary anxiety that such unfamiliarity creates. The conceptual models and the language of Kohut, Erikson and Anna Freud are different, but the underlying phenomena, of course, have much in common.

Ego psychology suggests that we all live in a mental universe in which mental conflict may be conceptualized by the discordant tug of the four lodestars diagrammed in Figure 1 (see p. 143): our desires, our conscience, the important people in our lives, and reality. By the term *desire* or *id* in Figure 1, I mean our emotions, our drives, our desires (hunger, grief, lust, rage, joy, and so on). Psychoanalysts call this lodestar *id*, moralists call it *sin*, cognitive psychologists call it *hot cognition*, and neuroanatomists label it the hypothalamic and limbic regions of the brain. Sigmund Freud lumped all desire under the term *libido*, but there are many desires. Grief, anger, dependency, and even at times joy loom quite as important as sex as sources of conflict. For the purpose of understanding intrapsychic conflict, the psychoanalytic term *affect* is a useful substitute for desire. (An affect is created when an instinct, drive, or desire is attached to an object, e.g., when hunger first smells and then attaches our attention to a sizzling hamburger.) Id is the lodestar about which the devotees of drive psychology have most to tell us.

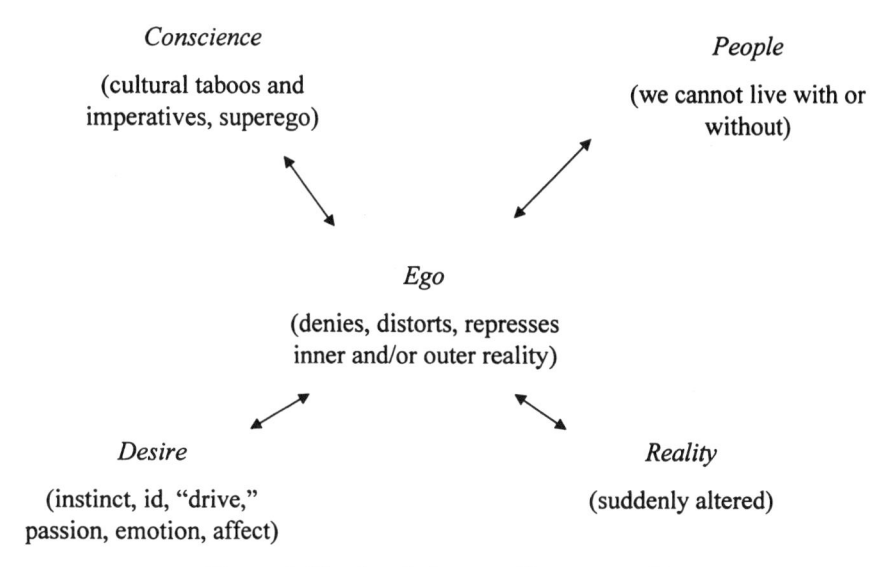

```
        Conscience                              People
   (cultural taboos and                  (we cannot live with or
    imperatives, superego)                      without)

                   ↘          ↗
                         Ego
                  (denies, distorts, represses
                     inner and/or outer reality)
                   ↗          ↘

        Desire                                 Reality
    (instinct, id, "drive,"                (suddenly altered)
    passion, emotion, affect)
```

Figure 1. The four lodestars of human conflict

By the term *conscience* – the superego of psychoanalysis – I do not mean just those precepts of our own mother and father that we absorbed before age 5. By *conscience* I mean our whole identification with our society, with our culture, and with our own ego ideals. Freud's *Civilization and its Discontents* (1930a), Erikson's *Childhood and Society* (1950), the "context" that Gardner asks us to ignore, have led even the most simplistic psychoanalyst to view the superego as far more than just the internalized parents of a young child. The roots of our conscience continue to evolve and undergo modification throughout our lives. In some ways Beck's cognitive-behavioural techniques and Kohut's staunch willingness to side with the self instead of the analyst have more to tell us about reducing guilt than the Freudians and the Kleinians.

People form the third lodestar. People become a source of conflict when we cannot live with them and cannot live without them. In other words, when the constancy of our object representation is threatened we feel depressed and anxious. The death of a beloved person is an obvious example. There are also individuals to whom we are peculiarly attached but with whom we are not at peace: the boss whom we strive to please but also hate, the scapegoat whom we abuse but would mourn were he to disappear, and the lover who terrifies us by exclaiming "Yes!!" to our rather tentative proposal of marriage. People are the lodestar about whom the object relations mavens have most to tell us.

By the term *reality*, the fourth lodestar, I mean those facets of our external environment that are capable of changing more rapidly than we can adapt. The drought of the Australian outback and the Amazonian damp are not stressful to those aboriginals for whom such drought and damp are predictable and unchanging. But five inches of snow – a mere flurry in Montreal or Moscow and a blessing at Aspen or St. Moritz – can paralyze Paris or Jerusalem. The fourth lodestar, external reality, was the last source of conflict to be fully appreciated by psychoanalysts.

Defensive operations arise when there is a sudden change in one or more of the four lodestars (e.g., puberty, an unexpected death, or a parent needing a nursing home). Defences allow us to stall for time until the self can adapt to the cognitive dissonance engendered by the change in the tug of the four lodestars. Until sudden change can be minimized by the ego (i.e., until adequate homeostatic defences can be deployed) the result is anxiety and/or depression. And there is not as much difference between anxiety and depression as the pharmaceutical houses would have us believe.

A basic property of defences is that they allow us the illusion of omnipotence. They distort internal and external reality and thus force the world to accept the terms of the Kohutian self. Defences may involve a rematching of working models (situations as they are perceived) and of enduring schemas (what is expected to be taking place). Because Melanie Klein's concept of image-distorting defences encompasses object relations more readily than Anna Freud's, her terms (e.g., *omnipotence* above) are superior to the simple Freudian defence terms in capturing the complexity and the subtlety of this process. One drawback to Kleinian semantics, however, is that a term like *projective identification* encompasses interpersonal processes so complex that no two clinicians define projective identification the same way. In addition, since for projective identification to work "it takes two to tango," and we can never know for sure whether projective identification does not rest in the eye of the beholder.

With this introduction let me focus on the Kohutian concept of *fragmentation*. The term offers a unitary semantic description that encompasses several very different psychic phenomena. The Kohutian term *fragmentation*, (i.e., the loss of coherence of the self organization), encompasses the vicissitudes of the embattled ego in Figure 1. Fragmentation also includes a loss of self cohesion (a.k.a. object constancy) due to the abrupt or chronic absence of self-esteem (e.g., being dumped by a lover). It also includes the disruption of cognition produced by under-modulated affect (e.g., a temper tantrum). Third, fragmentation can result from an unexpected change or novelty in one's environment, (e.g., a new operating system for one's word processor). Finally, fragmentation can result from the threat of merger and engulfment (e.g., loss of self/object boundaries during incest).

Let me go over this in more detail. First, fragmentation can come from disruption of self-esteem. Second, there is the loss of self that comes from sudden unexpected change in reality. Thus, Kohutian fragmentation can come from undermodulated Beckian cognition. Third, there is the loss of coherence of self and the identity diffusion that comes from finding ourselves overwhelmed by strong affect. Grief normally leading to comforting tears, or sexual excitement normally leading to a comforting cuddle, or fear normally leading to comforting flight can be replaced with overwhelming anxiety, depression, and learned helplessness. Finally, there is the loss of self that comes when we fear another is about to envelop or engulf us and when – whether it be from hypnosis or the reawakening of a very early intrusive role relationship model – we experience a loss of Kohutian self/other boundaries. The very defences religiously ignored by Kohut and dismissed as self-deception by cognitive scientists protect us from each of these different forms of self-fragmentation or loss of self-coherence.

If we consider the phenomenon of grief, there is not only the reality-based cognitive schema that the lost person seems to have abandoned the self forever, but there is also the enduring schema of the loved one with whom we cannot live without and who lives on forever in our hearts. The ego's task is to create a setting where both schemas can exist in harmony together by putting something – or someone – in the world who was not there before.

More than half a century ago, Frederic Bartlett (1932), a friend of Norbert Wiener, the father of artificial intelligence, declared, "Remembering is not the re-excitation of innumerable fixed, lifeless, and fragmentary traces. It is an imaginative reconstruction, or construction, built out of the relation of our attitude towards a whole active mass of past experience" (p. 213). Through a higher order of mental processes, analagous to play and creativity, defences and unconscious control mechanisms regulate the relationship of schemas of self to role relationship models and to passion. Admittedly, the term *unconscious regulatory process* is more accurate than the precybernetic term *defence mechanism*.

Let me describe a second set of mental transformations that involve the four world views that I am trying to integrate. Many glossaries of defence cite incorporation, introjection, imitation, internalization and identification (*i-words*) as defence mechanisms, but these i-words are homeostatic not in their transmutation of drives but in their transmutation of self. What is confusing to clinicians is that the i-words are used sometimes in the service of reversible defence and sometimes in the service of permanent transmutation of self. Thus the internalizing mental mechanisms – the i-words – are only sometimes regulatory processes; often they are metaphors for the enduring memories and attributional styles that reflect self schemas and mirror transferences.

I have excluded the i-words from my own discussions of defence mechanisms because the use of such transmuting processes like internalization and identification, unlike the always reversible defences of displacement and repression, can change the organism forever. The transmuting capacity of the i-words is equivalent to Kernberg's (1975) concept of "metabolizing the object." Consider the example of identification with the aggressor. When a person engages in this process, on the one hand, he may be organizing an act of creative homeostasis; on the other, he may be creating an enduring schema that takes place not only in fantasy or play but may colour her or his character for the rest of life.

Like the defences (Vaillant, 1977), the object metabolizing i-words can also be arranged chronologically to reflect human development. *Incorporation*, with its kinship to the mental mechanism of distortion, means literally taking the whole person inside. Incorporation is a vital part of the fantasy life of very young children and is present in the inner world of some psychotics. For most adults incorporation exists only in fable and song. *Introjection*, with its kinship to projection, hypochondriasis, and identification with the aggressor, is common in 3–10 year old development and in the frantic search by personality disordered individuals for ersatz object constancy. Introjection reflects role relationship models and inner representation of past objects that contributes to much psychosomatic symptomatology.

Imitation, with its kinship to hysterical identification and to Anna Freud's defence of reversal – namely of "pretending that you are the ghost that might meet you" – is central to 5–10 years old motivation. Imitation heralds the developmental transition of *being* the object rather than, as with incorporation and introjection, of *having* the object.

Internalization, characteristic of latency, bears kinship to reaction formation and passive aggression and contributes stable support to the coherence of self-organization. In self psychological terms internalization is intrinsic to permitting the processes of Kernbergian object metabolism and Kohutian mirroring memories to become permanent. Egosystonic internalization is epitomized in the song "Younger than spring time": "You touch my hand and my arm grows strong". This is in contrast to the more egodystonic introjection reflected by "I'm gonna wash that man right out of my hair".

The phenomena of *idealization, inspiration,* and *identity formation* are essential to adolescent development. In contrast to incorporation, idealization, if just as narcissistic, is not autistic. Finally, with the process of identification, as it occurs in adulthood, the alchemy of object metabolism is complete. It is no accident that Anna Freud's sublimation, the most permanent of the drive-regulating defences, is a close relative of Kleinian identification. With identification, the identity achieved is peculiarly one's own even if it is absorbed from others.

To conclude, a fundamental difference between the brain and a computing machine is the brain's inability to repeat itself precisely. Unless damaged, the human brain – unlike slavish disciples of Freud, of Klein, of Kohut, or of Beck – is incapable of being trite. Arnold Cooper, too, is incapable of being trite. We salute him.

Psychoanalysis and Empirical Research: A Reconciliation

LESTER LUBORSKY

There are good historical reasons for the long neglect of empirical research by psychoanalysts. From the point of view of psychoanalysis, empirical research has long been seen as an unnecessary, difficult to comprehend, and even unwelcome intruder. One pattern-setting example of this view occurred in the 1930s. A psychologist in St. Louis, Saul Rozenzweig, in a famous correspondence with Freud, sent Freud some reprints of empirical studies demonstrating the operation of repression. Freud replied that these were interesting, but that he had his own methods of doing things, and that the method presented by Rozenzweig was unnecessary: "I cannot put much value on these confirmations because the wealth of reliable observations . . . make them independent of experimental verification. Still, it can do no harm" (quoted in Luborsky & Spence, 1971, p. 408; Mackinnon & Duke, 1962). Consistent with Freud's response, the neglect of empirical research comes from psychoanalysis's traditional reliance on single case analyses and clinical-theoretical inferences based on what the patient says and does (and Freud may even have been right about these particular supposed analogues of repression called to his attention by Rozenzweig). Freud's style of investigation also offers an appealing basis to justify the neglect of empirical research on developmental stages as well as on mental functioning – after all, Freud made such world-shaking discoveries, it is natural to consider Freud's method as the *only* method; why then should one look elsewhere for a model of method?

As I will show, there needs to be a reconciliation between what are seen as opposites to some practitioners – psychoanalytic and empirical research. I have observed over the years that most psychoanalysts have paid relatively little attention to empirical research, especially on development and on mental functioning and I see that as a loss to our field, as does Erreich (in press) and others.

PRINCIPLES ABOUT PSYCHOANALYTIC TECHNIQUES FROM EMPIRICAL STUDIES

It does not seem likely that the field will discover general principles about psychoanalytic technique by studying any domain other than the psychoanalytic process itself, contrary to Grünbaum's (1984) suggestion to concentrate on extra-therapy research. Therefore, I think we should at least take a peek at what we would find if we looked in the direction of the principles of the psychoanalytic process, as these are implied by empirical studies, for there is much to find that could be of value to clinicians. First and foremost we would find treatment principles that happen to come mostly from research on psychoanalytic psychotherapy – although these principles would probably apply as well to psychoanalysis – only because the research is not there yet with psychoanalytic therapy. The following six principles, mostly from that research on psychoanalytic psychotherapy, will serve as good examples. Each one is first specified as a principle and then followed by some of the empirical research that supports it.

Principle 1: The greater the patient's psychiatric severity, the greater the restriction in therapeutic change.

This principle was first stated by Freud (1916–1917) and also restated by him (1937c) in terms of the associated amounts of ego distortion and consequent limitation in therapeutic change. The earliest empirical study of this principle concluded that higher (i.e., healthier) ratings on the Health-Sickness Rating Scale (Luborsky, 1962a) (which was constructed at the Menninger Foundation from about 1948) were shown to be associated with slightly greater benefits to the patient from treatment. There is a long history of subsequent empirical studies to support this principle, beginning with Luborsky (1962b). In this study, better psychological health, as measured by the Health-Sickness Rating Scale, was significantly correlated (.54) with more improvement in treatment as rated by an independent research team.

Another finding was that higher ego strength ratings were significantly correlated (.35) with better outcome (Kernberg et al., 1972). A more recent example is provided by Woody and colleagues (Woody et al., 1984). In this study, addicted patients with higher levels of initial psychiatric symptoms had poorer outcomes seven months after treatment started on seven outcome measures, including psychiatric functioning (mean correlation was .37). More of such studies are summarized in Luborsky and colleagues (Luborsky, Crits-Christoph, Mintz, & Auerbach, 1988).

Principle 2: The early therapeutic alliance predicts the benefits that patients eventually achieve in psychotherapy.

The idea in this principle also derives ultimately from a suggestion by Freud (1912b): therapeutic rapport between patient and therapist is necessary for treatment benefits to occur. There are more than a dozen studies that confirm this within psychoanalytically oriented psychotherapy, as well as 23 studies in a systematic review of many types of treatment (Horvath & Simmonds, 1991). A few representative examples follow: Morgan, Luborsky, Crits-Christoph, Curtis, & Solomon (1982) showed that higher helping alliance scores using the global rating method related to better outcome on two different outcome measures (a significant correlation of .44, and a very significant correlation of .58). Hartley and Strupp (1983) showed that higher scores on their Vanderbilt Therapeutic Alliance Scale assessed at the 25 percent point of completion of treatment correlated significantly with better treatment outcome.

Principle 3: A reliable and valid measure of the central relationship pattern, the Core Conflictual Relationship Theme (CCRT), is associated with the transference pattern.

The CCRT measure is based on the redundancies across relationship narratives told during psychotherapy and psychoanalytic sessions (Luborsky, 1977). In psychoanalysis and in psychoanalytic psychotherapy the theory of the technique of dynamic psychotherapy requires that the analyst must make a formulation of the transference pattern as a basis for fashioning appropriate interpretations (Luborsky, 1984; Luborsky & Crits-Christoph, 1998). Research has shown, however, that agreement among clinicians on the transference pattern is not usual, even by expert clinicians (DeWitt, Kaltreider, Weiss, & Horowitz, 1983; Seitz, 1966). In contrast, reliable and accurate clinical formulations of transference can be made with the guidance provided by the CCRT method. One of the main guidelines of the CCRT is that clinical formulation of transference should be based especially on the narratives patients tell in the course of psychoanalysis and psychotherapy. We have found that with the CCRT system in eight different samples of psychoanalytic psychotherapy, clinicians were able to agree well on their CCRT formulations (Luborsky & Diguer, 1998).

Principle 4: Mastery of conflict is a crucial component of change for improved patients in treatment.

The mastery of conflict at times was an important concept for Freud (1920g), for example in explaining children's repetitive games as an attempt to master traumatic memories. Mastery has been measured in terms of the acquisition of emotional self-control and self-understanding about relationship conflicts (Grenyer, 1994). The measure can be applied to changes in mastery during psychodynamic psychotherapy and probably even to psychoanalytic therapy (Grenyer & Luborsky, 1998). The concept of mastery implies that some changes in the course of therapy go beyond changes in the conflicts themselves; they are instead in the mastery of the conflicts. The scales in the mastery measure consist of six levels of mastery, from Level 1 as lack of impulse control, to Level 6 as self-control. For 41 patients in psychodynamic psychotherapy, greater gains in mastery were associated with greater gains on measures of general functioning and symptoms (for example, as measured by the Health-Sickness Rating Scale). In general, it was found that the three lower levels of mastery showed the most change during psychodynamic psychotherapy: lack of impulse control, introjection and projection of negative affects, and difficulties in understanding and control.

Principle 5: The level and quality of insight into one's conflicts parallels the improvement in treatment.

This principle sounds straightforward and confirmable, but it has mostly resisted empirical study. The evidence from studies so far has yielded only a few examples of promising results.

With the Penn Psychotherapy Project data, Crits-Christoph, Cooper, & Luborsky (1988) clearly have shown that greater accuracy of interpretations was associated with greater benefits for the patients. Accuracy is measured by independent judgements of the degree of agreement between each interpretation and the central relationship pattern as measured by the CCRT.

A similar result was obtained in the Mount Zion psychotherapy research (Norville, Sampson, & Weiss, 1996; Silberschatz, Sampson, & Weiss, 1986). They had defined self-understanding in a similar way, that is, convergence of the interpretations with their measure of the "plan diagnosis" – a measure analogous to the CCRT. In contrast to the Crits-Christoph et al. (1988) outcome of treatment measure, their measure was a sample of the session *just after the interpretation*, as rated by independent clinicians.

A questionnaire approach (Connolly et al., in press) called the Self-Understanding and Insight in Psychotherapy Questionnaire (SUIP) has also shown promising results in reliability and in prediction of treatment outcomes.

Principle 6: Consistent preconditions are regularly present just before recurrent symptoms appear in the course of psychoanalysis and psychotherapy.

Across seven different recurrent symptoms, the most pervasive preconditions were found to be (starting with the most): hopelessness, lack of control, feeling blocked, and helplessness. This knowledge comes from the only controlled empirical study of preconditions for recurring symptoms in psychoanalysis and psychotherapy (Luborsky, 1996; Luborsky, in press). That study in fact combines both a clinical-psychoanalytic approach and a clinical-quantitative approach.

DISCUSSION

Six principles related to psychoanalytic technique have been explicated; each one shows the value of a combined clinical and empirical research approach. The six topics for the principles are: the severity of the patient's psychiatric disorder, the therapeutic alliance, the changes in the transference pattern and a new reliable measure of it, the changes in mastery and a new measure of it, the changes in insight, and the preconditions of recurrent symptoms expressed during the course of treatment.

It remains now to further examine the operation of these six principles within a sample of psychoanalytic treatments. This can now be done because I have the data from the Penn Psychoanalytic Treatment Collection (Luborsky et al., in press). The plan for examining these principles in psychoanalyses would involve an analysis of that unique set of 17 completely tape recorded psychoanalyses. Each case was evaluated by two independent clinicians, who each assessed the early sessions and then the late stage sessions of each analysis and found that the assessment of change showed good agreement.

Much should be learned from the application of the principles in the sample of tape-recorded cases. However, the research tradition in psychoanalysis displays an unreadiness to attend to multi-case empirical research findings. In fact, there is now empirical evidence about the high pervasiveness of this unreadiness based on questionnaire studies (Schachter & Luborsky, 1998). In the questionnaires, analysts were given samples of two kinds of studies, empirical studies and clinical studies, and they were asked to make a choice about their inclination to read more about each of them. The clinical studies were by far the most preferred reading for most of the analyst respondents. However, in real life, as opposed to in a questionnaire study, a choice does not have to be made – a researcher who combines both clinical and empirical interests should be in the strongest, most informed position. As stated by Erreich (in press): "A fruitful synthesis of empirical and clinical findings should help us to separate the wheat from the chaff of psychoanalytic theory . . . and integrate psychoanalysis into the larger world of scholarship" (p. 17). This is a helpful guiding principle for all of us to adhere to in furthering the development of our field.

The Integration of Psychoanalytic and Neuroscientific Thought in the Realm of Personality

GLEN O. GABBARD

Unlike many psychoanalysts in the United States, Arnold Cooper has maintained his involvement with psychiatry throughout his career. For many years he directed the educational programs in the Cornell University Medical School Department of Psychiatry. He has always maintained that there are bridges between the neurosciences and psychoanalysis that could mutually enhance the two fields. In 1985 he published a much-cited paper, "Will Neurobiology Influence Psychoanalysis?" In his role as North American editor for the *International Journal of Psycho-Analysis*, he played a key role in developing a regular feature that would explore that interface.

In this chapter I would like to explore the potential for an integrated view of personality that takes into account data from both neuroscience research and psychoanalytic observation. Another area of Arnold Cooper's interest lies in character pathology, where he has made major contributions to our understanding of narcissistic and masochistic personality disorders (Cooper, 1982a; 1984a; 1985c; 1986a; 1988a; 1993; Groopman & Cooper, 1995). Hence this particular bridging effort encompasses two of Arnold Cooper's lifelong interests.

A BIOLOGICALLY INFORMED PSYCHODYNAMIC MODEL OF PERSONALITY DISORDER

For many years the psychoanalytic theory of character evolved independently of genetic and neuroscientific data. Psychoanalytic clinicians in our current era must take into account the information gleaned from studies of heritability and temperament. The psychobiological model of personality developed by Cloninger, Svrakic, and Pryzbeck (1993) provides a heuristically useful starting point. With solid support from sophisticated genetic research, these investigators have suggested that personality is composed of two domains: (a) temperament, which is largely influenced by biological variables; and (b) character, which evolves from environmental variables. Each dimension appears to contribute approximately 50 percent to the construct of personality. Temperament variables appear to play a key role in determining the subtype of personality disorder. However, the research of Cloninger and colleagues suggests that character variables distinguish whether or not an individual is sufficiently maladaptive in his behaviour to warrant being classified as a personality disorder.

The four dimensions of temperament within this model are: (a) *reward-dependence*, which is characterized by social attachment, dependence on approval of others, and sentimentality; (b) *novelty-seeking*, which involves active avoidance of frustration, impulsive decision-making, easy loss of temper, and exploratory activity in response to novel situations; (c) *harm-avoidance*, which is characterized by pessimistic worry about the future, shyness regarding strangers, rapid fatigability, and passive avoidant behaviour such as fear of uncertainty (this dimension has often been linked to the Eysenck construct of neuroticism); and (d) *persistence*, which is meant to characterize the capacity to persevere despite frustration and fatigability. Each of these four dimensions is heritable independently of one another, but only to an extent of 50 to 60 percent. Each also manifests itself early in life so that character is inevitably built on these temperamental foundations, much as Thomas and Chess (1984) have argued in their delineation of infant temperaments.

Specific personality types can, of course, be linked to various of the temperamental dimensions. For example, the isolative personalities, such as the paranoid and schizoid types, are strongly associated with a low rating on reward-dependence. Neurotic characters, such as those with obsessive-compulsive and phobic or avoidant tendencies tend to rate highly in the dimension of harm-avoidance. Psychopathic personalities, of course, would rate high in the dimension of novelty-seeking. Patients who have been diagnosed as borderline personality disorder are somewhat unique among the personality disorders in that they are high in both harm-avoidance and in novelty-seeking.

The other key component of personality in the Cloninger psychobiological model is character. Family and environmental influences are critical for character formation, and three dimensions have been identified by Cloninger and his colleagues: (a) self-directedness, (b) cooperativeness, and (c) self-transcendence. The former two are critically important for the diagnosis of a personality disorder. In fact, Cloninger and colleagues (1993) found that low ratings on self-directedness and on cooperativeness are associated with all categories of personality disorder in the *DSM-IV* system. On the other hand, self-transcendence does not appear to differentiate patients who have personality disorder from those who do not.

Self-directedness is regarded as a developmental process that has several discrete aspects: (a) identification of personally valued purposes and goals versus a lack of direction or goalless existence, (b) self-acceptance versus self-striving, (c) acceptance of responsibility for the choices one makes rather than externalizing responsibility onto others, and (d) development of skills and confidence in problem solving, which might be regarded as a dialectic between resourcefulness versus apathy.

Cooperativeness, the second dimension of character, involves the extent to which a person is hostile and self-centered versus agreeable and collaborative. Several dialectical aspects can be broken out of cooperativeness and studied: (a) helpfulness versus unhelpfulness, (b) compassion versus vengefulness, (c) empathy versus social disinterest, (d) social acceptance versus intolerance, and (e) pure-hearted principles versus those based on exploitation of others for self-advantage. While cooperative individuals involve themselves in mutually supportive and compassionate social networks, those who are uncooperative regard the world and external objects as adversarial and hostile, much like their internal object world.

The third dimension of character, self-transcendence, deals with the spiritual or religious dimension of humankind, so it is less relevant to personality disorders.

The recognition that biological temperament plays a role in personality and its pathology in no way diminishes the value of psychoanalytic and psychotherapeutic approaches in the clinical setting. On the contrary, this distinction allows the clinician to use psychoanalytic strategies more expertly, with specific areas targeted. Because the character variables determine whether or not a true personality disorder is present within this model, psychotherapeutic treatment is pivotal in addressing those problems that have led to the diagnosis of personality disorder. Temperament is relatively stable over time, even with psychotherapy, but may be toned down to some degree by medications (Svrakic, Whitehead, Pryzbeck, & Cloninger, 1993). Character, on the other hand, is malleable and is ever changing throughout adulthood. Long-term follow-up of antisocial personality disorders, for example, has suggested that these individuals may become more cooperative and more self-directed between the ages of 25 and 35, even though their fundamental biological temperament stays essentially the same (Robins, 1966).

Preliminary data on the use of specific psychopharmacologic agents, such as selective serotonin reuptake inhibitors (SSRIs), suggest that symptoms associated with temperament, like impulsivity and affect lability, may be diminished to a significant degree by medication (Coccaro & Kavoussi, 1997; Siever & Davis, 1991), which allows the patient's character problems to be addressed in psychoanalysis or psychotherapy. What I am suggesting in this integrative effort is that the character dimension identified within the Cloninger model can be more usefully adapted to psychoanalytic terminology. For example, the dimension of self-directedness is clearly linked to the psychoanalytic constructs of ego functions and self-representations. Cooperativeness, on the other hand, is essentially a dimension that reflects internal object relations as they are externalized and manifested in interpersonal relations.

Blatt and Ford (1994) have identified two fundamental tasks of personality development: (a) the achievement of a stable, differential, realistic, and positive identity and (b) the establishment of enduring, mutually gratifying relationships with others. The character dimensions of self-directedness and cooperativeness lend themselves to this distinction. Blatt and Ford propose that the two dimensions evolve in a dialectical and synergistic relationship to one another throughout the life cycle. They also feel that character pathology in general can be divided into two broad groups: (a) introjective types, who are primarily concerned about self-definition, and (b) anaclitic types, who are more concerned about relatedness.

Psychoanalytic clinicians, then, will note that certain patients appear to be more concerned about defining who they are while others are more focused on establishing relationships that are gratifying. Obviously, many people with personality pathology have considerable difficulty in both areas.

Sandler's (1981) view of character is a useful way of bridging the self and internal object relations within the construct of character. He regards character as manifested in the patient's ongoing attempt to actualize certain patterns of relatedness that reflect wishes in the patient's unconscious. Through the patient's typical behaviors, she or he subtly attempts to impose a certain way of experiencing and/or responding on the clinician. In other words, embedded in so-called fixed character traits is the unconscious attempt to actualize an internal object relationship that is part of a wish-fulfilling fantasy in the patient. From this perspective the transference–countertransference dimensions of the clinical interaction provide a privileged glimpse of the characteristic and problematic patterns of relatedness that have chronically caused difficulties in the patient's relationships with others.

In childhood an individual internalizes a self-representation in interaction with an object representation connected by an affect. These self-object-affect units ultimately form a kind of mosaic that comprises the individual's sense of self in a series of relational patterns with others. These internalized object-relations units are unconsciously repeated in interactions throughout adult life. Sandler suggests that these patterns are efforts to actualize one of the internal object relations as a way of fulfilling a wish. In this regard, even abusive relationships that involve a tormenting or "bad" object may be providing affirmation and safety for a variety of reasons. Sadism can be soothing, familiar, and predictable to patients who have known little else. Highly conflictual sadomasochistic relationships may certainly be preferable to having no object at all. Many such patients unconsciously assume that their capacity to feel connected to a significant object is dependent on maintaining an abuser–victim paradigm within the relationship. These relationships are not only reliable and predictable, but they also provide the patient with a sense of meaning and continuity (Gabbard, 1989a).

The repetitive interaction seen in personality-disordered patients may reflect actual relationships with objects from the past, but they may also involve wished-for relationships, such as those often seen in patients with childhood trauma who are seeking a rescuer. When the patient's interpersonal pressure causes the analyst to accept unconsciously the role in which he or she has been cast, American analysts are likely to refer to the phenomenon as *projective identification* (Gabbard, 1995; Ogden, 1979). In other words, the patient may "nudge" the therapist into assuming the role of an abuser in response to the patient's "victim" role, and the therapist may feel countertransference anger or hate and behave hostilely towards the patient. British analysts, on the other hand, would view projective identification as more of a fantasy – the therapist's complementary response is not a necessary part of the phenomenon.

Of course, many therapists may not accept the role that is projected onto them. They may ignore the role or defend against it by assuming an opposite or different stance. For example, when an analyst is feeling pressured into taking on a sadistic role towards a patient, he or she may respond by becoming overly empathic and kind as a reaction formation against the pressure to take on the sadistic role. Each clinician will respond differently based on his or her own set of internal object relations (Gabbard, 1995).

If the role evoked is highly ego dystonic, the analyst may well feel that an alien force has taken over. The analyst's reaction at such moments may be to feel that he or she is behaving irrationally and feeling "unlike myself." By contrast, if the wished-for interaction being actualized is that of an idealized parent who is loving and understanding, the analyst may experience the role thrust upon her by the patient as entirely ego syntonic and may therefore be unaware of any countertransference involvement. Regardless of which variant of countertransference involvement is present, a critically important aspect of this conceptual model of character is that the analyst must maintain a free-floating responsiveness (Sandler, 1981) to the patient's various provocations as a way of understanding the patient's usual mode of object relatedness *outside* of the treatment situation. The analyst's approach to these characterological dimensions include systematic clarification, confrontation, and interpretation of the patient's unconscious internal object relations, particularly as they are externalized in the transference–countertransference dimensions of the treatment and in extratransference relationships.

Another major component of character is the particular constellation of defences unique to each individual. Within the classical tradition, defences are regarded as intrapsychic mechanisms designed to prevent awareness of unconscious sexual or aggressive wishes. A more contemporary understanding of defence mechanisms is that they also serve as a way of preserving self-esteem in the face of narcissistic vulnerability and assure safety when one feels dangerously threatened by abandonment. Defences may also insulate one from external dangers through minimization or denial.

In the realm of character pathology, defences are most usefully conceptualized as embedded in relatedness. They may change the relationship between self and object and help manage unresolved conflicts with internal objects as well as with current figures in external reality. There is a time-honored tradition of associating particular defence mechanisms with specific personality disorders. A paranoid personality, for example, may use projection as a way of disavowing unacknowledged feelings and attributing them to others. These defences inevitably affect that individual's mode of relatedness. While defences are traditionally regarded as intrapsychic, they typically emerge in the treatment situation as *resistances* to the process.

Although resistance can be intrapsychic in some situations, there is ordinarily a strong interpersonal component involving the analyst as an object (Gabbard, 1994; Gill, 1994). The characteristic hopes and fears that are intimately linked to the patient's internal object relations and that patient's specific constellation of defence mechanisms frequently work synergistically to create a unique set of transferences that tend to evoke a related set of countertransferences in the analyst.

Using obsessive-compulsive personality disorder as an example, we can observe this synergy in vivo.

> Mr. A. came to each session filled with an array of topics to which he "free associated." He never lacked for analytic material, and eventually he confessed that he would make a list of items while in the waiting room to be sure that he knew what he wished to cover during the session. He often appeared to have considerable insight and psychological awareness, although his affect and vocal intonation was rather monotonous. He invariably showed up early for each session. When handed the bill, he would reliably write a check the very next day to cover the entire amount. He frequently noted that "I am a gentleman," and he eschewed anger or aggression as "inconsiderate" and "unnecessary." Indeed, he behaved within the analytic setting in such a way as to avoid any possible hint that he might have anger, aggression, or resentment towards the analyst. The reaction formation was partially designed to ward off attacks by the analyst, of course, whom he unconsciously regarded as a potentially critical authoritarian figure, in the same vein as his father. He also wanted to actualize a specific wished-for interaction, that of a good, dutiful child basking in the glow of an approving parent. This wished-for interaction itself could be regarded as a defence against a feared interaction in which the analyst or therapist would become an embodiment of the patient's harsh and critical superego.
>
> Mr. A. illustrated several defensive operations, principally isolation of affect, intellectualization, and reaction formation. His defences toned down affects and emphasized cognition instead. His intrapsychic defences manifested themselves as resistances within the session. They prevented Mr. A. from experiencing strong feelings, but they were also designed to avoid provoking anger or disapproval in the analyst. From his descriptions of himself as a child, his temperamental disposition would probably be rated high in the area of harm-avoidance and reward-dependence. Hence within this conceptual model, Mr. A.'s character traits represented the final common pathway of instinctual wishes, defences against those wishes, and modes of eliciting responses from significant objects in the environment or in the patient's intrapsychic world. This character was imposed upon a specific biologically based temperament.

A final implication of this integrative model of personality is that medications and psychoanalysis may be regarded as compatible elements of a comprehensive treatment plan for patients who have severe character pathology. Medications will not change fundamental concepts of self nor will they alter the patient's basic set of internal object relations. Nevertheless, medications may allow the patient to be more reflective and thoughtful about what is transpiring between the analyst and patient. Marcus (1990) has noted that defences may become less rigid as a result of pharmacologic effects of antidepressants and thus contribute to an increase in the patient's observing ego capacity.

Hence contemporary analysts are beginning to realize the dream of integration that Arnold Cooper has long advocated. With an increasing understanding of the difference between temperament and character, specific treatment approaches can target specific aspects of the patient's personality. There is perhaps a degree of irony in the notion that mind and brain may ultimately come together most clearly in the arena of personality.

Freud's Theory of the Mental and Modern Functional Imaging Experiments*

R. G. SHULMAN AND D. L. ROTHMAN

What relations are there between Freud's theories of the mind and modern functional brain imaging experiments? To anchor this question, we present two statements from an article by Mark Solms (1997) about consciousness in a recent *Journal of the American Psychoanalytic Association*.

First, Solms emphasized Freud's definition that "Mental processes are in themselves unconscious" (p. 683), arguing the relevance of this definition to modern controversies about brain/mind/consciousness. We are willing to accept a moderate form of this position, in which the unconscious is acknowledged to contribute significantly to mental processes.

The second quotation is less familiar: "psychoanalysis and PET scanning . . . study one and the same underlying object: the mental apparatus and its functions" (p. 691). We do not plan to discuss Solms's use of this identity in pursuit of consciousness. This statement is evocative and needful of comment particularly in a period of intense research in the neurosciences when functional magnetic resonance imaging (fMRI) and positron emission tomography (PET) methods have been experimentally localizing brain activities. These functional imaging methodologies map neurophysiological responses to cognitive, emotional, or sensory stimulations (Posner & Raichle, 1994; Raichle, 1998; Shulman, Blamire, Rothman, & McCarthy, 1993). The experiments are non-invasive and may be done repeatedly. The rapid progress made using these methods has encouraged widespread optimism about our ability to understand activities of the mind.

---

*This paper is reproduced from Brooks, P. & Woloch, A. (eds.), *Whose Freud?*, © 2000 by Yale University. Reprinted with permission.

In applying modern functional imaging methods to understanding the mind it is assumed that the imaging signal directly measures mental processes. That is, in fact, not true. The signals come from changes in blood flow and brain energy parameters. To interpret these energy signals in terms of mental processes, one must proceed cautiously since, as we shall show, inferences about the mental derived from functional imaging experiments have depended upon assumptions about mental activity. Hence before functional imaging methods may study "the mental apparatus and its functions", these assumptions must be examined. The psychological assumptions in the field today are so pervasive that their acceptance is usually unquestioned. The paradigm in the field is cognitive psychology, in which mental processes handle information by computational modules. Subjectivity is usually not acknowledged but when it is tested for, it too becomes a module of, for example, attention, working memory, or perhaps even mother love. However, since the basic premise of the field differs from Freud's view that mental processes have strong unconscious elements, psychologists and psychiatrists must be particularly precise about their assumptions when proposing and interpreting functional imaging experiments.

Functional imaging experiments are generally set up to measure directly or indirectly differences seen in the brain image between two behavioural tasks (Posner & Raichle, 1994; Raichle, 1998; Shulman et al., 1993). One task is usually the subject at rest, with minimum stimulation. Images collected during rest are subtracted from those during a task and the difference images are evaluated statistically to establish the probability they are not random. Difference images, as shown in many publications, are plots of regions in which the differences between images during the task and at rest are statistically significant. This presentation does not mean that imaging signals elsewhere are non-existent, but merely that they don't show on the difference image because their magnitudes do not change significantly between task and control.

To understand the meaning of these experiments we need to know the connection between the magnitude of these functional imaging signals and neuronal activity in the brain: in other words, the biological foundations of the signals. Functional imaging signals are caused by changes in neuronal activity and they are detected via changes in blood physiological parameters by changes in cerebral metabolic rate of glucose (CMRglc), cerebral metabolic rate of oxygen ($CMRO_2$) and the correlative changes in cerebral blood flow (CBF). Until recently, the relation between functional imaging signals (S) and neuronal activity (N) (which hitherto has been interpreted as changes in physiology parameters) was not known. However results of our recent experiments (Sibson et al., 1998) have established a quantitative relation between the *signal* S measured in functional imaging experiments and N, the neuronal activity that consists of neurotransmitter activity. In these experiments, neurotransmitter activity (N) was shown to consist almost entirely of glutamate to glutamine neurotransmitter cycling, and the energy measured in a functional imaging experiment, S, provided a measure of N. This recent calibration of the relation between S and N has been achieved in rats and humans by new methods that enable the neurotransmitter activity to be measured directly while at the same time energy consumption is measured. This is shown in Figure 1 (below) as a solid line.

Although the ability to measure cortical neurotransmitter flux (N) is important for mechanisms of brain activity in neuroscience, we pass over that, for the moment, to direct attention to its role in mental activity (M). The dashed line between N and M is the unanswered "hard problem", the relation between neuronal activity and mind that is the paradigm of neuro-

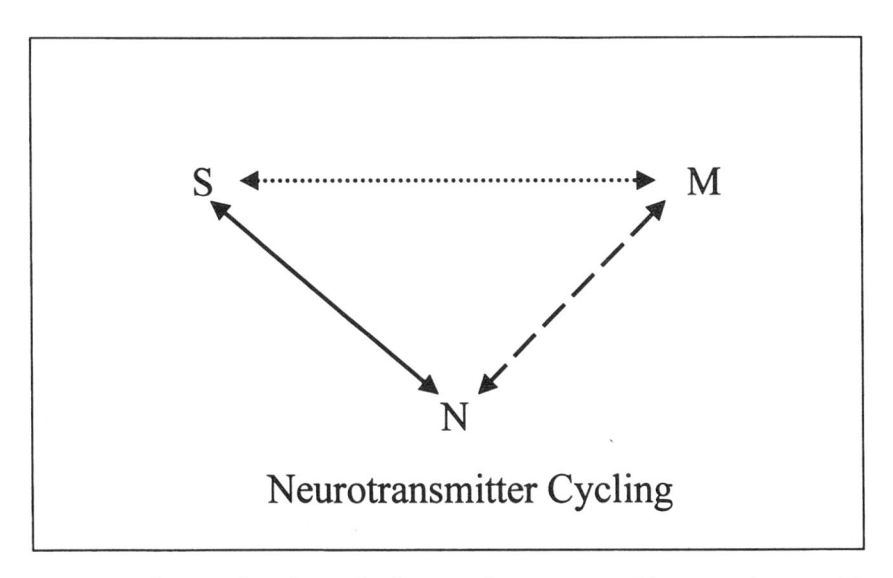

Figure 1. Schematic for relating the functional imaging signal S to mental activity M. In psychology this connection is made directly by interpreting S obtained during stimulation. In neuroscience, a biological interpretation (Sibson et al., 1998) shows that S arises from changes in the neuronal energy consumption determined by N. This shows up as changes in glucose or oxygen consumption, which may be accompanied be changes in blood flow. In this interpretation N still has to be related to M.

science that Francis Crick has summarized as "The scientific belief . . . that our minds – the behaviour of our brains – can be explained by the interaction of nerve cells (and other cells) and the molecules associated with them" (Crick, 1994, p. 7).

At this point we return to the functional imaging experiments that seem to represent the very cutting edge of scientific studies of brain activity. If functional imaging experiments had followed the neuroscience path of Figure 1, they would have sought a measure of N. Having done so, we would be facing the hard problem of neuroscience. How does N interact with M? But functional imaging has not proceeded this way! Generally functional imaging bypasses biology in favour of a top down cognitive psychology approach. In this approach, based upon psychology, not on neuroscience, the brain is modelled as consisting of separate functional modules each performing a discrete mental process. Since these processes are assumed to be functionally separable, any change in S is directly assigned to a mental process (M), reflected by the dotted line in Figure 1. The signals are being used to directly measure M with interpretations derived from a psychological methodology proposed by cognitive psychology.

To see how functional imaging bypasses neuroscience, consider how the mental operations are localized and measured in a typical experiment. The approaches of cognitive psychology were pioneered in PET studies by Posner, Raichle, and their colleagues (1994). In the Raichle and Posner view (described in general terms above), the computational module of brain activity is to be found in a PET-differencing experiment where images from two tasks are subtracted, one task presumed to stimulate the computational module, the other designed not to. Each difference scan is considered to have localized these postulated mental functions by measuring the magnitude and location of the computational module of mental activity required for the task. It is assumed that the difference signal between the two images represents all the brain activity needed to produce the mental activity. As pointed out previously it is further assumed that the difference in the task has been uniquely identified (Shulman, 1996; Shulman & Rothman, 1998). This is problematic and in fact circular since it ends up locating in the brain modules of activities, whose existence is merely postulated.

Figure 2 (see p. 167) presents a generalized description of the signals during a typical functional imaging experiment. From the recent metabolic studies (Sibson et al., 1998), it is now known that the height, S, represents the energy needed for neuronal activity, N. A large body of information has shown that the incremental activity ΔS is typically less than 10 percent

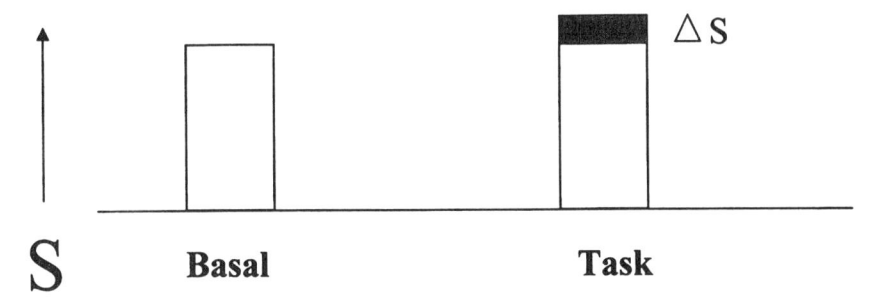

Figure 2. Schematic of the small changes in neuronal activity during a task showing how the differencing subtracts two large numbers.

of rest values during a cognitive task. In the cognitive psychology paradigm ΔS is assumed to measure the modular brain activity needed to do the computation required by the task. The baseline value of N is ignored since, based upon the assumption in the field, the mental module is not significantly active at rest. Put simply, this interpretation assumes that

$$\Delta S = \Delta N = M$$

The mental activity needed for the task in this interpretation is provided by the incremental signal ΔS which is assumed to measure incremental neuronal activity. But this interpretation is based upon the concept that the internal processes represented in the baseline neuronal activity (N) are separable from and not needed for the mental activity of the "module". How would other theories of mind, which consider subjective, conscious, or unconscious neuronal activities to be essential for mental activities, interpret these data? One of the early criticisms of cognitive psychology, from a biochemical viewpoint, was from Changeux (1985), who introduced the hypothesis that mental processes are internally induced by the subject. Changeux's view of the totality of mind activity being required for mental processes is shared with several major philosophical and psychological theories of mind. These theories (certainly including Freud's) accept the existence of unconscious activities, claiming for them an important role in mental processes and contributing to any computational activities of the type considered in cognitive psychology.

These differences have been sharply delineated by John Searle in his monumental critique *The Rediscovery of the Mind* (1992). He writes, "in the philosophy of mind, obvious facts about the mental, such as that we all really do have subjective, conscious mental states are routinely denied by many, perhaps most, of the advanced thinkers in the subject" (p. 3). In this position, Searle shares to some extent the view that mental processes include unconscious elements, although he does have a *very* different view of the unconscious. Similar criticisms of the computational basis of cognitive psychology have been made deftly by Edelman (1992) who, while presenting his own comprehensive view of the mind, critically dismisses the claims of cognitive psychology because "they are disregarding a large body of evidence that undermines the view that the brain is a kind of computer" (p. 14).

There are significant differences in these several schools of thought about the nature of mind and particularly of the nature of subjective, conscious, and unconscious activity. They are lumped together here because of their view of the holistic and comprehensive relation between brain activity and mind. They oppose the cognitive psychology position that mental activity can be considered as a series of computational processes that are separable from the subjective, personal activities of mind.

In other words, these holistic concepts of mind, from philosophy, psychiatry, and neuroscience share the view that

$$S = N = M$$

Our experimental results require the more holistic interpretation of functional imaging experiments. First, the calibration of functional imaging, which has been achieved by the recent ^{13}C MRS experiments (Shulman, 1996; Shulman & Rothman, 1998; Sibson et al., 1998) shows that fractional increases in N during cognitive tasks are less than 10 percent over baseline neuronal activity. These calibrations show that in the resting state neuronal activity accounts for nearly all of the brain energy consumption. From the cognitive psychology viewpoint, brain energy consumption during rest would not include neuronal activity because no computation was being performed. Accordingly the resting energy consumption, responsible for the signal S, could be subtracted from the signal during the task and yield the difference due to neuronal activity. However, the assumption of constant baseline activities in the differencing method has more uncertainties when the resting state has been shown to have almost the same magnitude of neuronal activity as the stimulated state, and to be performing the same neurochemical process of glutamate/glutamine cycling.

The second objection is experimental, coming from imaging science. If the subjective baseline activity were not needed for "mental" activity, then the incremental activity for a mental process should be independent of the baseline. There have been studies in rats in which sensory stimulations were performed at different degrees of anaesthesia. As shown previously (Sibson et al., 1998), neuronal activity of glutamate/glutamine cycling decreases in the anaesthetized states, falling monotonically to zero under deep pentobarbital anaesthesia. Under certain anaesthetics, animals will respond to sensory stimulations such as forepaw electrical stimulation, or vibratory sensory stimulation, and studies have reported the incremental rate of glucose consumption, which has been shown to be a direct measure of neuronal activity (Sibson et al., 1998). If the mental activity needed to perform the task were modular, it should add the *same* incremental signal in the anaesthetized and awake states. Starting from the anaesthetized state, ΔS should be the same as when stimulated from rest. If, on the other hand, the full neuronal activity is needed to perform the task then the final state during the task should be the same, regardless of the initial state, and the increment during the task will be larger under anaesthesia. A large number of animal experiments show that the latter is actually the case (Shulman, Rothman, & Hyder, 1999). During stimulation, S is observed to rise to approximately the same absolute level, independent of the state. These results support the holistic view of mind in which a particular *magnitude* of neuronal activity is required for a task, not a particular *increment*.

Since not all anaesthetized states allow the animal to respond, those experiments must be considered as models for cognitive human experiments. Humans with reduced basal activity, induced by anaesthesia or sleep, could be stimulated to perform cognitive tasks. Decisive choices between theories of mind could then be made, as suggested by these rat experiments. Where does this analysis position functional imaging with respect to psychiatry? Both functional imaging and psychoanalysis are presently being used as psychological investigations of mind. However because their starting assumptions about the mind differ significantly, their findings are incommensurate. We suggest that psychiatrists should not do functional imaging experiments based upon hypotheses of cognitive psychology without examining how these hypotheses fundamentally disagree with a more holistic concept of the mind. Furthermore we have shown how functional imaging now has the potential to study the mind in biological terms, by taking advantage of the relation between the signals and neurotransmitter activity. The present experimental paradigms are designed to exclude the subjective brain activity that is the essence of the psychoanalytic field. Rather psychiatrists should base their experiments upon concepts consistent with their own view – a view that embraces the subjective nature of mind.

Normative Sexuality in Contemporary Evolutionary Perspective

ROBERT A. PAUL

Like most of the people I know, I have changed my views about what constitutes the range of normal sexual behaviour. I share a general tolerance for a diverse array of possible choices for adults, and hold the view that – sexual happiness being both as important and as difficult to achieve as it is – people should be allowed, indeed expected and encouraged, to find it in whatever way suits them, as long as it does not bring harm to or interfere with the lives of others. My views on these matters have evolved relatively unselfconsciously, moving, as I look back on it, with the tide of widespread social and cultural developments. These developments include the challenge to accepted conventionality in the 1960s, and the feminist, gay rights, and other movements that have significantly recast the way we think and feel now compared to how we once did.

Given these changes, I can obviously no longer accept at face value, as I may once have done without thinking about it much, the position of the classical psychoanalytic libido theory, according to which only mutual orgasm achieved in heterosexual genital intercourse with a loved and appropriate partner is "normal", while other kinds of solutions to "the sexual problem" (as they used to put it) are not so much morally problematic as pathogenic or pathologic, liable to lead to neurosis, and/or to be symptoms of unhealthy psychodynamics. I have myself terminated what I consider to have been successful analyses in which the patients left analysis with their fondness for oral sex, or voyeurism (consuming "adult" entertainment), or masturbation intact, if better understood and modified. I certainly don't see it as my job to get these people to give up what they enjoy and to act as an enforcer of sexual "normalcy".

Is this change in attitude only a shift in socially permissible fashion? It would be intellectually more satisfying to be able to see one's abandoning of an unreflective norm as consistent not only with social changes but also with an evolutionary perspective. After all, while it may be that "compulsory heterosexuality" is a mere ideological norm that has flourished at a historical moment now largely over, nonetheless the case for regarding the privileged status granted to heterosexual genital intercourse as somehow grounded in "nature" does seem reasonable on the face of it. If the strength of the sexual drive, and the power of the motivation to feel the supremely pleasant gratification of it, leads humans to perform the one sexual act capable of leading to reproduction; and if successful reproduction is, in the Darwinian view, the bottom line in terms of natural selection; then, even if one refuses to leap from "is" to "ought", and to claim that genital intercourse is ethically right or good because it is natural, nonetheless, from the evolutionary point of view, one has to admit that as far as promoting reproductive fitness is concerned, heterosexual genital desire would indeed appear to be designed to get the job done.

It is this apparently obvious evolutionary assumption that Schafer, in a delineation of the evolution of his own views about normative sexuality in psychoanalytic theory (1995), attributes to Freud to account for the latter's adherence to the "compulsory heterosexuality" of his social milieu:

> A central part of my argument . . . is that Freud's Darwinism led him to adopt what I call an evolutionary ethic. Specifically he viewed the individual as the carrier of the reproductive organs and substances designed to guarantee the survival of the species. . . . From this point of view, it seemed to him to follow that psychosexual development should culminate in genital, heterosexual, reproductive orientations. Anything else would go against the plan of nature. [p. 193]

A number of quite recent findings from some fields outside psychoanalysis with a direct bearing upon the evolution of human sexual life seem to offer an interesting path forward here. As an anthropologist as well as a psychoanalyst, I turn then to the emerging picture of the evolutionary relationship between humans and our two closest kindred primate species, the chimpanzee (*Pan troglodytes*) and the bonobo (*Pan paniscus*). Although they are classified under the genus *Pan* and we under the genus *Homo*, many evolutionary thinkers now hold to the view that this distinction is only maintained because of humanity's *amour propre*. In terms of genetic relatedness (we share over 98 percent of the genes in our DNA with these other creatures), as well as in terms of the minute amount of evolutionary time since the three of us diverged from each other – *Homo* separated off about 5 million years ago, and chimps and bonobos parted ways about 3 million years ago – it would make more biological sense to include the three species in a single genus. While recognizing that chimps and bonobos are not our ancestors, it is nonetheless not illegitimate to draw conclusions about our species' evolutionary history by "triangulation" with these close relatives.

Though chimpanzees were regarded not long ago as peaceable vegetarians, like our only slightly more distant cousins the gorillas, it has now been reliably observed that they do hunt for game to eat under some circumstances, and, more startling, that they engage in raiding, when chimps from one territory, if they sense a numerical advantage, will form coalitions to invade and kill off rivals in nearby territories (Stanford, 1996; Wrangham & Peterson, 1996). At the same time, chimps emerge from field observations as highly skilled social and political operators, capable of forming alliances and factions, with a complex set of behaviours designed to maintain intergroup, and especially male–male, cooperation, including extensive mutual grooming, selective food sharing, and other forms of calculated reciprocity, and an elaborate hierarchical system of dominance and rank. Perhaps somewhat violating the strict Darwinian rule, chimpanzees are said to operate as if they understood that the coalition itself is their most valuable weapon, and therefore they take care to preserve it as one of their own, at first apparently "altruistic", vital interests (de Waal, 1996). This sort of cooperation among males is practically unheard of among most sexually reproducing organisms, because competition among males for access to the much more costly reproductive time, energy, and physiology of females is simply too great.

Chimps live in multi-male, multi-female groups, but male–male rivalry is kept under control by the short, clearly marked oestrus period of fertility and receptivity in females, which leaves the rest of the time relatively unstressed, and by the strictly observed dominance hierarchy, which gives mating priority to the ruling coalition who can maintain their position with force until unseated. Such coalitions are maintained by what is called *reciprocal altruism* (Trivers, 1971), a strategy that requires the sufficiently high intelligence we share with chimps, in order to recognize others as individuals and recall what they have (or have not) done for us lately.

Bonobos, which until recently were not even recognized as a separate species, and which by virtue of their small numbers and reclusive forest habits were hardly known, present a startling contrast to the chimpanzees (de Waal

& Lanting, 1997; Kano, 1992). They also live in multi-male, multi-female groups, but among them, collective aggression is absent, and it is the females, not the males, who form the alliances that determine social order. While males do, like chimps, establish rank orders among themselves, they do not unite as fighting teams, whereas females form a number of dyadic bonds with other females that serve to maintain political order in the group.

What is most striking about these apes, however, is their exuberant use of sexuality as the main form of social bonding and affiliation. In addition to heterosexual genital intercourse, bonobos regularly perform sexual acts involving manual-genital, oral-genital, and genital-genital contact. The last named, informally dubbed "G-G rubbing" by specialists, is the preferred form of demonstrating and enacting alliance and friendship between two females, whose genital swellings extend far beyond their fertile periods (unlike chimps). Sexual contact is frequent between members of the same sex as well as between sexes, and also across generations, including with juveniles. As most observers agree, this sexuality is to be thought of as "prosocial", that is, as functioning first and foremost to cement friendships and alliances, to reestablish harmony after disputes, and to maintain a sense of mutual cooperation within and commitment to the group as a whole and to its individual component members.

What we learn from these briefly sketched examples is that there is precedent among our closest kin in the primate world both for coalitions of males able to keep destructive competition among themselves under control, while also capable of uniting in violent and lethal aggression against others; and for the use of sexual pleasure to establish and maintain attachment among individuals, with nothing whatsoever to do with reproduction. This behaviour nonetheless can be said to be adaptive, and to enhance the reproductive fitness of each individual in the group, insofar as the group itself, and its ability to cooperate, is a large part of each individual's system of adaptation to the environment. If it can be managed – and this occurs very rarely in the animal world – organization itself is the most powerful weapon of all (see Mann, 1986).

Bonobos can manage this because there is a low level of aggression among them, the males being reduced to bickering with each other over rank in the dominance order but unable, or unmotivated, to unite to assert themselves over the superior organization of the females. Chimps, on the other hand, who are much more aggressive, are forced to forego the lively sex lives of the bonobos in the interests of keeping order among the organized coalitions of males.

We can surmise that for the ancestors of humans, who emerged from the equatorial forests to become bipedal predators and scavengers of the savannah, the importance of the whole group, as well as of the organized coalition of strategizing, hunting, and raiding males, was greatly enhanced under increased selective pressures. These would include the necessity for males, differentially, to provision pregnant and lactating females with high-protein meat sources, a dietary requirement made necessary in turn by bipedal posture which enforced the "premature" delivery of infants from the womb and led to greater mother–child interaction and dependence. Males became specialized in predation and lethal aggression, whether in hunting or war. Their greatest weapon was not only projectile and stabbing implements, but the intelligent foresight and symbol use that made possible coordinated group action, including aggression.

While humans, like chimpanzees, were once thought to be naturally peaceable animals only given to warfare under certain social conditions, that view is giving way to a more sobering picture of war and all-male weapon-bearing war coalitions as intrinsic features of human social life (Keeley, 1996). Those few groups in the ethnographic record who can be described as non-violent turn out to be either only temporarily so, as defeated or pacified populations, or to live in tiny groups of only a few hundred either scattered in huge territories so that hardly any contact occurs (such as the Copper Eskimos or the notorious Semai and other forest people of Malaysia) or else confined to tiny islands, such as Ifaluk, where any conflict, once started, would immediately decimate everyone (as seems indeed to have happened on Easter Island).

This picture is consistent with that drawn by Eleanor Maccoby (1998) in her recent book capping a lifetime of research into the development of sex differences. She concludes that while few differences appear between individuals, or when individuals are in mixed-gender groups, all-male groups and all-female groups do differ significantly in the higher level of aggression manifested in the former, even among boys who don't seem any different from girls when observed outside this particular social arrangement.

The conclusion to which all these considerations point is one which, as so often happens, Freud himself anticipated, in this case in *Civilization and Its Discontents,* a work often read and commented upon but in my estimation rarely understood. If I may boil down the essence of Freud's argument in that book, it is that when humans lost the oestrus cycle and began to live in more or less long-lasting or permanent erotically bonded pairs, the problem of male competition among themselves became the chief obstacle to stable social organization. Were it not for that factor, humans might well live in the erotic paradise of the bonobos, bonded in friendship and able to cooperate without risk of killing each other. In a world without able-bodied men, indeed, women, children, and old people could probably still do this. But because of the endemic threat posed to social harmony by male–male competition, a trait we share not with the bonobos but with the chimps, radical measures have had to be taken. The most typically human of these has been the diverting of sexuality away from reproductive uses, which employ erotic ties to bind men to their domestic partners and offspring, and into prosocial erotic bonds with other men and with the group as a whole. It is for this reason that human sexuality is conflicted and inhibited; the conflict built into its heart is that it must serve two antithetical purposes, one to bind male–female couples together in reproducing domestic units, the other to serve as the all-purpose social glue, at odds with the tendency to break off into mating couples, but necessary to hold together both the whole group, as well as the male fighting force. The latter has to suppress the tendency to lethal aggression within itself, while remaining able, when appropriate, to muster organized lethal violence against similarly organized outsiders.

These considerations, finally, help us to understand the otherwise mysterious psychoanalytic observation, so well grounded empirically but otherwise so apparently puzzling, that genital sexuality is only one among an array of activities in the human erotic repertoire. Freud, as we have seen, took it for granted that the achievement of the desire and capacity for heterosexual genital sexuality was the natural biological norm, even while he himself initiated the radical deconstruction of its normative status in social terms (1905d). Therefore, he saw preferences for the "component" instincts and "partial drives" as fixations in a stalled progressive development. It would be better to drop that implied view, and instead view the nonreproductive forms of human sexuality as constituting a different phenomenon with a different evolutionary teleology, phylogeny, and ontogeny. In this prosocial form of sexuality, oral and anal sexuality, pleasure in seeing and touching others, same-sex as well as cross-sex desire and activity, and other features would be understood for the part they play, whether through overt enactment or in sublimated form, in the adaptive process of group formation, cohesion, and protection from internal self-destruction as well as from external threat.

Not only would this proposed prosocial sexuality serve to create bonds of affection within a group, but it would also serve the stronger purpose of binding aggression within the group and containing it within erotic casing, so to speak. Thus it would in general manifest a dimension of sadomasochism, and would lend the distinctive heightened aspect of excitement to sexual arousal (Stoller, 1975). The mastery of aggression by Eros was, according to Freud, one of its greatest achievements. Dominance and submission, so typical of sadomasochistic relations, would be psychological correlates of the dominance hierarchies that are a major mechanism for managing intragroup hostility among all primates. The "perversions", insofar as they are actually "perverse", would be those in which the aggressive component is inadequately contained or transmuted by the erotic and turned into a form of libidinal bonding (Cooper, 1991b; Kaplan, 1991; Stoller, 1975). Some of the major defences, too, including reaction formation, turning against the self, and reversal, would all have been evolved to serve the purpose of transforming aggression into intragroup peace.

In addition, an expectable feature of any sort of prosocial erotism would be its "narcissism", in the sense that it would be invested in those with whom one identified oneself as like rather than different – that indeed being its primary raison d'être. Its "promiscuity", too, would be an expression of the fact that its adaptive purpose is precisely to offset the fragmentation of society into isolated domestic pair bonds and to establish links among many different individuals.

Totem and Taboo *and Professional Correctness*
ELIZABETH BOTT SPILLIUS

I have long been an admirer of Arnie Cooper's work as a psychoanalyst, as a leading member of the American Psychoanalytic Association at an important and difficult time, and as an editor, and so I was keen to contribute to a *Festschrift* on applied psychoanalysis in his honour. But how could I do this when, unlike Arnie himself, I have always felt rather uneasy about applying the findings of psychoanalysis to any field other than that of clinical psychoanalysis? Then, however, I thought about *Totem and Taboo* (1913), one of Freud's favourite books, a major excursion into anthropology. And so a suitable subject presented itself. What has been the fate of this particular and very famous case of applied psychoanalysis?

Freud appears to have attached as much importance to his cultural and literary studies as to clinical and theoretical psychoanalysis, as if he thought of psychoanalysis as all of a piece, not divided into two sorts, psychoanalysis "proper" and psychoanalysis "applied." Jones (1957) says that the works by which Freud most wished to be remembered were: "(1) The seventh chapter of *The Interpretation of Dreams*, (2) the last chapter of *Totem and Taboo*, and (3) the essay on "The Unconscious" in his metapsychological series" (pp. 40–41). Even if, as seems likely, Freud made this choice from his writings up until the end of the metapsychological papers, I think it is hardly the choice we would make today. What about the rest of *The Interpretation of Dreams*, "Three Essays on the Theory of Sexuality," "Formulations on the Two Principles of Mental Functioning," "On Narcissism," "Mourning and Melancholia," the papers on technique, and the case histories?

In this brief essay I consider why *Totem and Taboo* was so important to Freud, how it has been received by anthropologists, and how it has come about that it seems almost to have disappeared from the psychoanalytic canon. What does the fate *of Totem and Taboo* tell us not only about the ideas of the book itself but about applied psychoanalysis generally?

A short answer to the question of why *Totem and Taboo* was badly received and has ceased to be considered important is that Freud wrote it some twenty or thirty years too late. In the nineteenth century the great question of how civilization began was being enthusiastically debated. By 1913, however, the various gentleman scholars were beginning to form themselves into separate professions, each jealous of its own territory and each concerned with what I shall call "professional correctness", that is, with the profession's right to its own separate method and ideas, each profession maintaining a respectful distance from the others. Freud's cultural interests ran counter to this trend. He was gripped by the puzzle of human life and culture: What started us off on the path to civilization? How, as an anthropologist has phrased Freud's search, ". . . *did homo* come to be *sapiens*. What sets man off from Nature while leaving him part of Nature?" (Fox, 1967, p. 161). In pursuing answers to these fundamental questions Freud used not only his background knowledge of Western civilization, but also set about reading the standard anthropological works, even though the method of these works was in the process of being superseded. Most of these late nineteenth and early twentieth century works were compendia of customs reported by travellers from various parts of the world. The prevailing view was that current primitive peoples represented early stages of contemporary European civilization, that is, that societies could be arranged in a pyramid of increasing complexity and moral superiority with European civilization at the top. Freud accepted this view at least initially, and, like these anthropologists, he was looking for a general theory of the development of civilization. A contributory interest was a wish to demonstrate to Jung and others the superiority of his theory of infantile sexuality and the Oedipus complex over what Freud regarded as Jung's mysticism (Mahony, 1987a). Mahony also suggests that *Totem and Taboo* was an expression of the intense fraternal and father/son rivalries within and between Vienna and Zurich for dominance in the young psychoanalytic discipline.

Totem and Taboo consists of four essays, the first three laying the ground for the grand thesis of the fourth. The first essay, "The Horror of Incest", establishes that the Australian aborigines have much more complex rules of incest and proscribed (and prescribed) marriage than those of civilized society. Freud notes that incest was defined not in terms of consanguineal kinship based on the nuclear family but in terms of clan (totem) membership; he also notes the extension of kinship terms (mother, father, sister, brother, etc.) outside the family to more distant relatives. Freud points out that in a matrilineal clan system it would not be incestuous for a man to have intercourse with his daughter, and that in a patrilineal system it would not be incestuous for a woman to have intercourse with her son. He states, however, that totem (clan) prohibitions include prohibitions against "real incest", that is, intercourse between members of the nuclear family, but as "a special case" (Freud, 1913, p. 6). It is typical of Freud's acute observation and reasoning that he so readily grasped the principles of unilineal descent, something that most anthropologists, even recent anthropologists, had not realised that he understood (Fox, 1967, pp. 164–167; Leach, 1967, pp. vii–xix).

Freud also describes the way in which each clan was not only exogamous, that is, its members had to marry outside the clan, but each clan had its own totem, an animal species that was revered and could not be eaten except at a special ritual totem feast. In totemic theory the clan members are descended from the totem animal, and Freud suggests that the totem animal represents the father.

The second essay, "Taboo and Emotional Ambivalence", compares cultural taboos and the rituals of obsessional neurotics, showing the role of ambivalence, a concept introduced by Bleuler (1910), in both types of behaviour. Freud had used the concept of ambivalence intensively in analysing Little Hans (1909b) and the Rat Man (1909d).

In the third essay, "Animism, Magic, and the Omnipotence of Thoughts", Freud notes that both the "savage" and the obsessional neurotic act as if they believed that wishes were equivalent to deeds.

The notorious fourth essay, "The Return of Totemism in Childhood", actually says only a little about childhood but much about the childhood of the human race, including an assumed momentous historical event that was the beginning of civilization and religion. Freud brings various strands together in a grand historical reconstruction: Darwin's idea of the primal horde; his own idea of the Oedipus complex; omnipotence of thought; totemic taboos as described in the anthropological literature; Robertson-Smith's (1889) ideas on the commemorative totemic feast; ambivalence in the form of murder of the primal father followed by remorse; a banding together of the guilty brothers; clan exogamy and the inheritance of the historical event and its sequelae. One can see why Freud was excited: it was a very comprehensive explanation.

In Freud's reconstruction of the distant past, humans were organized, as gorillas were thought to be organized, into a primal horde dominated by a leading male who monopolized the women. The sons, in jealous hatred, banded together, killed and ate the father, thus taking in his admired qualities. Then, overcome by guilt and remorse, they worshipped the totem as the father-ancestor, gave up their sexual rights to the women of the clan, their "mothers" and "sisters", and henceforth practised clan (totem) exogamy. The totem could not be eaten except on ritual occasions, when the totem feast commemorated unconsciously the original murder and cannibalism. This event, combined with the pact to maintain fraternal solidarity, the relinquishment of the women, and the beginning of religion in the form of taboos towards the totem, were the first steps towards civilized society. "I should like to insist," says Freud, ". . . that the beginnings of religion, morals, society and art converge in the Oedipus complex" (1913, p. 156).

There is little doubt that Freud thought of the primal horde and the murder of the father as historical events. In the last pages of *Totem and Taboo* he hesitates, raising the possibility that ". . . the mere existence of a wishful *phantasy* of killing and devouring [the father] would have been enough to produce the moral reaction that created totemism and taboo" (pp. 159–160). In the end, however, and for reasons that are not entirely clear, Freud reasserts his earlier view: "I think that in the case before us it may safely be assumed that 'in the beginning was the Deed'" (see also Jones, 1956, p. 35).

Freud assumes that this historical event was somehow passed on to successive generations and that it is part of our collective mind. It is similar to the inheritance of "primal phantasies" (castration, seduction, primal scene), which he discusses in Lecture XXIII of the *Introductory Lectures on Psychoanalysis* (1916–1917) and which has led to criticisms of his Lamarckian attitudes. Freud was not unaware of the difficulties of explaining how such cultural and in some cases personal inheritance was to take place. As he says in *Totem and Taboo*:

> . . . how much can we attribute to psychical continuity in the sequence of generations? And what are the ways and means employed by one generation in order to hand on its mental states to the next one? I shall not pretend that these problems are sufficiently explained or that direct communication and tradition – which are the first things that occur to one – are enough to account for the process. . . . A part of the problem seems

to be met by the inheritance of psychical dispositions which, however, need to be given some sort of impetus in the life of the individual before they can be roused into actual operation. [1913, p. 158]

This considered formulation has some affinity with Klein's (1952; 1959) idea that there is some inherent knowledge of bodily functions and with Bion's similar idea of preconceptions awaiting realisation (1962). Robert Paul (1992) and William Grossman (1998) make somewhat similar statements, Paul about our biological propensities, Grossman about mental potentialities. But Freud's idea of an actual experience being inherited is, I believe, more problematic, and many analysts as well as anthropologists and other readers have remained critical of it.

THE REACTION OF ANTHROPOLOGISTS

Freud predicted that *Totem and Taboo* would not be well received. He wrote to Ferenczi:

> ... not since *The Interpretation of Dreams* ... have I worked at anything with the same feeling of certainty and elation. The reception will be comparable: a storm of indignation, except among my closest supporters. It comes at a very opportune time in the struggle with Zurich; it will separate us the way an acid does a salt. [Freud & Ferenczi, 1993, pp. 485–486]

In fact the book had a mixed reception (see Kiell, 1988, pp. 398–402; Wallace, 1983). It was the experts in particular who rejected Freud's conjectures, especially anthropologists, and it was Chapter 4 they disliked most, with its assumptions about the murder of the primal father. Some readers, however, found much to admire in the first three essays.

From the point of view of Freud's thesis being accepted by professional anthropologists – and by 1913 they were becoming a recognized profession – *Totem and Taboo* could hardly have been published at a worse time. The great push of the late nineteenth and early twentieth century towards cultural generalization was giving way to a much more detailed study of particular societies, each regarded as a relatively well-integrated set of interdependent roles and customs. Sweeping treatises like that of Frazer on totemism using bits of material from many different societies were being replaced by careful empirical studies. Present-day "primitive" societies were no longer automatically regarded as relics of earlier phases of Western European civilization, nor was it thought possible to arrange societies in a simple developmental hierarchy. Hence Freud's speculations about a supposed historical event of which there was no direct evidence was viewed at best with scepticism, at worst with contempt (Wax, 1990).

The definitive anthropological review was made by A. L. Kroeber (1920) in *The American Anthropologist*. Though scholarly and polite, Kroeber presented eleven items of disagreement with Freud's thesis, his main arguments being that Freud's construction of the primal horde and father-murder was entirely conjectural, and, further, that there was no clear evidence that exogamy and totem abstinence were the essential features of totemism. In fact, it was becoming established that totemism could exist without clans and that clans could exist without totemism, that some tribes had clans called after animals that were not totems, and that others had religious beliefs in which animals played a large part but through the mediation of shamans, not social groups (see Lévi-Strauss, 1964). Kroeber was as scathing about Freud's sources as about Freud himself: Reinach, Wundt, Spencer and Gillen, Lang, Robertson-Smith, Durkheim, Keane, Avebury, and, above all, Frazer. He requested Freud and other psychologists to realize that since we know nothing directly about the origin of totemism ". . . our business is first to understand as thoroughly as possible the nature of these existing phenomena" in the ethnological present. But even though Kroeber thought Freud got it wrong, he accepted that anthropology should not try to free itself from the psychology that underlies it. In this he differed from many later anthropologists who wanted to free themselves entirely from any sort of psychology.

In 1916 and the 1920s Malinowski challenged Freud's contention of the universality of the Oedipus complex in a series of papers and books – "Baloma: The Spirits of the Dead" (1916), *Sex and Repression in Savage Society* (1927), *The Sexual Life of Savages* (1929) – in which he claimed that the matrilineal Trobriand Islanders, whom he had studied intensively, felt only affection for the father and hatred for the mother's brother. Jones (1925) attempted to defend Freud, asserting that the classical Oedipus complex must be basic in all societies and that the "avunculate" (love for the sister and hatred of the mother's brother) was a defence against it. Roheim (1949) emphasized, among other things, that the Trobriand Islanders were patrilocal so that the child always lived with the father and mother until about the age of 6 or 7 – crucial years for the Oedipus complex – before being removed to the location and authority of the mother's brother. A later generation of anthropologists revisited the Trobriands and decided in favour of Freud and the Oedipus complex rather than Malinowski and the mother's brother (Wax, 1990), but by that time general interest in the debate had diminished. Neu (1992) examines the Malinowski–Jones debate from a philosophical point of view, showing the immense problems created by Freud's Lamarckian assumptions, by the relation between the level of analysis of individual psychology and that of society, and by the relative roles assigned to biology and to social structure in explaining the Oedipus complex.

In 1939 Kroeber published another paper, "*Totem and Taboo* in Retrospect" in *The American Journal of Sociology*, in which he stated that if Freud had given up the claim to the historical authenticity of the great event with which culture was supposed to have begun, and if instead he had confined himself to the psychology that might underlie certain recurrent institutions like totemism, his theory might be worthy of consideration. "Put in some such form as this," Kroeber wrote, "Freud's hypothesis might long before this have proved fertile in the realm of cultural understanding instead of being mainly rejected or ignored as a brilliant fantasy" (1939, p. 448). Kroeber also spoke of himself as having:

> ... spread out [*Totem and Taboo*'s] gossamer texture and then laboriously torn it to shreds. It is a procedure too suggestive of breaking a butterfly on the wheel. An iridescent fantasy deserves a more delicate touch even in the act of demonstration of its unreality. [1939, p. 446]

As Wax (1990, p. 54) points out, one wonders what Freud would have thought of this patronizing characterization of a book he valued so highly. Nevertheless, most anthropologists have followed Kroeber in refusing to accept Freud's conjectural history or the idea of the inheritance of an historical event and its consequences.

Although anthropological opinion, particularly among the "culture and personality" school of anthropology in the United States, became a bit more favourable to *Totem and Taboo* after the Second World War (Wallace, 1983), it was still regarded as an interesting historical relic rather than a work of serious concern to the profession as a whole. Certainly by the time I was studying anthropology (1945–1960), *Totem and Taboo* was regarded as a bit of a joke, as an ingenious but irrelevant attempt to psychologize anthropology by appeal to imaginary history. No anthropology student was expected to read it unless he was especially interested in the prehistory of the culture-and-personality school of thought in anthropology. When I actually read it I was surprised to find how useful was Freud's understanding of ambivalence in my own anthropological field work, and later I was impressed by his understanding of the principles of unilineal descent. But our training in empirical fieldwork meant that Freud's conjectural history was virtually meaningless to my generation of social anthropologists. *Totem and Taboo* was beyond the pale, not at all professionally correct.

In the 1950s and 1960s there was a resurgence of interest in cross-cultural anthropology and in generalization about the human mind, largely because of the "structuralist" approach of Claude Lévi-Strauss. But this brought no awakening of interest in Freud and *Totem and Taboo,* for Lévi-Strauss and his followers were resolutely opposed to any understanding of the mind or of totemism that emphasized the emotions rather than the intellect (1964). There has, however, been a significant paper by Robin Fox (1967) that has restored some anthropological interest in *Totem and Taboo*. Fox approaches it by a logical, structural analysis of its central thesis as a "scientific myth", examining some of the affectual reasons for the genesis, change and persistence of various systems of kinship and descent, among them Freud's totemic, matrilineal, and "father-denying" system. Fox's structural analysis includes affective as well as intellectual attributes of the human mind.

Generally speaking, however, *Totem and Taboo* is still regarded by anthropologists and all those influenced by them either as an interesting but irrelevant survival of an alien mode of anthropological thought current in the nineteenth century, or as an invalid and archaic attempt to psychologize culture and social structure. For the most part the book is ignored by social anthropologists.

TOTEM AND TABOO AND PSYCHOANALYSTS

Freud's immediate circle was enthusiastic about *Totem and Taboo.* Jones continued to regard it as one of Freud's greatest works, not surprisingly perhaps because Jones was steeped in the same nineteenth-century anthropological point of view as Freud. Gradually, however, *Totem and Taboo* has come to be almost disregarded. Recently, however, there has been a mild resurgence of interest in it (Grossman, 1998; Paul, 1992; Wallace, 1983), especially in seeing how its ideas influenced Freud's other work, but for the most part it is hardly known. Certainly I do not think any contemporary analyst would place it among Freud's greatest works, and in asking various analytic colleagues about the content of the book I found that most of them had only the vaguest idea of what it was about.

Why has the book fallen out of favour? First, I think that psychoanalysis has been influenced by the general trend of contemporary thought in favour of close empirical study as contrasted with grand conjectural reconstructions of imaginary history and generalizations about the human mind. This is especially true of Anglo-Saxon psychoanalysis as well as Anglo-Saxon anthropology, perhaps also of Anglo-Saxon social science in general and of Anglo-Saxon literary criticism as well. Even within psychoanalysis itself I think that there are some schools of thought that are more sceptical of reconstructions even of an *individual's* life history than Freud and his colleagues would have been; in such schools of thought a patient's "history" is likely to be viewed as his projection into the past of his inner world in the present (see, for example, Caper, 1997). Second, infantile sexuality and the Oedipus complex are universally accepted today whereas in 1913 both were considered problematic. Freud wrote *Totem and Taboo* at least in part as a challenge to Jung, whereas today the idea of the Oedipus complex no longer needs to be defended against rival schools of psychoanalysis, and the use of the Oedipus complex to explain the origin of civilization would do it more harm than good. Third, the idea of inherited predispositions is more or less accepted now, but the idea of inherited memory of specific prehistorical events has become even less acceptable than when Freud wrote about it.

Although I think psychoanalysts have never lost a desire to develop a general theory of the workings of the human mind, nor, perhaps, a hope that the psychoanalytic theory of the mind might apply to everyone in every society, most of today's psychoanalysts are understandably cautious about making generalizations that will appear ridiculous to people of other disciplines. Each discipline is now much more aware than it used to be that when it "applies" itself to another discipline it is applying its insights rather than its method (Wallace, 1983) and that this is likely to be regarded as professionally incorrect. So analysts today are more careful about applied psychoanalysis than Freud was, for in his day I think there was much less sense of difference between clinical and applied psychoanalysis than there is today. Perhaps at the present time analysts are more willing to speculate about literature than about the social sciences – sometimes much to the annoyance of literary critics – for everyone tends to feel that he knows something about literature because it is part of his own familiar culture. In the case of the social sciences, however, most psychoanalysts now feel that it is really only wise to apply psychoanalytic thinking to such a field if one already has some specialized knowledge of it oneself. This is a pointer to the way scientific culture can and has changed. What was plausible or even "fact" to scholars in the late nineteenth century and to Freud and his "closest supporters" is not at all plausible to most of today's psychoanalytic and anthropological scholars.

And so in our search for accuracy we have become more professionally correct, but we have lost the great sweep of imagination of Freud and his generation.

Words, Ideas, and Psychoanalysis
THEODORE SHAPIRO

T. S. Eliot (1930) in the voice of apeneck Sweeney notes, "I've gotta use words when I talk to you!" That brief sentence, uttered in frustration, could as well be applied to the patient and analyst when they are in interaction. There are, of course, other aspects of the discourse of psychoanalysis, but at its heart it is word-centred, leading to understanding and change. Psychoanalysts do not subscribe to epiphanies or sticking pins into fetishes as vehicles of change. They talk about their patients' lives, ideas, feelings, and attitudes, and try to arrive at a coherent image of their past as remembered in words. They then assess its relevance to their current behaviour and how that relates to their misery and suffering as well as the cruelty that they do to others.

The centrality of words in Freud's model of understanding and treatment and his zeal for understanding the formerly mystical by translation of mental images and dreams into words has always fascinated me. Indeed, the very unconscious fantasies that he discovered as the underpinning of behaviour must yield to narratives about conflict that are voiced in words. Other therapies may embrace hugging, beatific smiles, or ritualized mantras, but none other tries to make behaviour understandable from the vantage of words as they relate to the unconscious fantasies that are displayed in the transference, in life, and in symptoms. These very words become handy tools to be brought into action whenever we meet an old enemy from within that can now be named and with that name can be mastered. Thus from exposition to interpretation it is words all the way (Shapiro, 1970).

Having set the theme of this tribute to Arnold Cooper, let me now tell about how my thinking evolved and why my turn of mind may have been well suited for this zeitgeist and for the integration of language study in relation to psychoanalysis. I was early interested in literature and history in terms of their narrative power in harnessing emotion and understanding. However, it was not until I studied philosophy that I became aware that large systematic programmes existed that could offer paradigms that could encompass how we think and what we can know. While each system left unanswered questions, the idea of grasping so much with but a few paradigms fascinated me. Moreover, when I read Kant I realized how much of the structure that we assume is in the world most likely derives from the way our minds are structured and how we think. We are responsible for placing the order in nature – the limiting factor being the reach of our human understanding.

During psychoanalytic training, the papers of Freud that caught my special attention were Chapter 7 of the Dream book (1900a), "On Negation" (1925h), "The Antithetical Meaning of Primal Words" (1910e), "Constructions in Psychoanalysis" (1937d), and "Screen Memories" (1899a). These, each in its own way, fascinated me because Freud distinguished himself in them as a major philosophical thinker concerned with the way we symbolize, represent, and express our thoughts. Freud also addressed the impact of affect on our representational world and animated the bland epistemologies of cognitive science and rationalist, empiricist philosophy with real drive and emotion. He emerges as a major student of the psychology of representation, not only of personal symptoms but of cultural symbols linking ritual and iconography to psychopathologic symbolic expression and perversions. I am continually amazed at the prescience of his constructions concerning the use of myth as a response to natural danger and the inexplicable.

During this intellectual odyssey I came across the new work in linguistics. Chomsky wrote his magnum opus in 1957, and his work and that of other linguists became more highly disseminated in the '60s. Victor Rosen (1977), one of my most esteemed teachers, introduced a course on language and ego function in the curriculum while I was in psychoanalytic training, and I was hooked. I joined his linguistic study group, which infected my perspective and coloured my work from then on. Following Rosen's death I led the study group for another three years. It was relatively early in my career, so that not much had hardened in the way of my practice or my attitudes and beliefs about psychoanalysis. Parenthetically,

I had maintained my academic/clinical work, where I became fascinated with the language of autistic children, and the study of linguistics seemed apt for the continuation of my work with developmentally disordered children as well as with psychoanalytic patients. I also introduced myself to Professor George Miller at the Rockefeller Institute, where I attended a weekly study group to find out how the real linguists work. During the following years I developed two panels at the American Psychoanalytic Association in which we discussed the interface of language study and psychoanalysis. I introduced Thomas Bever, a developmental linguist, and Bernard Kaplan, a developmental psychologist, to the psychoanalytic audience (Shapiro, 1971).

From the beginning Freud was focused on mental transformations as represented by language and symbol. His ideas, with some modifications introduced by recent knowledge about linguistics, should lead to a new intellectual focus for psychoanalysis in the study of linguistics and communication. For example, the recent interest in the intersubjectivity between patient and analyst might be demystified if we attend to what is known about the uses of language in human interaction, and developmental contributions to the formation of personal symbols within a natural language and in the context of cultural and community symbols. Since I cannot address the entire interface of psychoanalysis with linguistics let me point to a few key areas: (1) syntactic organization and drives; (2) semantic and semiotic factors in relation to the construction of symbols; and (3) the pragmatics of the psychoanalytic conversation as compared to natural conversation.

Freud's earliest description of unconscious functioning suggested that the unconscious is chaotic with the mobility of energic cathexis, described as primary process. Freud's aim in this description was to explain the slippage in designation that permits one thing or image or word to represent another, and to link the representational flux to what he had written about earlier in the Project (1895) as neuronal structuring without designative specificity. He postulated some neurons as leaky and others as stable, retaining their charge or cathexes. At about the same time de Saussure (1911), the father of modern linguistics (and, incidentally, of a prominent psychoanalyst), was describing the relation of the signified to the signifier and establishing a basic structural description of language as a code. Those who study Lacan will recognize the familiarity of the language used by de Saussure. Lacan (1956) claimed de Saussure and Freud as his intellectual precursors and the dominant influences on his theory. In addition, Lacan believed that the most important theories of Freud emerged in his early years, with little of significance appearing after he gave up the topographic theory. This judgement is based largely on Freud's struggle with the issue of the transformation of thought into words, the protolinguistic idea of the antithetical meaning of primal words, the change from visual image to verbal representation, and the recovery of dream thoughts in dream analysis, all in those early years.

This became moot in 1923 as Freud turned to the structural theory, which in itself offers no theory of transformation from one vehicle of representation to another. Instead, the structural theory gave us a means to see symbols as composites. The elements of drive representation in compromise with the ego defence are the decomposed elements of each representation. The theory also taught us to look for the superego representations in the narratives. However, Freud never again approached the representational process as the relationship between signifier and signified except to discuss the issue of veracity of memory seen in the now hotly debated issue of repressed memories and their historical truth.

In later writing by Freud (1926d), followed by Schur (1966), he did not give up the idea of primary process, but he did introduce the idea of a more organized unconscious in which there is a flux of changing dynamisms and wishes as the child develops and as the various experiences with body and community unconsciously take hold in the mind. I would add that the syntactic underpinnings of wishes as represented are already present in the earliest theories insofar as Freud noted that the psychological dimensions of the drives, that is, object and aim (source being seen as better studied by biology), when represented in our wishes, must be organized in the form of active and passive desires directed toward our objects. These formats then serve as syntactic algorithms that can be represented as sentences such as, "I wish to do x to y" or "I wish y to do x to me." Thus, when we interpret the unconscious we interpret in sentence form what was until then a virtual representation and only had been translated into action dispositions in life and in the transference. Now the stated verbalization would reside as a recovered thought that would serve as an action-modulator in the face of known realistic consequences. "Where there was id, there shall ego be!"

Chomsky's universal generative grammar was exploited by Edelson (1972) to describe the use of unconscious structures for dream formation, and I (Shapiro, 1988) wrote about the need in a structuralist model such as psychoanalytic theory to have a few base structures and rules for transformation to create innumerable heterologous structures for surface representation. Psychoanalysis and linguistics share a common structural heritage. Chomsky proffered that in-built linguistic structures are exploited by any given language to provide a small number of deep structures that, with the aid of a small number of operators, can be converted into innumerable possible surface structures using any specific lexicon. One can see in this model a usable parallel to Freud's idea that we construct our many fantasies about certain deep structural universal algorithms – the Oedipus complex is the central such deep structure according to psychoanalysis. The active and passive permutations and combinations that are possible become the surface structures we deal with on the couch and in our consulting rooms (Shapiro, 1977; 1986).

Semiotics and *semantics* refer to the relationships that accrue between sign and signified. Psychoanalysis is above all a science of semiotics, with one part of the represented out of awareness, or unconscious. While we may no longer believe that the simple rendering of the unconscious conscious leads to cure, we nevertheless believe that we may defend against unconscious fantasies by acting them out and/or enacting them in the transference. Thus, verbal representation and naming the enemy go hand in hand with understanding the manner of defence and the compromise enactments in the transference (Shapiro, 1970). We still turn our attention toward the manner in which unconscious fantasies, formed when our cognitive style was marked by magic in childhood, direct our actions even in adult years. Understanding the community language and the cultural myths only takes us to the commonplace and not to the connotative and idiolectic personal significance of the individual's fantasies. Studying the patient from the vantage of personal meaning systems frozen in childhood remains the rewarding gold we seek as we encounter the surface symbols that point toward deeper meanings. We must bring out all the tropes, known in the trade as dream mechanisms and transformations, to divine the rock-bottom fantasies that have become contorted by the defensive process. This is the work of analysis, but it would gain in force and intellectual vigour if tied to the theory of signs as described by the linguists and to the knowledge about the ontogenesis of signs within development. Most recently the vigour of neuroimaging in relation to verbal stimuli has brought us closer to the earliest of Freud's dreams, that is, the localization of the represented in the brain itself (see Posner & Raichle, 1994). However, we are a long way off from deciphering the significance of these locales for unconscious residues.

However, before we enter that arena we still are semiotic translators for our patients. We offer plausible constructions about their fantasies as we discover them in our patients' free associations, actions, and enactments.

Indeed, the recent struggle about the constructivist view of the creative elements of psychoanalysis becomes moot against the clinical data concerning the repetitive senseless behaviour about which patients complain. If we are not approaching what is already there that forces repetitive and tedious and sometimes destructive and redundant behaviour, what are we doing for our patients? This is an argument for some form of historical truth rather than a here-and-now relativism. It is an argument for the persistence of our childhood constructions, which appear senselessly in adulthood as anachronisms and have to be exposed to our patients as the core fantasies that corrupt their aims and capacity to live more adaptively. As I see it, the persistent force of unconscious fantasies poisons our best laid conscious plans and keeps us slaves to an unknown or undiscovered past that is already there.

Pragmatics refers to the use of words in communication. The usual mode of communication is the conversation. Recent attention to intersubjectivity and the interpersonal setting of the analytic situation puts us in mind of the Sullivanian focus on the dyad and Sullivan's (1940) devotion to Sapir and to the social psychologist George Herbert Mead. Emde (1988) recently reissued George Klein's call for a *wego* (a socially derived ego) in psychoanalysis. This will not decentre us from the intrapsychic if we accept that psychoanalysis has always been conducted as a two-person adventure and we have only neglected the person of the analyst, because we mistakenly thought if he were well-analysed the patient would be safe. However, recent years have brought a spate of literature concerning countertransference and the analyst's fantasies. We have always known that the analyst's actions can interfere or at least influence the process, but at no prior time have analysts come forth as readily to present how and when their fantasies, conscious and unconscious, promote a specific line of inquiry and discourse (see Greenberg & Mitchell, 1983; Jacobs, 1986). The most recent form of the debate concerns how much the analyst should tell about what he fantasizes and how to determine the effect of the telling on the process of analysis. While I refer to the structures as fantasies in keeping with my central theme, these fantasies are cast as words linked by syntactic rules.

I have approached the dialogue of psychoanalytic inquiry as conversation (Makari & Shapiro, 1993; Shapiro, 1995), as has Arlow (1997). There are excellent linguistic analyses of conversational discourse in terms of topic maintenance, turn taking, and sincerity of exchange that have not yet been used to address psychoanalytic dialogues. An analysis of the differences in the conversational rules that apply to those who conduct a relatively one-sided conversation, as in the classical descriptions of psychoanalysis, and those who offer more give-and-take analyses would be of interest. I am convinced that most analysts converse more as the analysis progresses and also that the nature of the patient's needs determines the austerity of the technique. These are empirical issues that may be answered by the study of taped analyses.

Dahl (1978) has demonstrated how syntax is altered in the analytic settings. We tend to use subjunctive conditional language to explain a past that we construct from the language of the current analysis.

Linguistic science has tools that psychoanalysts can use to replace some of the nineteenth-century models offered by Freud. These new tools, under the rubrics of syntaxis, semantics, and pragmatics, have been exploited by some of our computer-minded researchers, such as Teller and Dahl (1995), Bucci (1985), Spence (1993), and Kächele and Thomä (1995). Our rich discussions of cases are difficult to bring to resolution when we lack a veridical test of our hypotheses. Studies of language use by patient and analyst during analyses holds some hope for better tests of truth about our theories.

Notes on Linguistic Activity and Psychoanalysis

JORGE CANESTRI

In a book with the impressive title *Psychoanalysis: Toward the Second Century*, Arnold M. Cooper (1989c) wrote: "Psychoanalysis may be characterized as an attempt to decode, that is, interpret, a patient's communications according to a loosely drawn set of transformational rules concerning underlying meanings, motivations, and unities of thought" (p. 202). Further on he stated: ". . . it is important that analytic theories not be out of touch with developing new knowledge in areas adjoining our area of interest, lest they become idiosyncratic and isolated from the mainstreams of science and the humanities" (p. 203).

Both these statements merit reflection. In these brief notes, it is my intention to mention certain ideas that may be of interest in psychoanalytic theory and that come from a field adjoining ours – the study of the linguistic activity of individuals. The area implied in this title is very wide, but also fairly well circumscribed. Although it borrows concepts from the disciplines of linguistics and the philosophy of language, it is limited to a specific object intimately linked to the activity of the analyst – the linguistic activity of individuals – and not to the somewhat ideal and idealized realm of language. I am sure the reader will understand that in the space allowed me here I can only make a brief summary of themes without being able to discuss them in detail or illustrate them.

The philosopher Karl Otto Apel (1994), at the beginning of his book *Le Logos Propre au Langage Humain*, recalls that his reflections were suggested to him by a comment of Karl Popper. Following a lecture of Apel's, in which he attempted to outline the programme of a pragmatic-transcendental theory of communication, Popper said that it is not necessary to pay so much attention to communication inasmuch as it is what we have in common with animals, and that what is important in human language are the propositions.

Apel writes that Popper's comment refers to the classical paradigm running through the philosophy of language like a scarlet thread from Aristotle to the referential semantics derived from Frege. The classical or propositional paradigm is the semantic-logical-referential of the *logos*. Through a panoramic vision of the tradition of *logos*, Apel is able to state that the platonic root of *logos* was dialogic (*logos* as language and discourse in conversation); if it is objectified it takes the meaning of a proposition, of a true or false statement. The next step is taken by Aristotle, who introduced a distinction between *semantikòs* logos and *apofantikòs* logos. The semantic logos of language must therefore be conceived as having a wider meaning than that of the representative function of language, which would be able to reach the truth. From this point of view, the *apofantikòs* logos is dependent on the *semantikòs* logos, which develops its functions of communicative agreement on the world in dialogue.

From the viewpoint of this philosophy of language, there would be a division and an opposition between referential semantics and simple pragmatics of the communicative functions of language. Let me take as an example (following Apel's exposition) Karl Bühler's theory of the linguistic sign – a theory that in some ways is nearer to our own experience to the extent that it includes the functions of expression and of appeal of the linguistic sign. In fact, Bühler distinguishes three fundamental semiotic functions of language in his well known theory of the linguistic sign: (a) the representative semiotic function of signs, inasmuch as they are symbols (the symbolic function corresponds to the denotative function of nouns and to the descriptive-representative function of propositions); b) the expressive function of signs as symptoms; and (c) the semiotic function of appeal of signs as signals. But these three functions are not on the same level. The functions of expression and of appeal do not possess a semantic character; rather, they have pragmatic functions that, in this theory, are clearly distinguishable from the semantic statement of contents of linguistic symbols.

That is the reason why, in contesting Apel, Popper (1962) distinguishes two "inferior" functions of language (Bühler's b and c) and a "superior" one (Bühler's a). The classical paradigm does not consider that pragmatics contributes to the semantic logos, to the intersubjectively valid meaning of the signs of language and to the meaning of theories. Pragmatics, in this meaning of logical empiricism, is the place for all the problems of a psychological-subjective kind that are beyond the logical justification of meaning, that is, beyond the context of the justification, as opposed to the context of the discovery. The epistemological consequences of this attitude are well known in the psychoanalytic field and I will not be dealing with them in this paper (Canestri, 1993; 1994b).

In his turn, Apel questions the incompleteness of the "new" paradigm: the consequence of the "pragmatic turn" operated in the philosophy of language, underlining the need to understand it in a pragmatic-transcendental perspective. From the psychoanalytic point of view, it is not necessary to be in agreement with Apel's philosophical exigencies, but I think it is essential to accept his reasoning about the limitations of the semantic-logical-referential paradigm of the logos. A conception of linguistic activity that does not recognize the contribution of pragmatics to the construction of the meaning, that is, its semantic contribution, would be extremely limiting in analytic practice and would contradict our experience.

Although it is well known that linguistic analysis is present throughout the whole history of philosophy, it is through the philosophers of language and their research (their analytical philosophy) that philosophy of language fully acquires the meaning that is of interest to us. From the common starting point of neo-positivist logic, several different points of view may be distinguished. What is most relevant for us is perhaps the field of research of the "philosophers of ordinary language", and their most significant contribution is the "pragmatic turn", particularly the theory of the "speech acts" deriving from the works of J. L. Austin (1962) and of J. R. Searle (1969). This current of thought is one of the bases of the "alternative paradigm" that Apel opposes to the classic paradigm. Their works are classics today, and I do not need to dwell longer on them, but I must mention here, for the sake of clarity, that speech act theory is not the sole aspect of pragmatics, as we shall see later on.

For our discussion, it is sufficient to point out that what appears as an essential dimension of this new pragmatic paradigm, in opposition to the classic paradigm, is now the link with a theory of meaning. In this sense, a good definition of pragmatics could be: a performance theory at the semantic level. The pragmatic approach places in the forefront the process of production of the linguistic object. There is no doubt, and the fact is underlined frequently by many researchers in this area, that by changing the paradigm a kind of overflowing is created by which the extension of pragmatics grows beyond measure, sometimes without convincing theoretical support. It remains true, however, at least from my point of view, that the advantages of the new paradigm (to use Apel's terminology) overcome the disadvantages, above all in our field. This new paradigm has consequences not only within the study of the linguistic activity of the individual, but also in the epistemological field. In other words, not even scientific theories can leave out of consideration the pragmatic dimension of the meaning.

The psychoanalyst who is involved in clinical work and is unaccustomed to reflecting about language, could think that this alteration in paradigm does not essentially change anything in his clinical practice. It should, however, be pointed out that (a) every psychoanalyst works with a specific but sometimes approximate philosophy of language, even though he is often not aware of it, and (b) that even in the history of psychoanalysis and in the theoretical writings of the classical authors and in their published clinical cases, it is possible to demonstrate the sometimes remarkable differences in orientation of their philosophies of language. For example, Ferenczi's orientation is considerably different from that of Freud, and the concept of linguistic activity that can be deduced from the cases of Melanie Klein, especially from the published analysis of Richard, is considerably different from that of Freud or Ferenczi. But the same differences can also be seen in contemporary authors. This is not the place to go into all these differences in detail, but it could be an extremely useful exercise for our clinical work inasmuch as it would throw light on what M. and W. Baranger (1969) have called "the problem of the specific action of the word", and on how each analyst conceives this specificity.

Putting the accent on the linguistic production of the individual, rather than on the ideality of the language, favours the growth of an area of research entitled "analysis of the discourse", which privileges the structure of spoken language as manifested in current use: conversation, interviews, and such. Language is studied as a dynamic, social, intersubjective phenomenon, intrinsically dialogic, in the original meaning of platonic *logos* or in the more recent meaning resulting from the studies of Mikhail M. Bakhtin. A first field of research for psychoanalysis would be the description and careful study of the specific characteristics of the psychoanalytic discourse that is so profoundly different in rules, structure, and codification from any other discourse of ordinary communication. To offer a few examples: the endofasic internal discourse of patient and analyst that elsewhere I have called "internal flux" (Canestri, 1994a) does not have to take pragmatics into account, but pragmatics reappears in the uttered sentences of both. Nevertheless, the existence of the fundamental rule of free association and free-floating attention allows both participants of the experience to transgress canonical rules in the analytic communication. In analysis the word expresses the drive and is also a drive object that must be interpreted (Fónagy, 1983); there are a great many enveloped registers (preverbal, organic, paralinguistic), conditioned in their turn by the context (internal transcriptions, transmutations of code, etc.).

In the analytic experience, depending on the expedients of the analytic setting, there is a different use of non-verbal means to communicate; these means follow a digital codification and not an analogic one as happens in ordinary face-to-face communication. Moreover, the expedients of the analytic setting attempt to shift the balance between the word itself as revelation and the communicative intention of the discourse towards the former, as if to say that the communication takes second place, while the value of the word itself as revelation passes into the forefront. It is not a question of denying or diminishing the value and the communicative aim of the analytic discourse, at least as "primary intentionality" of the patient and of the analyst, but of underlining the fact that this is not the only or the primordial function of language in analysis. Of course, the list of relevant facts characterizing the analytic discourse could be much longer.

The analysis of the discourse brings to the forefront the production of utterances. The different forms that the presence of this act of production can take, and also the degrees of its importance, enables a typology of the discourses to be created. From the point of view of the analytic discourse, the study of the elements of the utterance that allude to its production is particularly significant, because they are part of the actual sense of the utterance. Some of these allusions are represented by grammatical categories such as personal or demonstrative pronouns, relative adverbs and adjectives, or tenses of verbs (i.e., deictic categories); other allusions are represented by semantic categories such as the time and the place of the utterance.

I have tried to show elsewhere (Canestri, 1994c) that the alterations and modalities that the normal dialogism of the discourse in analysis undergoes are very significant. In the follow-up of the analytic process we can obtain a great amount of knowledge about psychic change by analysing the discourse of the patient. This implies considering who the patient speaks to (transference) and how he perceives himself, not only through the analysis of the content of his unconscious fantasies. It is important also to observe the linguistic means that he uses (and that are normally unknown to the speaker), for example, personal pronouns, to represent all this in the discourse. Within this vast field of research we should mention the work of the psychoanalyst and linguist L. Danon-Boileau (1987), who, as well as offering a rich and productive interweaving of the two disciplines, presents a well-articulated panorama of what has been explored in psychoanalytic reflections about language

In the linguistic activity of individuals, language becomes a complex and heterogeneous object; all the more so in the analytic discourse where the three classical channels described by semiotics are co-present and cannot be dis-articulated. I refer to the first channel of articulation (segmental) that includes, in order of increasing complexity, phonology, morphology, syntax, and stylistics; a second channel (or supersegmental level) that includes a wide range of phenomena coming under the classification of prosody (tone, accents, pauses, silences, intonation, and expressive connotations); and a third channel or level including non-verbal elements such as gestures, facial mimicry, movements, and positions of the body. If we can say that the activity of the analyst relies to a large extent on his/her capacity to contain and adequately transform the unbearable experiences of the patient through a correct decodification of the patient's communications, as Cooper emphasizes, then the importance of a conception that takes into account the complexity of the individual's linguistic activity and of the whole range of semiotic systems both for production and for recognition becomes all the more evident.

Returning now to Cooper's paragraph that served as an introduction to these notes, we can suggest another argument along the lines previously indicated. Cooper identifies analytic activity with an ". . . attempt to decode, that is, to interpret, a patient's communications according to a loosely drawn set of transformational rules concerning underlying meanings, motivations, and unities of thought" (p. 202). I have attempted to put forward certain concepts about linguistic activity that could help us in this task. But perhaps we can take another step forward along the lines suggested by Cooper by reflecting on the meaning of identity: "to decode, that is, to interpret" and on the nature of the transformational rules. Keeping within the area that I have tried to define, I think that the work of H. P. Grice (1989) can be of assistance to us. Grice formed part of the Austin group, and after the rejection of neo-positivism that led the "Oxford Philosophy" to abandon all types of formalization, he was the one who, in the field of the philosophy of language, was able to develop theories. Here I should like to mention just four very important distinctions introduced by Grice: (a) between the natural meaning and the non-natural meaning; (b) between what the words mean and what the speakers mean; (c) between what is "said" and what is only "implied"; and (d) between the conventional meaning and the non-conventional meaning.

Grice tries to explain (and here I am obviously summarizing) what a single speaker in a given circumstance means by a word or a gesture. It is this concept of meaning, which Grice calls "the meaning of the speaker", that precedes the concept of the linguistic meaning and not vice-versa. It is not the concept of conventionality (distinction between natural signs and conventional signs) that distinguishes the non-natural meaning from the natural meaning, but the concept of intentionality (connection between meaning and intentions, between semantics and psychology). If I mean something, I must intend to obtain a given effect on my interlocutor, at least in part through his recognizing my intentions. This is where a vast field of possibilities opens up from the psychoanalytical viewpoint. The intentionality that concerns us as psychoanalysts is not the conscious one; the effect that a patient tries to obtain does not correspond to a conscious but to an unconscious wish (and a good example could be the way projective identification operates). In Grice's theory the meaning of a sentence ultimately depends on what the speakers mean when they utter it, as long as the linguistic use is correct. When we converse, we often mean more than what the words mean literally, or we mean something different from their literal meaning. Grice here introduced the concept of *implicature*; the implicature has the task of systematically linking what is said to what is implied, therefore explaining how it is possible to do what we do continually when speaking, that is, communicating more than our words mean literally. A corollary of this statement is that a proposition is certainly conveyed by an utterance, but this depends not only on the utterance pronounced, but also on the circumstances of the utterance and on a series of general rules governing the conversation and the use of the language.

Another step forward has been made by D. Sperber and D. Wilson (1986). The starting point of these authors is a reflection on the classic model that tries to explain how communication takes place. According to the classic model or *code model*, coding and decoding messages is communicating. Grice's theories suggest a different model, the *inferential model*, where communication consists of the production and interpretation of facts. These two models are not incompatible and can be combined in various ways. Verbal communication brings into play at the same time both inferential processes and codifying processes. A code is a system that associates messages with signals and requires a codifier and a decodifier. The inferential model must include central processes at the entrance and at the exit, a set similar to: thought processes → acoustic codified signal → acoustic signal received and decodified → thought processes. From this point of view, the semantic representation of a sentence does not coincide with the thoughts that can be communicated by pronouncing the sentence. We pass from semantic representation to communicated thought not through an addition to the code but by means of inferentials.

It is clear that the distinction between sentence and utterance is essential; an utterance possesses a set of characteristics; some of them are linguistic, others not. The study of the interpretation of utterances belongs to pragmatics; utterances express propositional attitudes, they carry out linguistic actions, or else they have "illocutionary force".

Summarizing, from this viewpoint, communication succeeds not only when the speakers recognize the linguistic meaning of the utterance, but also, and sometimes predominantly, when they infer the "meaning" of the utterer. It is worth reflecting on how and when this operates in psychoanalytic practice. In his "Introduction" to a Panel on Language and Psychoanalysis for the 26th International Psycho-Analytical Congress, almost thirty years ago (1969), V. H. Rosen said: "If we direct some of the questions posed herein to a re-examination of the process of free association [and, I would add, the process of interpretation] from the point of view of language theory as well as psychoanalysis, we may find that our patients communicate more than we are aware of and less than we often think that we discover" (p. 115). Returning to Cooper's statements, we could say that the ideas of Grice, Sperber, and Wilson and the developments in pragmatics could enrich the set of transformational rules.

I should like to add a last point in this regard. For lack of space, I shall be brief and cannot do justice to all the psychoanalysts who have worked on this topic. A. Culioli (1990), a French linguist, has outlined three different levels in the treatment of representation. The first is the level of mental representations, whose conceptualization will obviously depend on the discipline involved. Access to this level is not direct. The second level is that of linguistic representations, or second grade representations. They carry traces of the activity of the first level, but no biunivocal relation can be hypothesized between the two levels because the representations are heterogeneous. The third level is that of metalinguistic representations. It is reasonable to presuppose a level of neuronal activity that precedes the first level and in this case also we hypothesize a heterogeneity in respect to the first level.

This outline confirms – if this were necessary – the clear-sightedness of Freud's distinction between thing presentation (*Dingvorstellung*) and word presentation (*Wortvorstellung*), and leaves open to reflection the vast field of the relationship between thought and word, of verbalization, of the "internal language", of the Freudian concept of sign and symbol – all matters that fall outside the limits of this brief contribution.

The work of the psychoanalyst is certainly different from that of the linguist or the philosopher of language; he moves between the first and the second levels, and is not concerned with the level of neuronal activity or with metalinguistic representations. However, these notes of mine point in the direction indicated by Cooper – that is, not to isolate psychoanalysis from those disciplines with which it shares certain boundaries.

Reasons, Causes, and the Domain of the First-Person

MARCIA CAVELL

Early in the seventies, Arnold Cooper and I decided to teach an elective course together at the Columbia University Psychoanalytic Center in New York City. He was a senior analyst and faculty member; I was a philosopher and psychoanalytic research candidate. We were friends. We knew very little about the subject we proposed to teach, existential psychoanalysis, and thought we should know more. Friendship, curiosity, our joined areas of experience would, we naively figured, see us through.

We began the course, on my suggestion, with the subject of reasons and causes. I argued, taking a line recently in favour in philosophy, that to explain a bit of human behaviour that is an *action,* that is, something done intentionally – for example, raising one's arm in order to make a salute versus being the hapless sufferer of a muscular spasm – we invoke reasons, not causes. The argument saw reason-explanations – explanations in terms of the person's beliefs, desires, and other mental states – as antithetical to causal explanations. And though it did not explicitly put human beings outside the natural order, it seemed to open a disturbing breach.

Arnie was not convinced. He agreed that actions are done for reasons, conscious and unconscious, but he couldn't see why that rules out causality. From this muddy base we launched ourselves into the morass of Binswanger, Sartre, and freedom.

Perhaps I can now be a bit clearer about the issues of our old elective, and in a way sympathetic to a conviction Arnie and I share: human activity is a part of the natural order, though a special part, and one that psychoanalysis illumines in a way nothing else does. Holding onto the peculiarities of reason-explanations, while insisting, as I did not back then, that reasons are a kind of cause, honours this complex vision.

Here are just two peculiarities of reason-explanations. Understanding why someone has decided to give up smoking, for example, requires a kind of empathic imagination on our part, but understanding the link between smoking and lung cancer does not. Reason-explanations are teleological in character (what is the agent's purpose?); causal explanations, as we post-Aristotelians understand them, are not. But most philosophers are now persuaded that while reason-explanations are special, they are nevertheless a kind of causal explanation (Davidson, 1980).

I won't rehearse this contemporary philosophical position, but we glimpse it in thinking about rationalization in the psychoanalytic sense. When we say that someone's reason is a *rationalization*, are we saying that no reason of any sort elucidates what he did? That anything more than a strictly neuro-physiological account forays into fiction? No. We mean that though the rationalization might be, in itself, a good reason for doing what the person did, it was not *his* reason; it was not the reason that *caused* him to do it. Or while it was among his reasons, it was not sufficient by itself to cause him to act, and there are other more pressing reasons about which he is keeping silent. *Rationalization* suggests that the reason he offers masks some other reason that makes him anxious, or would, if he were aware of it. An explanation of what he did via those reasons that genuinely caused his action is not a *rationalization* in the specifically psychoanalytic sense. (Such an explanation will always be partial, not only because reasons are multiple, but also because any one reason alludes to many others.) In short, the causes of an action are reasons, and reasons *are* causes, as the *because* indicates in ordinary everyday explanations like, "I am going to Egypt because I've always wanted to see the Pyramids."

If we were to describe what someone did in a strictly physicalist language, we would assume it had causes of a physicalist sort; insisting that an action is caused by reasons does not deny that the same bit of behaviour can be seen under a physicalist description. Yet reason-explanations are irreducible to explanations of a strictly neuro-physiological character. (I take this for granted here.) That is, the language of mind cannot be adequately replaced by the language of neuro-physiology. Of course whether or not x can adequately replace y in some explanation, depends on who's asking. An explanation is adequate or inadequate only in relation to the needs and purposes of the explainer. So to say the language of mind is not reducible to the language of body is to say something about *us*, something like this:

none of us is either willing, or able, to give up explaining her *own* actions in terms of things like beliefs and desires, in short, reasons. (For example: I am writing this paper because I want to honour an esteemed friend and colleague.) We are also unable to give up thinking of the beliefs we hold as *true,* assessing them as justified or unjustified, rational or irrational in the light of other things we believe, and so on. And these concepts of rationality, truth, and justification that we implicitly invoke in being first-person thinkers are irreducible to a non-evaluative language. As more or less rational creatures, each of us has a first-person point of view in the light of which she forms plans, projects, intentions; each of us forms beliefs that she sometimes calls into question, appraises as rational or irrational, justified, foolish, wise, and so on. So long as we are ourselves such creatures, we are going to try to explain the behaviour of creatures like ourselves in similar, essentially psychological terms. (This seems to suggest, wrongly, that first we understand our own minds, then look into others'. In fact I believe our coming to have minds in the first place and our coming to see others as minded, are co-dependent.)

How does the reason-cause issue take us to existentialism? Let's back up to actions, things done intentionally. We don't worry about the freedom of molecules, or even infants. Freedom comes up only for creatures some of whose behaviour has to be explained in the complex way that the concept of an action invokes. An action is by definition something we do for a reason, because in some sense we want to do it; it is by definition something volitional, chosen, that is, not merely guided by instinct or impulse, but by desires that can themselves be subject to rational integration with one's other desires, values, and beliefs. Very generally, we are free when we do what we want to do – where "wanting" is more conceptually laden than either "instinct" or "drive" – and because we want to do it.

Yet though embodiment is not an impediment to freedom, as causal "determinists" seem to think, freedom knows constraints within the domain of the mental itself. We are not free when our own unresolved conflicts somehow prevent us from doing what we would like to do, or think we would like to do: we would like to stop stealing, or being voyeurs, or exploding at our children, but "despite ourselves" we go on in the same old way. Or when unconscious conflicts prevent us from knowing what we want, or from acting to realize it. These are the sorts of volitional knots that often bring people into therapy. Untying these knots is a matter, in part, of resolving the internal conflicts that get in the way of knowing what one wants, and doing it, of helping the person more genuinely to think about the world and himself. Beliefs and desires are caused by, at least, one's other beliefs, desires, and perceptions, but because of the sorts of things that beliefs and perceptions are, factors of rationality, also of choice and decision, enter into this causation in ways that make for just the interesting differences between human behaviour and the behaviour of other creatures. Freud was trying to articulate this difference when he said that we are the only animals subject to neurosis. For the same reason we are the only creatures who can act with degrees of freedom. As human possibilities, freedom and inhibition go together.

It is a mistake, then, to think either that we are never free, that freedom is cancelled by our membership in a natural order where *cause* holds, or that we are angels of spontaneity. Freud was one sort of absolutist, some of the time; Sartre another: we cannot escape our freedom, Sartre said. It comes with consciousness, which he described as a *Néant,* a Nothing or a Nothingness. Things are caused, Sartre claimed, whereas consciousness is not a thing but an attitude towards things. Consciousness is un-caused; therefore it is necessarily free. (Kant said something similar without the talk about *being* and *nothingness.*) Absolutist positions about freedom wrongly assume that reasons and causes are incompatible. Freud opted, some of the time, for causes, Sartre for reasons.

But if instead of the mysterious *Néant* we give Sartre the rather obvious idea that consciousness is not any kind of thing, we can see something of what he is after. First, the idea of *the self* is a reification. There are embodied creatures in the world who think in the first-person ("I think that . . . ," "I believe that . . . ," "I want . . ."), with all that this presumes. This is a great deal, and it distinguishes us from other creatures: among other things, we can reflect on our pasts, experience a range of emotions that come only with concepts, make choices and decisions about our future. But there is no Self who stands behind these activities. Second, this first-person point of view has characteristics that a third-person point of view, even though it uses the language of mind, lacks. It is as important to note these differences in saying what we mean by freedom as it is to untangle the issue of reason and causes.

A first-person avowal of belief, for instance, in which I say (or think) "I believe that . . . ," is not just an essentially third-person description of me with the pronoun changed. It might look as if your sentence, "Marcia Cavell believes there's a lectern in Dwinelle 207", and mine, "I believe there's a lectern in Dwinelle 207", attribute a certain belief to me, the same belief, and that the difference between the sentences is merely grammatical. But "the grammar" goes deep. For your saying about me that I have this belief about the lectern in Dwinelle does not commit *you* to holding that this belief about the lectern is true, whereas my saying I believe it does. When I consciously hold that *p*, I am, necessarily, endorsing *p*, committing myself to its truth; that's part of what saying I believe it means. (This is so however we go on to analyse the concept of truth itself.)

We might put this difference in terms of a Cartesian idea about self-knowledge. How do I know that I believe there's a lectern in Dwinelle 207? The Cartesian answers: by turning my mind inward and seeing there, in the theatre of the mind, the idea, "There's a lectern in Dwinelle 207." This answer suggests that the essential difference between a thought being *my* thought and a thought being *your* thought is that mine is visible uniquely to me. But my knowing what I think – when I do – is typically not a matter of my passively observing what I think, but of actively endorsing the truth or rationality of that belief. You can observe that I (seem to) believe there's a lectern in Dwinelle 207, and simultaneously also believe that I am mistaken: you just saw the janitor remove it. But I cannot sensibly think that there's a lectern in Dwinelle 207, and *at the same time* (in the same "part" of my mind, so to speak) hold that this belief is false. By endorsing *p* I mean that I take a position toward it, a position that is by nature open to evidence, question, and challenge. (I restrict my remarks here to beliefs that are conscious, since with unconscious beliefs and fantasies the matter is more complex.)

If I think a belief of yours is wrong I can try to change your mind, and my failure to do so does not mean that I am irrational. But I can hold on to a belief of my own that I think is wrong only at the cost of a split in my very self, the kind of split that our concepts of repression, disavowal, and self-deception invoke. My relation to your mind is then essentially different from my relation to my own, in a way that the concept of self-knowledge belies.

The fact that in forming beliefs or intentions we are making judgements about what *to* believe, what action we *will* perform, means that there is a self-constituting aspect to first-person thinking: when I assess what I should believe, given the evidence I have and my other beliefs, or what it is I want or intend, I am not simply being acted upon, but acting, *judging* what I should believe, evaluating what I want to do. "Knowing my own mind" is also making up my mind (Moran, 1988). When Luther said, "Here I stand! I can do no other," he was not passively describing a fact about himself, but declaring the person he intended to be.

Sartre spoke of the *vertigo of consciousness*, by which he meant our uneasy awareness that the self of which we are aware as fully conscious believers, desirers, doers, is not a knowable thing but a kind of openness toward the world, an endless array of possibilities among which we choose. It is an awareness we try to mute, typically, Sartre said, by thinking of ourselves in an "inauthentic" way as not "free" but as having the sort of determinate, determined nature that other kinds of things in the universe have; we attempt to cast ourselves as the tellers of tales, he says, that in effect have already been told. (When the analytic patient says, "I know, I'm doing it again, but that's just the sort of person I am", we feel she is shrugging off responsibility.) We construe the self as a special kind of entity, behind and directing our various acts of consciousness, as Sartre put it, because we don't want to acknowledge that who and what we are is up to us. "Perhaps," he writes, "the essential function of the Ego is not so much theoretical as practical . . . to mask from consciousness its very spontaneity" (Sartre, 1960, p. 100).

There are then two different irreducibilities that I allude to in this paper. First, the language of mind cannot be reduced to, or adequately replaced by, a strictly neuro-physiological language. Second, even within the language of mind, a first-person point of view is irreducible to a third-person point of view. Sartre is calling attention to both.

Yet he overplays his hand in two respects. First, he thinks that the idea of "a consciousness" that, as he puts it, is not implicitly self-conscious is a self-contradiction. This is wrong: unconsciousness is an attribute of the mental, not of consciousness. Second, he suggests that belief and desire know no constraints. This too is wrong: a person can't help believing that it's raining outside if she sees that it is; though of course she can see *that* it's raining only if she has a certain conceptual mastery. (Among other things, she needs the concept of rain and of judgement itself, namely the idea that a belief about the world might be true or false.) One can't help believing that the rain may get her get wet, not if she means by "rain" what we think she does. The world, the real objective world, enters into our perceptions and beliefs in ways over which we have little control, *even though the world seen by us is the world interpreted by us*, and by each of us differently (see Sellars, 1956). Thinking is constrained both by the world and by the other thoughts of any particular "thinker".

We human beings have a hard time coming to terms with the fact that even in making our choices, determining who we want to be, we have to work with certain *faits accompli*, facts about us as creatures in the world.

"Narrativity" theorists also sometimes overlook the fact that who we are now is in part a consequence of this unchangeable past. They are joined by post-modernists who assume that we cannot both acknowledge, on the one hand, our debt to a real, objective world, and on the other, hold on to the idea that what happens in that world is always interpreted by us. But we do not have to choose between external reality and psychic reality. In fact, without the first idea, the second makes no sense. Present interpretations of the past cannot change the past itself, not even the past as it was then interpreted; yet they can change our attitudes towards it now, so change its future effects.

One of the goals of psychoanalytic therapy is to free the thinking process itself, partly a matter of removing blinders to seeing what is present, partly of letting oneself know that one sees it. Freud calls the ability to acknowledge what one sees the *reality principle*. Its presence, he says, is the distinctive mark of *das Ich*, the *I*. But reality is often painful, so we have ways, conscious and not-so-conscious, more and less successful but never wholly so, of closing it off. When we do, reason and reasoning, in the broadest sense of those words – thinking – become distorted. We shrink the domain of what Freud calls the *ego*, and what I am calling the domain of the first-person.

Oedipus Reckoned

PATRICK J. MAHONY

If we were asked to name one text from which psychoanalysis arose, we would have to answer *The Interpretation of Dreams*. And if we were asked to identify the pair of most significant passages in that seminal book, we would name the Irma dream and Freud's prescient discussion of *Oedipus Rex* and *Hamlet*.[1] I have already analysed the Irma dream for its thematic richness, especially as embedded in the German text (Mahony, 1977). On the present occasion, I shall examine Freud's famous, oft-read pages on *Oedipus Rex* and *Hamlet* (pp. 261–266). In the face of daunting scholarship on those pages and their primary referents, I shall offer some fresh thoughts that will be unevenly distributed upon three pertinent areas of focus: theme (here I shall examine only *Oedipus Rex*), performative textuality, and translation.

THE WHATNOT OF OEDIPUS'S KNOWLEDGE

To introduce the thematic consideration of knowledge, I shall share one of my linguistic reflections about Oedipus (etymologically, "swollen foot"). In Greek, the first three letters of Oedipus are *oid*, the same letters as in

---

1. Henceforth in the main text, page numbers will refer to the English *Standard Edition*. Where the original German is cited, the page numbers from the *Gesammelte Werke* (*G.W.*) will also be given. Most of the citations refer to Freud's commentary on *Oedipus Rex* and *Hamlet* in *Standard Edition*, 4:261–266 and *G.W.* 2/3:267–273.

oidao and *oida*. The verb *oidao* means "I swell up" (either physically, as in the foot, or mentally, as in hubris). The Greek past tense verb *oida*, "I saw", also means "I know" – a gloss that ironically comments on Oedipus's internal and subsequently external blindness. I propose, therefore, that a *three*-lettered signifier is at the centre of the play and indeed contains seeds of the play's meaning that sprout out in various directions: Oedipus, swelling up, seeing, knowing. As well, the three-lettered nature of the key signifier fits in the play's triadic pattern: Oedipus's triangular involvement with his parents, the parental abandonment of Oedipus when he is three days old, the parricidal site where three roads meet, and the consultation of the Delphic Oracle three times.

Along with many classicists, Freud ignored the profound insights about knowledge that are condensed in the episode about the Sphinx (its etymological root, *sphingein*, "to bind tight", is related to the root of "anxiety", *ankhein*, "to press tight, to strangle"). To quickly review: in the Sophoclean drama, we read that the Sphinx, residing on a mountain not far from Thebes, slew all the passers-by who could not answer the riddle, "What walks on four legs in the morning, on two at noon, and on three in the evening?" Finally, to the Sphinx's suicidal despair, Oedipus correctly replied that it was man in the three stages of his life: the crawling infant, the grown man, and the old man leaning on a staff.

In *The Interpretation of Dreams* Freud does not make much out of Oedipus's solving the riddle of the Sphinx per se. He merely says that the Thebans, consequently grateful that their city was relieved of the monstrous threat, proceeded to make Oedipus king and grant him Jocasta's hand. Despite Freud's contention elsewhere in his corpus (1905d, p. 195; 1907c, p. 135; 1909d, p. 133; 1916–1917, p. 318; 1925d, p. 37) that the latent meaning of the Oedipal legend refers to the origin of babies, there is nothing in the play itself to justify the critical application of such latent meaning. Oedipus's knowledge of the Sphinx's riddle is a conscious knowledge of the identity of man in general. That kind of general knowledge is personally non-redemptive and does not prevent Oedipus from being tortured by the Oracle's pronouncement, which concerns the specific knowledge about Oedipus himself as a particular man. Oedipus knows "man," but does not know who his father or mother are, even if, unwittingly of course, he has known the latter carnally.

Although not heeding the two different kinds of knowledge involved in the Sphinx and Oracle episodes, Freud does highlight its dramatic process: "The action of the play consists in nothing other than the process of revealing, with cunning delays and ever-mounting excitement – a process that can be likened to the work of a psychoanalysis" (1900a, pp. 261–262). In effect, Sophocles' play deals not only with knowing but with the process of knowing, which, if precipitous, may devastate rather than liberate Oedipus. His gradually approaching the truth occasions his ever greater denial – approach and flight are antonymous and synonymous – and ironically, his very attempts to avoid his fate deterministically drive him into fulfilling the Oracle's pronouncement.

Outwitted by his smartness, Oedipus does not know that he is confronting two different kinds of knowledge, and even that triumphancy in one kind can hubristically indispose him to pursue the other kind and to readily face the mounting evidence for it. If his knowledge of general man, if his facile, immediate solution of the Sphinx's riddle proved salvific for Thebes, likewise it was personally anti-productive: it increased his hubristic resistance toward forbidden and repressed knowledge. Pre-oedipal grandiosity, one may say, also contributed to Oedipus's eponymous defeat.

The Aeschylean motif of suffering into knowledge (*pathei mathos*) anticipates Freud's brief definition of transference as a "school of suffering" (*Schule Leidens*) (1909d, p. 209, G.W. Vol 7. p. 429). Oedipus's journey to wisdom by way of self-mutilation reminds us of some of our patients, who, were they to confront their incestuous guilt without the aid of a timely analysed transference, might mutilate themselves. Yet so different from the partial resolution of transference that helps patients sublimate their struggle with forbidden knowledge, the self-help of Oedipus was limited: the return of the repressed contaminating any sublimated quest for self-knowledge, he reacted to the informative Tiresias and the herdsman as persecutors.

Tied into knowledge as process in *Oedipus Rex* is knowledge as narrative transaction. Storytelling and listening to stories, whether they be interpersonal or intrapersonal activities, are a fundamental part of human nature. Since the beginning of humanity, no culture has existed without its myths. The quintessential sequentiality of primal fantasies and our innate mental capacity to perceive sequence already define us. We are narrative animals, driven either to uncover or to construct order and self-identity throughout the duration of our lives (in a typographical lapsus, I wrote "loves"). The repetition of stories, with or without change, along with their varied forms of rhythmic structuring, gratifies our desire for pleasure. We innately want more stories and seek that pleasure, which, especially in its sexual form (Freud, 1905d, p. 222; 1930a, p. 105), is insatiable. As Ricoeur (1978) has stressed more generally, in its insatiable desire, humanity had to create art just as it had to create dreams, for endless substitution defines the very activity of memory and fantasy.

Oedipus Rex foregrounds the problems of storytelling and listening, ranging from empathic attunement to individual or collusive resistance. The transferential entanglement of knowledge, desire, and power undermines their communicability, which at times is death-threatening. Like a neurotic under treatment whom Freud defines as initially incapable of giving a coherent and accurate autobiography (Mahony, 1996b), Oedipus starts out as a sighted listener who resists listening to Tiresias, the herdsman, and Jocasta, who in their turn are resistant storytellers.

Eventually Oedipus becomes a competent and insightful blind listener, permitting himself to hear the unheard-of, and he becomes too a narrator of the unspeakable. And so ends Sophocles's drama, picturing Oedipus like a cured patient, who can adequately tell so much of his life story. Or so it seems, for the play ends with the most tragic realization in all world literature. Given the potential catastrophes that hover ever about us, no one can be sure about the happiness of his life until he dies. In his drama, Sophocles underlines the pertinence of such a realization:

> Look at Oedipus –
> proof that none of us mortals
> can truly be thought of as happy
> until he is granted deliverance from life,
> and must suffer no more.

WHAT FREUD'S TEXT DOES

The greater part of so-called exploratory writing is only so in a secondary sense: that kind of writing, set in the past tense, reports previous exploration. Correspondingly, of lesser frequency is the writing that reports ongoing exploration. Such exploratory writing in a primary sense is divisible into two kinds: the first kind reports an ongoing exploration that is contemporaneous with yet external to the act of writing; the second, much rarer kind of exploratory writing, in a primary sense, functions performatively as the very means of exploring.

Much of *The Interpretation of Dreams* is of an immediately exploratory and performative nature. Freud tried writing his Dreambook but quickly fell into a writing block, which then precipitated him into a systematic self-analysis. He conducted his self-analysis, focusing mainly on his dreams, in writing, an instrumental circumstance that was so much more performatively significant in that he did not bring about one talking cure during the whole time of the Dreambook's composition (Mahony, 1994).

Several other relevant data should be kept in mind. Identifying the maternal object and dream, Freud twice referred to its unfathomable core as its navel or *Nabel* (1900a, pp. 111, 525; G.W. pp. 116, 530). In the same vein, holding that Nature and landscape symbolize woman and mother, Freud narrativized his epistemological investigation in the Dreambook as a journey through nature. Thus, symbolically, Freud carries out his psychoanalytic venture as an exploration and conquest of the maternal body. It follows that, in examining Sophocles' play, Freud focused on the son's oedipal complex, not the father's, nor the father's homosexuality, nor, *inter alia*, Jocasta's suicide.

Let us look more closely at the organization of *The Interpretation of Dreams*. Its first chapter functions non-symbolically as a survey of oneiric literature; Chapter Two on the Irma dream, which steers clear of explicit analysis of infantile sexuality, is retrospectively portrayed as a passage through a narrow defile (p. 122); the first descent in the hell of the unconscious occurs in Chapter Five, where Freud evokes Oedipus as traveller! Then, as the oedipal conquistador, Freud proceeds to the pre-oedipal in Chapter Seven. There, at the very outset, Freud uses his maternally symbolic imagery to express the limits of his performative writing to attain the pre-oedipal depths:

> Hitherto, unless I am greatly mistaken, all the paths along which we have travelled have led us toward the light – towards elucidation and fuller understanding. But as soon as we endeavour to penetrate more deeply into the mental process involved in dreaming, every path will end in darkness. There is no possibility of *explaining* dreams as a psychical process, since to explain a thing means to trace it back to something already known, and there is at the present time no established psychological knowledge under which we could subsume what the psychological examination of dreams enables us to infer as a basis for their explanation. [p. 511. See also Mahony, 1987b]

Clearly, Freud's self-cure had its achievements, but it also had its limits, marked by some collusion between writing and dreaming (Mahony, 1994). The epistemological fragility of Freud's opus was contained only in a private admission that Freud made to Fliess: "So far I have always known where the next dream-night would continue" (1985, p. 268). To Fliess's insistence that a certain dream be omitted from the classic monograph, Freud yielded, adding that whatever were the objectionable elements in the dream, he would eliminate them in one of his future dreams, "for he could have dreams like that made to order" (1985, p. 315). Freud's book about dreams, then, was also a dream to a certain extent: the dreams and book were mutual wishes and fulfillments; the dreams were texts and pre-texts. Further indicative of the discursive pressure marking the composition of his opus, in one passage Freud lapsed into positing that childhood was "innocent of sexual desires" (1900a, p. 130), a monumental self-contradiction that Jung brought to his attention (letter of February 14, 1911; see Freud & Jung, 1974). All in all, then, the composition of the Dreambook was a "writing through," a "writing-out," or neologistically, a "writing through-out."

Performative writing culminates in its publication, as Freud indicates in a series of dispersed comments. First, during his self-analysis Freud became bitterly disenchanted over the enormous gap between Fliess's unpublished research and its validatable write-up. Second, Freud called attention to the fact that Shakespeare wrote (and by implication, staged) *Hamlet*[2] immediately after the death of his father and therefore during the period of familial mourning (Freud, 1900a, p. 265). Third, the autobiographical reflection of Freud's reference to Shakespeare's filial mourning emerges in one of the greatest of belated realizations. In a preface to the second edition of the Dreambook in 1908, Freud acknowledged this postponed discovery (p. xxvi).[3]

WHAT TRANSLATION DOESN'T SAY

Freud applies the label of translation (*Übersetzung*) to a whole range of analytic phenomena, ranging from parapraxes, fetishes, symptomatology, and dreams, to the analyst's interpretations (these translate or paraphrase and simultaneously bring about a transposition of unconscious material

---

2. In dealing with Hamlet, Freud evinced a sensitivity to the historical change that a universal fantasy might undergo. Thus he alludes to transformations of the oedipal myth as it evolves from Hellenic Greece to Elizabethan England and onto contemporary Europe.

3. Or as Freud said many years afterwards, his soul was "revolutionized" by his father's death (1993, p. 370).

into the conscious). Indeed, in his expanding conception of translation, Freud ranks as one of its outstanding theoreticians in history (Mahony, 1980).

I turn now to a relevant passage about the very act of translating in the Dreambook. After having interpreted some of Hamlet's prohibited wishes and defensive reactions, Freud writes: "Here I have translated [*übersetzt*] into conscious terms what was bound to remain unconscious in Hamlet's mind" (1900a, p. 265; G.W. p. 272).

Freud's dramatic reflection should be glossed by his epistolary insight: "A failure in translation – this is what is clinically known as 'repression'" (1985, p. 298). In German, the verb *übersetzen* may mean to transpose (in a spatial sense) or to translate (as from one language to another). The choice of meaning becomes clear either owing to context or, as in the above instance, because of other linguistic features. When *übersetzen* means translate, the *ü* is accented, and the verb's past participle is simply *übersetzt*; when, however, *übersetzen* means to transpose, the *setz* is accented, and the verb's past participle is *übergesetzt*. In the first half of his sentence cited above, Freud uses *translate* in the sense of putting into another language, but the second half of the sentence refers to space and in so doing makes the German speaker think of the alternate meaning of translation.

Close attention to Freud's German also makes one aware of the various synonyms of knowledge that Freud utilized. One of them, *erkennen*, is highly charged, as Freud explained in a letter to Jones: ". . . you remember that 'Erkennen' [to know] means 'Coitiren' [to have intercourse] in the Bible. (Und Adam erkannte sein Weib [and Adam knew his wife])" (1993, p. 77). Freud could have added that, in German, the tree of knowledge is *der Baum der Erkenntnis*.

Bearing the carnal note of *erkennen* in mind, the English reader of the Dreambook will better appreciate Freud's explanations of Oedipus:

> While the poet, as he unravels the past, brings to light the guilt of Oedipus, he is at the same time compelling us to recognize [*zur Erkenntnis*] our own inner minds. [1900a, p. 263; G. W. p. 269]

> This discovery of knowledge [*dieser Erkenntnis* – actually, Strachey does not translate these two words] is confirmed by a legend that has come down to us from classical antiquity (p. 261; G. W. p. 267]

It is also interesting to observe that in one of the three citations from the Greek classic, Freud uses a German translation that has Oedipus asking where the hardly knowable (*erkennbar*: p. 261, G. W. p. 268) trace of the old crime can be found. Strachey relies on an English translation that speaks simply of a "fading record". Let it be said, however, that the suggestivity of the German *erkennbar* is not to be found in the original Greek *dustekmarton*, which means, literally, "difficult to discern or discover".

Another of Freud's terms in the Oedipal passages, *Regung*, has the greatest pertinence for the understanding of psychodynamics and psychoanalytic technique (see Mahony, 1996a). *Regung* signifies the beginning of a movement, that is, a stirring. For intensifications of movement such as excitement, *Erregung* and *Aufregung* would be used, and for stimulation and impulse, *Anregung*. The nuances differentiating the previous terms have weighty implications: analytic training makes one alert to stirrings, whereas such sophistication is ordinarily not necessary to perceive the signs of impulse and stimulation. Apart from a single correct rendering of *Regungen* by "stirrings" (p. 264, G.W. p. 270), Strachey typically amplifies the term into "impulse(s)" (pp. 261, 262, 266; G.W. pp. 267, 269, 272). Strachey's mistranslations obscure the fact that *Regung*, occurring in the singular and plural well over 400 times in the *Gesammelte Werke*, is a cardinal Freudian concept.

The serious drift of this essay justifies my conclusion in a lighter note. I have a fantasy about a witty dream that Freud would have if we were living today and in which he would retrospect on the oedipal wrecks of post-Freudian psychoanalysis. Musing on Klein's earlier dating and oral version of the oedipal complex, he might jibe at her edible complex. And musing on the analysts who exclusively choose either topological or structural theory, he might mock their edifice complex.

An Indiscretion on Psychoanalytic Fiction
GEORGE STADE

I might as well confess from the outset that my interest in literature is a prurient interest and always has been. I began to read compulsively during my twelfth year, when I thought all women were as blank between the legs as the goddesses in the Classical wing of the Metropolitan Museum of Art. I would spend hours mooning over those fine figures of women and then run home to read – as I now see it – in search of solutions to the problems posed by that uncanny blankness. If I had not discovered in Poe's stories a fascination in the verbal equivalent to my own state of mind – ". . . much of Madness and more of Sin, And Horror the Soul of the Plot" – to quote Poe (1843) himself; if I had not discovered in *Huckleberry Finn* the absorbing fable of innocent males escaping dreadful women only to become voyeurs; if I had not discovered in the jungle tales of Tarzan a model of manliness triumphant not by overcoming its animal nature but by succumbing to it, and along with that the pipe dream of a captive and goddess-like Jane who has no grounds for invidious comparisons, the only other males around being apes; if I had not discovered these works I might simply have joined the line for Dirty Francine instead of becoming a compulsive reader.

"Compulsive" is the word for it. I read anything with a plot, good, bad, or abominable, that I could steal from the paperback racks on old man Stephanovitch's candy store, and I read at a terrific rate of speed. A test I took my senior year in high school exposed me as someone who read faster then 99 percent of college freshmen, but did not reveal why. By the time I was myself a college freshman my morbid curiosity turned restlessly towards non-fiction, although that is not how I read it. This was in the early fifties, and I devoured books of sociology as you might gobble corn chips while watching a soap opera; I had hopes of a peep at what had made me a member of the lonely crowd and hopes of a peek at what the rest of the crowd was doing behind the drawn curtains of the picture windows in Levittown and Middletown, USA. During a binge of some years on anthropology I tracked down traces of the primal scene in primitive man. During a truly reckless toot on astrophysics I spied on the darkness of interstellar space for glimmers of what Mama and Papa did at night. My long-term addictions to linguistics and biology are similar attempts to catch a glimpse of ontogeny recapitulating philology.

And so it went, until one day I awoke to find myself dim of eye, stiff of neck, and chronically dyspeptic – I had stumbled into middle age and still I was ignorant. I had failed to learn anything, not in spite of my reading but because of it. I had never read what I was reading for what I was reading, but for something else. I had never found what I was looking for and I had never looked at what was actually there to be found. I was as empty as a man trying to feed on air plankton while holding his breath.

For the first time in twenty years I took a good look around – probably for help. But what I saw, of course, was a reflection of my own neurosis. I saw people on subways hooked on the narratives of crime, chicanery, and casual slaughter in their newspapers. I saw people of a more modest literacy finding romance in little hard-cover comic books, and I saw students high above any kind of literacy finding the colours of outer space in the old-fashioned soft-cover kind. I saw people spending four hours a day before their television sets or radios watching or listening to stories that were interrupted by other stories, by cautionary tales of how your children will get rickets if they don't eat a certain white bread with the latest additives or inspirational tales of how a despairing housewife found happiness with new Fab. I saw people extricate themselves from their television sets only long enough to get wrapped up in the plots of movies, plays, operas, and ballets. I saw gossips telling tales over backyard fences, and I saw thugs on street corners or hunters in bars telling still taller tales of their hits and near misses. I saw a plague of gurus and politicians fabricating their own hagiographies of temptations overcome and vocations overtaken, and I saw their disciples spreading fabulous gospels of small miracles and large promises. Everywhere I looked someone was either telling a story or listening to one – as you and I are right now. I saw that what passes for conversation is usually a series of anecdotes with the teller as hero or a series of anecdotal jokes with someone else as the butt. I heard of professors who had to read some detective novel or other piece of schlock every night before they could go to sleep. In fact, I am one of them. I read somewhere that of the 4,000 human societies known to anthropologists not one of them is without literature, written or oral. It was clear that telling and listening to tales is as species-specific to humans as opposable thumbs and rounded buttocks.

The vision of humanity in the grips of a repetition compulsion, driven by an appetite that can never be satisfied because it grows on what it feeds, brought me up short. My morbid curiosity became reflexive. I developed a prurient interest in my prurient interest, and it directed me to psychoanalysis, towards which a man with a problem like mine was bound sooner or later to turn. I took out my Freud, this time determined not just to read, but to understand – enough! where id was, there let ego be. Freud's starting point is that we write and perhaps read as we produce fantasies, and for the same reasons. By now this is no longer news, even to me, nor is it very specific, but it was the right kind of start, as were the books on dreams and jokes, the essays on the uncanny, on the three caskets, on the Medusa's head, and the rest. They were more useful, however, as models of what genius might achieve than as expositions of a method I could adopt to other materials, more useful as accounts of what this work or that might mean than as explanations of why we read in general or why we read this or that in particular. Freud, moreover, confessed bafflement over the component of art in literary art, and as Jack J. Spector (1972) has said; "Aside from some fruitful implications of his ideas for criticism and art, no final system can ever be built out of Freud's ideas" (p. ix).

It was a final system I was now after in those days of besotted optimism, now thank God gone forever, so I turned to Freud's followers, who as critics are mainly of three types. One type diagnoses the author through his texts, which are read as symptoms. The knowledge so obtained is by no means despised and, once you have read a good psychoanalytic biography of a writer, all other kinds seem to leave out the essentials; but it was not the author's symptoms I was after. A second type diagnoses not the author but his characters. It was helpful to learn that Othello, Macbeth, Lear, Romeo, Julius Caesar, and Mark Anthony had each a different complex of his own, for I sympathized and was moved by all of them. Did that mean I was a walking compendium of every possible psychopathic-tragic flaw? The third type reads texts as allegories of psychoanalytic doctrine. For example, the house in the Tom and Jerry cartoon, with its clutter of appliances, its overstuffed furniture and black maid and cornucopic refrigerator, a showplace of suburban acquisitiveness and the scene of the action, is the ego. The mouse, who is repressed, denied, abhorred, a denizen of holes, a nocturnal and chthonic appetite so sexy that women lift their skirts to him, is the id. The cat, implacable warden and tormentor of the mouse, dark of colour, long of tail, sharp of tooth and claw, is the super-ego. I was not ready to deny such readings, but I had a suspicion that at least some works were more than diagrams of psychoanalytic doctrine. In any case, I already knew the rudiments.

But Norman N. Holland was of a different type altogether. In 1964 he wrote that "a comprehensive psychoanalytic theory for the response to literature remains to be written," and in three subsequent works he tried to write it. His work on the dynamics of literary response (1968) for a while revived my flagging optimism. I was convinced by his demonstration that technique is to the latent content of literature what defences are to drives in people: ways, that is, of managing what we fear or abhor but cannot do without. His readings of individual works, however, were so lame, tame, and strained as to seem in themselves defences against the hidden terrors and forbidden pleasures they were meant to display ("the single most common fantasy structure in literature," Holland says, "is phallic assertiveness balanced against oral engulfment" [p. 43]). So I spun around with some of my old frenzy from Ferenczi to Fenichel, from Reik to Reich, from Hans Sachs to Hanna Segal, from Karl Abraham to Abraham Kaplan, from Ernst Kris to Christ knows what else, until I was like a certain Mercy Rogers who, according to a newspaper account of 1922, read 100 books on psychoanalysis and then stuck her head in the oven.

The outcome was that a horrible thought took possession of my mind. I refused to entertain it, but it would not be denied. I know you will forgive me – it was just a passing aberration – the thought was this: that psychoanalysis was itself a form of literature, that it was a fiction for obsessed critics to examine, rather than a critical method for examining our obsessions with fiction. As I say, this madness passed, but it left a residue. I do not now often read psychoanalytic criticism, although I read it more than most other kinds. But I read some Freud nearly every day. Only his sombre pessimism and double-edged ironies seem equal to the occasion. Psychoanalysis did not cure me of my obsessions, but did make it easier for me to live with them, and even, in a shy kind of way, to like them.

As for the project of working out a complete psychobiological explanation of our prurient interest in fiction, I gladly bequeath it to someone who has not yet been exhausted by his vices.

Part IV

Setting the Frame for the Future

Through the Looking Glass – Psychoanalysis, Conceptual Integration, and the Problem of the Innate

MERVYN M. PESKIN

Psychoanalysis is in a period of punctuated equilibrium, a time of change. Energetic subspecies have developed within the psychoanalytic niche, once dominated by classical ego psychology. Of even greater import, the allopatric evolution of psychoanalysis is undergoing transformation due to the encroachment of neighbouring scientific elaborations of the functioning of the mind. Noting that "it is inherent in the nature of science to be refreshed by discourse in other disciplines" (Cooper, 1997, p. 9), Cooper has persuasively argued (1990a; 1991a; 1997) that psychoanalysis cannot remain isolated from these elaborations and still maintain its scientific status. I agree, and read him to be arguing not only for the inspirational but for the constraining effect of neighbouring ideas – for the powerful heuristic guidance and, if necessary, reorientation brought about by conceptual integration, or at least conceptual compatibility, with neighbouring scientific endeavours. In this chapter, part of my ongoing dialogue with him, I will focus on the implications of the curious fact that moving toward conceptual integration leads us back into the theoretical wilderness of mirrors surrounding the innate and instinctual dispositions, which so many advances and revisions of psychoanalytic theory have recently led us out of.

The issue of conceptual integration has grown both more realistic and more pressing in the recent past with the rise of cognitivism and the demise of behaviourism in scientific psychology. For cognitivism, unlike behaviourism, accepts that there are hidden causes of behaviour located in the mind/brain (Plotkin, 1998). A purview of the neighbouring fields of cognitive psychology, developmental psychology, and linguistics makes it clear that they are burgeoning with studies relevant to our interests. However, it also reveals that they are in the grip of a great debate. For the difficult, protracted acceptance of hidden causes was largely catalyzed by the arguments and evidence for *innate complex mechanisms* in the mind, notably the telling arguments and persuasive evidence for an innate language acquisition device (Chomsky, 1980). Studies in memory and perception have repeatedly demonstrated that output is richer and more organized than can be accounted for by input alone, implying the working of unobservable causes. This "poverty of the stimulus" argument is a basic tenet of modern cognitivism (Fodor, 1983; Plotkin, 1998). It is not surprising that the acceptance of hidden causes has reactivated in psychology and in mind/brain studies the great debate as to the roles of the innate and of early experience in human behaviour. Furthermore, acceptance of hidden causes has inevitably opened the way for ideas from the branch of biology particularly knowledgeable about innate mechanisms, that is, evolutionary biology, into the new, comprehensive elaboration of human psychology. Concomitantly, evolutionary theory itself has increasingly turned to a consideration of adaptedness and behaviour in our species. A new division of psychology, evolutionary psychology, incorporating evolutionary studies with cognitive psychology has emerged as a result.

Of course, psychoanalysis is no stranger to these matters. Indeed, classical Freudian theory in its inclusion of early experience, hidden causes, and innate dispositions was nearly a century ahead of current developments. However, the formulation of instinct theory was problematic and has been revised in all newer psychoanalytic models (Brenner, 1982; Kernberg, 1992; Kohut, 1977; Lichtenberg, 1989a; Sandler, 1989; Schafer, 1976). Though the nature and degree of the revision has varied, I think it is accurate to say that all new models and in particular the "revisionist" theories, comprising self psychology and the clade of (non-Kleinian) object relational, interpersonal, intersubjectivist, and social constructivist theories, which some regard as representing a new species, a new paradigm, of psychoanalytic theory, are distinguished by the degree to which they have freed themselves of traditional drive theory, which is an essential feature of the classical psychoanalytic theory of the innate. This at a time when the data of cognitive psychology and the resurgent influence of evolutionary studies have turned scientific psychology toward a greater appreciation of the innate. Thus the necessary quest for conceptual integration with neighbouring scientific endeavours will, *inter alia*, lead us to a reconfrontation with the old ghosts of biological disposition and instincts (or evolved psychological mechanisms as they are carefully called), which still roam, unburied, in the labyrinthine halls of mind science for the sound reason that they are not dead.

An important focus of the current debate in mind studies is centred on the degree to which our evolved mentality consists of domain specific, specialized psychological mechanisms as opposed to all purpose, contentless, generalized mechanisms (see Symons, 1987). As it has become increasingly untenable in mind studies to espouse a position eschewing innate mechanisms, the anti-nativist stance has shifted to the acceptance of general purpose learning devices, or connectionist neural networks as the basis for all human cognition (Elman et al., 1996). This is in contrast to the more domain- and content-specific psychological mechanisms proposed by theorists who advocate a stronger position for evolved adaptations fashioned by natural selection (Tooby & Cosmides, 1992). It is worth noting that the term *instinct*, all but abandoned scientifically following the naive excesses of early twentieth century instinct theorists, seems to be regaining respectability (Symons, 1997, personal communication; Pinker, 1994) in describing a biological predisposition that is preformed and ready to operate prior to any experience. Harking back to William James's contention (1890), Tooby and Cosmides note that the human mind is distinguished, not by its lack, but by its proliferation of "instincts" – that is, content-specific problem-solving specializations" (1992, p. 113). These include motivational problems. They note that the general purpose mind would be faced with an infinity of possibilities and that desirable outcomes from the human adaptive perspective represent a very small subset of possibilities. As noted by Lorenz (1965) over a generation ago, learning itself depends on a set of evolved dispositions.

Even proponents of general purpose neurostructure such as Elman accept that these networks are predisposed to operate in certain ways. The most coherent scientific account is that these predispositions are innately, that is, genetically determined, that they are the consequences of natural selection, and are biased to operate in certain constrained ways (see Dawkins, 1982; Dennett, 1995; Plotkin, 1998). Although I agree with Tooby and Cosmides (1992) that there has been a general acceptance of innate evolved processes, I believe this overt acceptance is misleading. If by evolved psychological mechanism we mean the differential selection, over evolutionary time-scales, of that mechanism rather than others, due to its being causally related to an overall advantage in individual survival and reproductive success, then there are and always have been challenges to this interpretation of evolution from various scientific quarters, including from within evolutionary biology itself (Gould, 1980; 1982; see Peskin, 1997). More recent challenges have been based on theories of self-organizing processes in complex, dynamic, non-linear systems (Kauffman, 1993). Also, although the refutation of the relevance of evolved predisposition has a long pedigree in developmental psychology, recent opposition has also come to be based on dynamic systems theory (Oyama, 1985; Thelen & Smith, 1994). In Thelen and Smith's view, behaviour and development have nothing to do with evolved design: "There are no structures [and] no rules. There is complexity. There is a multiple, parallel, and continuously dynamic interplay of perception and action, and a system that, by its thermodynamic nature, seeks certain stable solutions. These solutions emerge from relations, not from design" (p. xix). This reflects an extreme developmentalist position. In general, however, there has been a move toward a more correlated conception of the interaction between innate disposition and experience in epigenesis, the complex cascade of intricate, mutual interactions between genetic information, phenotypic development, and the environment. However, despite this general acceptance of flexibility and anti-reductionist complexity, the dispute shows little sign of ending.

I have focused on the innateness dispute from the perspective of evolved cognitive mechanisms, as they constitute an important active interface between cognitive, developmental, and evolutionary studies. It should be noted that evolutionary science has actively and productively been pursuing another approach, that of elaborating, via optimality theory and game theory, the behaviours and strategies associated with inclusive fitness. This is an individual's reproductive success plus the effect he or she has on the reproductive success of relatives (each measured by a coefficient of relatedness). In these approaches, using mathematical modelling, the full adaptive advantage of self-enhancing behaviours and motivations is clear and predictive (Dawkins, 1980; Maynard Smith, 1978; 1979). These behaviours include altruism and the models encompass the conflict regarded as inherent in all relationships, including the parent–offspring relationship (Trivers, 1971; 1974). As the genetic interest of no two individuals is congruent (despite great coincidence, as in the mother–child relationship, where 50 percent of the genotype is shared and there are many mutually coadapted mechanisms at work) relational conflict is inevitable. Furthermore, the recent focus on the gene as the target of selection (a reciprocal view to regarding the individual as the target) highlights the importance of manipulation and counter-manipulation, deception and the ability to detect deception, in adaptive success. As human Darwinian fitness depends profoundly on social success, a general motivational tension between "selfish" and "mutualistic" aims is predicted. Indeed, both consciousness itself and unconscious motivation (self-deception) are postulated to be evolved adaptations associated with interrelational, competitive advantage and sexual success (Humphrey, 1986; Nesse & Lloyd, 1992). In this regard, domain-specific specialized mechanisms are a set of functions, functionally related to each other but ultimately causally related to the overall essential function of survival and reproduction (see Pinker & Bloom, 1992). From the perspective of evolved specific mechanisms, drives for sex and aggression (or a drive for attachment) can be regarded as generalizations and condensations of more specific, functionally related component mechanisms.

The adaptationist argument, as outlined, has remained central to the theory of Darwinian natural selection and central to many of the rejections and revisions of the theory. In fact, a revolution or new paradigm in evolutionary theory is sometimes said to be occurring. Arguably the most significant and most widely quoted authority for this view, from within the field itself, is Gould. In his repeated challenges to adaptationism and gradualism and his promotion of the theory of punctuated equilibrium (1980; 1993), in which evolutionary change is concentrated into relatively brief periods punctuating long spans of equilibrium, he has in effect raised the claim that evolutionary change is not caused by natural selection operating on differences between members of a population. In this approach, evolutionary change would depend on the differential selection of one *species* over another, based on factors that make extinction less probable and splitting of lineages more probable. Individual survival and reproduction are replaced by extinction and lineage splitting, and selection between individuals by that between species. (However, species selectionism is a weak force of selection compared to that between individuals, in part as the "birth and death" of species is orders of magnitude less frequent than that of individuals: see Maynard Smith, 1989). Gould has also written approvingly regarding the possibility of a large phenotypic shift or macro-mutation (a "hopeful monster" in its extreme form): "it relegates selection to a negative role (eliminating the unfit) and assigns the major creative aspect of evolution to variation itself" (1982, pp. 343–344). What is specifically rejected in this view is the presumed "major creative aspect" of natural selection – selecting the fit. Both the revival of group selectionism and the espousal of macro-mutations reject the current primacy in natural selection of competition between individuals. My reading of Gould suggests this is a central theme of his work.

I believe disagreement over this primacy lies at the core of the continuing dispute over the degree to which innate evolved mechanisms play a determinative role in developed motivation, as opposed to being merely a necessary substrate that is metabolized away in development to something different. Furthermore this rejection and this dispute are mirrored in facets of the many revisions to classical drive theory and the subsequent psychoanalytic reconceptualizations of motivation. The latter represent a significant part of the evolution of psychoanalysis itself and in the following succinct remarks I hope for maximum specificity with minimum injustice to this corpus of work. In broad purview the drive concept has embodied two features: first, those relating to psychic energy, and second, the component of an instinctual motivation. The component of psychic energy has been the focus of much of the compelling criticism of the drive concept and I will not deal with it here. However, the second component of the drive concept, that of endogenous motivations arising out of "instinctual dispositions", to use Freud's term (1920g, p. 171), remains theoretically relevant and central to current contentions. Dual drive theory (death instinct excepted) maintained the centrality of the Darwinian adaptationist argument; natural selection favours behaviours and motivations that are causally related to ensuring survival and reproduction, and I would contend that this accounts significantly for its resiliency. Ironically, it was the heirs apparent of ego psychology, Hartmann, Kris, and Loewenstein, who, troubled by Freud's phylogenetic oversimplifications, turned decisively away from evolutionary connections, despite their very focus on adaptation. The analysts who turned strongly toward evolutionary principles were relational attachment theorists, Bowlby (1969) and Erikson (1964). (Erikson's concept of psychosocial equilibrium is derived from the group selectionist thinking prominent at the time.) Furthermore, current relational models function as if they had a powerful drive for attachment at their core (Greenberg, 1991; Peskin, 1997; Slavin & Kriegman, 1992). However other important attachment theorists (e.g., Fairbairn, Winnicott) focused their work on the early mother–child relationship without a basis in evolutionary theory. A more prevalent theoretical tendency was to move away from "biology" altogether, as manifest in self psychology (see Bacal, 1990). This trend was of course not confined to relational theorists (Klein, 1976; Schafer, 1976). A powerful new reconceptualization was that of the strong developmentalist position in which drives and motivation are seen as *arising out of* early development; a very different conception to that in which early experience plays a critical role in the contextualized, *drive-derived* unit of motivation, the wish.

As enunciated by Loewald: "[I]nstinctual drives . . . are not forces immanent in an autonomous, separate, primitive psyche, but are the resultant of tensions within the mother–child psychic matrix" (1972, p. 242). Here, evolved motivational dispositions are excluded and drives as psychic forces are "determined by the characteristics of that matrix-field" (Loewald, 1970, p. 291). I believe this developmentalist position has remained a key feature of relational models and was of course presaged by Fairbairn's recasting of libido as object seeking. Darwinian innate motivations of self-interest are rejected in favour of object-seeking mutualistic motivations. Conflict is the result of relational (empathic or self-object) failure, rather than inherent in all relationships *a priori*.

Currently the search for conceptual validation from related sciences is proliferating. Much of this hunting and gathering is partial and selective. Mitchell (1988) approves a preadapted potential in the infant for being social suggesting a "motivational property *within* the organism" (emphasis in original, p. 24) but rejects any other preadapted potentials. Stolorow (1997) seeks validation for the intersubjectivist, anti-nativist position in Thelen and Smith's (1994) non-Darwinian attempt to base development on non-linear thermodynamics. Modell (1993) finds support for the need to maintain a coherent sense of self in a Darwinian theory, not of evolutionarily determined innate motivations, but in neuronal group selectionism (Edelman, 1987), essentially a developmental theory. In this brief overview I cannot deal with the many compelling appeals to neurophysioendocrinology. But it should be remembered that neurophysioendocrinology, a necessary part of the comprehensive elaboration of the innate, is itself a probabilistic manifestation of natural selection. Unlike evolutionary explanations it thus constitutes a proximate explanation. Traditional drive theorists, for their part, have remained largely detached from the powerful Darwinian connection, holding to the precarious base of physio-mental energic transformations, for which there is no emerging scientific validation and which is likely misconceived. A more significant approach has been to base sexual and aggressive drives on psychoanalytic observation alone, that is, generalizations that can be made from the wishes of many patients (Brenner, 1982). This is a proposition that is, in principle, testable.

Is there something for everybody in the garden of conceptual integration? There is no doubt that the more selective the search the more convenient the harvest. However, the manner and degree to which evolutionarily determined, genetic endowment determines behaviour and strategy, and, from the psychological perspective, determines motivation, has become a burgeoning, organized field of study in evolutionary science and in the new field of evolutionary psychology. Concepts that are central to psychoanalytic theory, such as consciousness, motivation, unconscious motivation, deception and self-deception (defence), altruism, attachment, sexuality, and conflict are all central in the developing formulations. It is thus remarkable that more comprehensive correlations with evolutionary studies are so rare from within psychoanalysis (for exceptions see Nesse & Lloyd, 1992; Peskin, 1997; Slavin & Kriegman, 1992). A more profound issue at this stage is that, as discussed, disagreements as to motivation, analogous to those in psychoanalytic theory, are reflected from within evolutionary theory as well. These focus around the postulated alternatives, promoted as a new paradigm in both cases, to the central Darwinian adaptationist perspective of enhancing individual self-interest and competition between individuals. Further reflected similarities between psychoanalytic theory and other related sciences lie in the approaches that bypass this Darwinian perspective on the innate, via developmentalist solutions, in which innate evolved behavioural dispositions are confined to general purpose capacities, out of which, in the early object tie, motivation arises; or approaches that bypass Darwinian natural selection altogether by invoking relationally organized complexity as the origin of mental structure.

We should remember that psychoanalysis, which offers a unique in-depth perspective on the psychology of human motivation, has contributions to make as well as receive in the gathering scientific integration (see Olds & Cooper, 1997). Let me mention one consistent psychoanalytic finding: the ubiquity of conflict in the functioning of the mind. Is this simply a reflection of the inevitable imperfection of the early relational world? Is it merely the expected result of the complexity of a multiplicity of motivations? Or does it offer a way through the looking glass, by constituting something more specific and more profound – a substantiation by psychoanalytic data of the *inherent and inevitable* intrapsychic tension, integral to the deployment of self-interest, between mutualism and exploitation, predicted in the main body of evolutionary theory; a substantiation detailing the beautifully intricate involvement of early relationships in the mental representation of this tension; and a substantiation, moreover, by data derived from our unique perspective in depth on the human mind at this stage of evolution.

Theoretical Pluralism and the Construction of Psychoanalytic Knowledge
DAVID TUCKETT

More than a hundred years after its foundation, what psychoanalysis is, what a psychoanalytic treatment is, and how and on whom it works are very much in doubt, within the discipline and without. When spelled out in detail, few psychoanalytic propositions are treated consensually, even among psychoanalysts, as having a value as "real" in the sense that to ignore them is consequential. Nor are they agreed as useful truths, so that they necessarily limit the scope for competing beliefs and constitute a secure fund of knowledge from which any other proposition must take off.

As an example, the central concept of *transference* is a subject for dispute, being visited and re-visited with little clear consensus. Other key concepts for some – for instance, the *therapeutic alliance*, the *castration complex*, or the *après coup* – are almost irrelevant to others. Indeed, my impression (see also Hamilton, 1993; Schafer, 1983) is that few psychoanalysts would confidently feel able to set out a list of the core propositions of the discipline as a whole and at the same time expect, *on close inspection and definition*, close associates in their own country, let alone more distant colleagues, to agree.

Several questions seem pertinent. Why are there so many different groups and apparently isolated points of view in psychoanalysis? How do new ideas get adopted and why are they often so uncritically accepted or rejected? What can be said about the institutional arrangements in the field that hinder or facilitate the development of a secure and consensually agreed fund of knowledge?

THE SOCIAL CONSTRUCTION AND LEGITIMISATION OF PSYCHOANALYTIC KNOWLEDGE

The study of the fund of psychoanalytic knowledge is a special case of the study more generally of knowledge in society. Knowledge, insofar as it is claimed or transmitted so that what one person believes to be true is accepted by another, is a social entity. Agreement depends on the processes of argumentation and inference that take place within a social grouping, and is subject to the beliefs, rules of procedure, and evidence found there. These include more or less well-defined ways to deal with the possibility that certain situations – for instance, the proposition that the earth is round, or that smoking is a cause of major illness – are beyond the immediate comprehension of personal experience and require some form of specialized argumentation.

Several ideas, adapted from the sociology of knowledge to my purpose, seem to me likely to enlighten the study of the social construction of psychoanalytic knowledge.

Social groups normally demonstrate a degree of orderly basic agreement on key questions, which maintains their existence and prevents their collapse. Order is not usually the result of coercion or legal forms but arises because the individuals within groups share (more or less descriptively unconscious) sets of assumptions as to what it is (and is not) considered right and proper to think and do. Social groups that are unable to establish a core set of shared and (to them) meaningful and plausible explanations of what their members observe to be happening in and around them tend to disintegrate. Similarly groups that fail to maintain their separate identity by controlling deviation or those who become reliant on coercion to achieve this end, are vulnerable to disintegration. I will be referring to *strongly* and *weakly* ordered groups (conceived along a continuum) to distinguish those psychoanalytic groupings where there is more or less shared understanding and practice at some depth on key questions. Groups that have agreement only at more superficial levels will be designated *weakly ordered*.

Maintaining orderly conceptions of knowledge of reality within the membership of a social group over time depends to a considerable extent on the system for transmitting knowledge to new initiates, termed the process of *socialisation*. It is noticeable that historically the transmission of knowledge in psychoanalytic groups has consistently shown signs of oligarchy, prescription, and politicization and has remained strongly influenced by private personal sponsorship and idealization. It has not often been able to move towards transparent universalistic achievement-based criteria, and in some instances has relied heavily on coercion (see, for instance, Kernberg, 1996).

Another question to be asked about any group is how it settles puzzling questions or potential crises of meaning. The way legitimate authority is exercised to resolve matters is important in this respect. Authority in social groups can be characterized as conferred legitimately along traditional, charismatic or reasoned rule-bound lines (Weber, 1923). Put in more ordinary language, we could say that who is legitimately and consensually regarded as speaking the truth can be determined on the basis of what we have always known, what a charismatic or dictatorial leader says, or can be subject to processes of reason and regulation formally independent of individual whim. I think it highly significant that authority in psychoanalysis has usually been charismatic (referring questions to the authority of a revered leader) and occasionally traditional. It has rarely been rule-bound in the sense I shall be using this phrase, meaning "independent of individual whim". All systems of authority are associated with legitimating formulae that are used to settle day-to-day questions. In charismatic systems these formulae involve association with the charismatic figure – for example, the quotation in support of a knowledge claim of his or her text, or the wearing of associated robes. In traditional systems there are sets of complex rules and tests conducted in agreed ways that are followed because they are the way things are done. Among the Azande, for example, questions as to the causes and appropriate remedies for misfortune were resolved through a complex system for divining witchcraft (Evans Pritchard, 1937). In rule-bound systems like most modern science there are agreed methodological procedures based on reasoned argument and counter-argument. To become rule-bound successfully it is necessary to begin to specify theoretical knowledge and rules of inference and evidence at an experience-near level sufficient to allow situations requiring adjudication to permit a group to reach uncompelled consensus. Cavell (1988) suggests that "to know that you and I disagree, I must know what you are saying in the first place". This has been the difficulty in agreeing on such questions as what is a valid psychoanalytic technique, and is one that is side-stepped by attempts to resolve argument by traditional or charismatic authority. Legitimating formulae in psychoanalysis have been personalized rather than based on clear rules of evidence, with a great deal of energy going into seeking authority by quoting selected texts authored by charismatically accepted sources or citing revered names.

Economic, technical, ideological, temporal, and spatial considerations mean that new ideas and situations inevitably confront all social groups and their systems of authority and legitimation. With time, because more and more deviant ideas must be confronted, more is demanded from socialisation processes and from legitimating formulae. Insofar as theories and concepts are not well specified, do not capture the individual's experience, or do not transmit the experience of the discovery, this is likely to be particularly marked (Tuckett, 1993; Tuckett, Boulton, & Williams, 1985). Ideas not well specified are less likely to withstand robust counter-argument.

SOME PROBLEMS OF LEGITIMATION IN PSYCHOANALYTIC GROUPS: STRONGLY AND WEAKLY ORDERED GROUPS

I wish to use the notion of legitimating formulae, and the extent to which concepts are well specified in terms of transmittable experience, to consider some features of the adaptability of psychoanalytic groups according to whether they are strongly or weakly ordered.

At one end of a continuum one might envisage groups that are strongly ordered in fairly well-defined and apparently rigorously understood sets of theory and practice. They operate with traditional, charismatic, or rule-governed structures of legitimation. Their effective legitimating formulae are reasonably well specified and hence transmittable. In these groups deviants defect or face expulsion with little effect on the viability of the group. No group can avoid new ideas but in the encounter with them the members of strongly ordered groups refine their ideas and develop them.

At the other end of a continuum there might be groups that are relatively weakly ordered in the sense that the ideas they share are quite general or difficult to specify. (I have suggested this model may apply to the current psychoanalytic movement as a whole.) These groups are ones in which, because it is difficult for them to develop well-defined and robust legitimating formulae of an evidential rule-based kind, there is particular reliance on other factors, such as charisma, ideology, prejudice and personal affiliation. Such groups might be characterized by suppressed conflict and a strong tendency to fragment, as well as by sub-groups that engage in the rapid and uncritical take-over of new ideas.

My impression of many psychoanalytic groups is that they seek to remain relatively ignorant of ideas in other groups beyond characterizing them in "straw man" or stereotypical terms. Stereotyping is a common form of group identity and boundary maintenance that can be used to keep out threatening ideas and so create the feeling of group superiority and cohesion. For many years the "new" ideas of the London Kleinians were treated in this way in North American training institutes. The degree of stereotyping has become evident in recent years as policy has changed. Many analysts in these groups have responded to presentations by leading Kleinian analysts by feeling them much less alien than they expected and characterizing the presenters as "not" Kleinian. The presenters in question – Segal, Joseph, Feldman, Steiner, Spillius, and Britton – were the leading contemporary exponents of their group and seem to have been experienced and labelled "non-Kleinian" solely in their failure to live up to the stereotype. I do not cite this example from a belief that North American colleagues are any more likely or less likely to stereotype than others; it is just an obvious example of a widespread phenomenon.

While stereotyping is common in all psychoanalytic groups it seems to me more problematic in common with two other factors: the formation of group identity largely on negative identification, and reliance on tolerance rather than precise legitimating formulae. In such situations members tend not to share a common and rigorously applied technical or theoretical approach. A consequence is that they cannot reliably compare their data except superficially. This in turn means they cannot keep their theories closely grounded in clinical observation. Because theories are not required to be well specified, there is often unchecked theoretical promiscuity. Typically such groups cohere around ideology and espouse anti-authority and anti-elitist positions. This will be further consequential if that ideology protects them from the need to undertake systematic research into the effect of different approaches.

The combination of open-mindedness, lack of grounded legitimating formulae, and negative identification makes weakly ordered groups particularly vulnerable to uncritically and superficially accepting fashionable new ideas. Indeed, there are a number of such groups that have embraced in quick succession aspects of Winnicott, Klein, self-psychology, and Lacanian structuralism. Such groups are unlikely to contribute to building a secure and deepening fund of psychoanalytic knowledge.

Of course, it is possible the flexible capacities present in weakly ordered groups could prove adaptive in a process of change. I consider this is likely only insofar as it is possible to facilitate robust and well-specified dialogue within them. This condition is particularly unlikely to be present in such groups.

SOME POSSIBLE COMPONENTS OF ADAPTIVE CAPACITY IN PSYCHOANALYTIC GROUPS

Some preliminary ideas about the component structures that might facilitate adaptive capacity in psychoanalytic groupings faced by new ideas and new situations can, I think, be gleaned by comparison. I will look at the London Kleinians, the French school, and the North American ego psychologists, albeit that the three groups are by no mean homogenous.

Each of these groups seems to me to have developed a strongly ordered psychoanalytic identity of its own. They developed some degree of shared legitimating formulae by successfully codifying the contribution of their founding charismatic leaders to develop rule-bound structures. I suggest that in two cases new ideas rest on legitimating formulae mainly dependent on tests that indicate mastery of a transmittable theoretical language. In the other the test is mainly dependent on mastery of a clinical technique.

Thus, on the one hand, the French and the North Americans developed a powerful theoretical language legitimated in (actually quite different) detailed readings of Freud's text. This reading appeared to illuminate and create the basis for legitimization in matters of theory, method, and practice. Practice was considered theoretically driven. A good theoretical understanding of the relevant and precisely transmittable *langue d'initiés* determined credibility. Published work and new ideas in these groups mainly debated this theoretical language and extended it or refined it. New ideas were judged with reference to their relevance to these theories and would be rigorously scrutinized in those terms. In these groups clinical reporting was not highly valued and what was actually said or felt within the context of an interaction, and how the analyst arrived at his or her inferences, when mentioned at all, was not transparent. Legitimate authority within these groups came to rest on creative mastery of the theoretical language.

By contrast, the London Kleinians, in common with British colleagues from the other groups too but more so, seemed rather to develop a theory and method derived from argument about practice. For the Kleinians mastery of their practice – based on specific ideas about the conceptualisation and interpretation of the *here-and-now* unconscious relationship of analyst and patient – was the foundation of legitimation. Their published work was notoriously thin on systematic theory building. References to work outside their own group almost entirely served the purpose of trying to legitimate their ideas in relation to Freud. But papers nearly always contained dense and detailed illustrative reporting of patient–analyst interactions with graphic details of the interpretation of primitive part-object phantasies and enactments. Although the ground for inferring meaning from process material was not always transparent, it was detailed enough to have debate around it.

Around the 1970s legitimate authority in the Kleinian group had become routinized and closer to being rule-governed. I mean this in the sense that a significant number of colleagues became legitimating authorities on the basis of their demonstrable mastery of the technique. They could impress *their* colleagues with clinical sensitivity and the capacity to see the internal conflicts, which Klein formulated, enacted in the here-and-now analytic situation. The capacity members of this group developed to illustrate clinical work and to spell out the relevance of their theory for their clinical work and that of others has made Kleinian knowledge transmittable and exportable to all continents.

The pressure of the requirement that ideas be derived from the clinical situation has, I suggest, been highly conducive to the way the Kleinian group has adapted and deepened the fund of psychoanalytic knowledge. Ideas in this group became gradually and significantly refined and altered so that while knowledge changed, the group's basic approach and procedures for legitimating it did not.

Kleinian theory and clinical practice have adapted to new findings and new ideas. First, there is a broader and more detailed conceptualisation of the oedipal situation and its relation to the primal scene and paranoid-schizoid and depressive positions. Second, there is the theory of the container and contained, and associated modifications to the theory of projective identification, enactment, counter-transference, and the idea of transference as "total situation". Finally there is the concept of defensive organisation. (See Schafer, 1994b, for one discussion of these modifications.)

The Kleinian group seems to provide one model of the way strongly ordered groups might adapt effectively by allowing ideas to develop within a robust dialogic context – inside and outside their group. The emphasis on clinical data was also congruent with local cultural values.

Social groups of all kinds may adapt and grow, or they may become ossified because, for example, legitimation practices become too dependent on a *langue d'initiés* that ceases to be credible outside the small circle. Similarly, weakly ordered groups could be a precursor to a creative adaptation or could be ones that cannot maintain identity and collapse altogether. The history of psychoanalysis in Europe and in some parts of North and South America provides an opportunity to reflect on these possibilities. The French and the Argentine schools are two candidates for scholarly comparison but in the space available I will mention only some aspects of the development usually called North American ego psychology.

For a long time strongly ordered as a largely single group characterized by ego psychology and strong legitimating formulae based on a *langue d'initiés* of great sophistication and clarity, the North American group has recently become quite diverse, pluralistic. Ego psychology presently contends with interpersonal psychoanalysis, self psychology, interactional psychoanalysis, and various varieties of object relations and developmental psychoanalysis. However, many of the ideas in these groups are significantly contradictory with each other. To deal with this situation, organized American psychoanalysis has become relatively weakly ordered and tolerant. This may herald the creation of several rigorously differentiated groups that spur each other to clarification or a quite major crisis of confidence in the discipline as a coherent whole.

One possible explanation for the advance from ego psychology into pluralism (if that is how it should be characterized) is that legitimating formulae, in what seems to have been a quite coercive form of exercising traditionalist authority, became discredited. The core viewpoint could not be effectively transmitted within the changing socio-temporal and sociocultural parameters with which it had to contend.

Ego psychology managed the transition from the early pioneering days very successfully. The personalized authority of the early pioneers gave way to a more rule-bound system of legitimization less dependent on individual whim. Heinz Hartmann (1939; 1964), and David Rapaport (1951; 1967), among others, undertook a systemization, rephrasing, and in some aspects a revision of Freud's theories. They attempted to make them more consistent with the intellectual culture of the host environment: North American medicine and psychiatry undergoing the post-Flexner (1910) revolution. Legitimate authority seems to have become based on the mastery of this theory that drove technique and clinical observation, even to the extent that professional certification came to depend on being able to demonstrate the capacity to treat cases that fitted.

In publications, unlike in France where (consistent with local intellectual culture) quite often there was no clinical reporting at all, clinical accounts were usual but of the vignette kind. Process material, which for all its limitations offers some scope for the uninitiated reader to see and to debate the grounds for the inferences an analyst is making, was relatively absent. One consequence appears to have been that agreement with *the* theory could then be consistent with marked variation at the level of day-to-day practice. As Donald Spence (1982b; 1994; 1998) has observed, the typical publication in this tradition took a great deal for granted. Concepts like that of the "good analytic hour" (Kris, 1956), which made sense to the initiates, for instance, and may still resonate, were presented with exemplification that did not include what patient or analyst actually said. As soon as someone not sharing basic assumptions asked questions, there was difficulty (Spence, 1994).

An ego psychological approach in the hands of skilled adherents has been widely considered responsible for discovering new and interesting ideas and illuminating clinical findings. At the same time the tendency to fit facts to theories, when supported by a method of reporting that was opaque, may have damaged the capacity of this tradition to engage in robust debate and to transmit ideas successfully and credibly to neophytes. Indeed, it has been suggested that some psychoanalysts trained in this tradition and supporting it came to develop official and unofficial theories of practice that were seriously out of line with one another (Lloyd Meyer, 1996, p. 175 et seq). Where this is the case, the legitimating formulae within a group will be damaged, particularly if authority in the group is used coercively and openly excludes, by authority rather than by robust and informed counter-argument, alternatives to orthodoxy. In the long run and unchecked this is unlikely to be adaptive. The new emphasis on empirical research in North America may be considered an attempt to revitalise legitimating formulae in a manner more congruent with prevailing cultural norms.

CONCLUSION

The main purpose of this chapter has been to introduce the concepts of legitimate authority and legitimating formulae. I have wished to use them to provoke consideration of the grounds on which the fund of psychoanalytic knowledge rests and some of the difficulties in the way of developing a discipline that is capable of the sort of robust dialogue on which real consensus can be based.

Over the last five years Arnold Cooper has stimulated me to think long and hard about these matters and about the task we have shared of evaluating psychoanalytic manuscripts. The task of peer review on which we have concentrated a great deal of attention (Tuckett, 1998) is to encourage a dialogic process. We have considered (within broad limits, anyway) that what someone is arguing is less our concern than whether it has substance and clarified consequences. More importantly, we think the focus of evaluation should be on how arguments are made and the reasons given to us.

Against Post-modernism

PETER GAY

Are psychoanalysts susceptible to post-modernism? The evidence is not overwhelming, but there are some disturbing symptoms, and I have written this paper to diagnose them. Other than checking triumphalism, this French invasion is a road to deep shallowness pointing away from the psychoanalyst's essential business.

Post-modernism is an orgy of subjectivity. It privileges language over substance, coherent stories over empirical investigations, competing narratives over a single truth. Post-modernists maintain that what they call the Enlightenment "project" with its supposed dream of universal reason and triumphant science has proved bankrupt. Hence they have assailed long-honoured categories of inquiry like truth, causation, or reality, which separate the observer from objects of observation, "unmasked" reality as a fairy tale, and, since everything is at heart a fiction, "discredited" the distinction between fiction and fact. Since, post-modernists say, every observer confronts the world with presuppositions, with blinkers or distorting spectacles, the stories anyone tells about the past, the present, and other minds, never deserve absolute authority. Every "fact" is laden with theory; Donald Spence puts scare quotation marks around the word. Pure perception is a myth.

It follows for post-modern psychoanalysts that, the sooner analysts and analysands acknowledge this, the more clearly they may understand, perhaps rescue, the patient's inner world. I appreciate Spence's and Schafer's bravery. They have entered the sacred domain of Freudian edicts without their shoes on. We owe both a debt. We can no longer be sure that in psychoanalytic theory and therapy everything continually gets better and better, more and more scientific. These are achievements – all the more reason that they should not be spared criticism in turn.

I begin with Donald Spence's *Narrative Truth and Historical Truth* (1982a), which more or less started it. It dates from 1982, and caused considerable stir on its publication. A highly critical review of *Narrative Truth* by Rosemarie Sand in *Reviews of Psychoanalytic Books* was twenty-two worried pages long. According to Spence, the psychoanalyst must learn to accept the coexistence of two truths battling for supremacy in the psychoanalytic situation. *Historical truth* is what we customarily call "truth", an assertion that corresponds (more or less) to some external past event: a memory of abandonment, a moment of intense pleasure, a trauma.

Spence defines *narrative truth*, in contrast, as a story that is "compelling, persuasive, and seemingly complete". Freud, he notes, was a master at delineating this kind of truth; he "made us aware of the persuasive power of a coherent narrative". Spence is certain that "a well-constructed story possesses a kind of narrative truth that is real and immediate" (p. 21).

Postulating two truths is an epistemological trap. Once you have two, why not more? In fact, Spence actually comes up with a third, *artistic truth*. Critical realists like Freud have always argued that where there is smoke there is fire.[1] But post-modernists have asserted that (to vary the saying)

---

1. It must be admitted, even though Spence does not mobilize this fact, that late in life Freud himself briefly played the game of two truths, but he gave it far less weight than Spence throws into the scales. In *Moses and Monotheism*, Freud (1939a) suggests that, in antiquity, devout believers made a god for themselves by taking an outsize figure, perhaps a charismatic legislator, and raised him to a divinity. "We too believe," Freud comments, "that the pious solution contains the truth – but the *historical* truth and not the *material* truth" (p. 129). That is, the invention of god drew on an external reality, however vastly elaborated. This thought, that when there is smoke there's fire, even if the fire may be very small, was of course one of Freud's essential tenets as a critical realist; he refused to decide whether the Wolf Man had witnessed his parents' intercourse or transformed his perception of animals copulating into a fantasy about witnessing his parents' sexual congress. He refused to decide, but it had to be the one or the other; Freud always suspected a sliver of what he called historical truth, even if it was remote from material truth, in anything a person said, thought, or felt. He would have been more precise, more elegant epistemologically, if he had recognized that what he called "historical truths" really are beliefs ("true" in short for the believer only), convictions that appear to be true and are therefore an element in historical inquiry as in the psychoanalytic process, but may be distorted or altogether false.

where there is smoke, there is someone operating a smoke machine, and the person operating the machine is more interesting than its product.

By multiplying truths, Spence accompanies the post-modernists a long way. To place old-fashioned historical truth in the centre of psychoanalytic practice is to his mind a seductive but aberrant procedure. It imposes a rigid model on the "conventional" analyst, who fishes for the "truth" with evenly hovering attention assisted by his analysand's free associations. As the two dig and dig, they approach repressed truths, and, once uncovered and worked through, they can pronounce the analysis a success.

Spence dismisses this positivist agenda as a self-delusion that slavishly echoes Freud's natural-science aspirations. There are no free associations, there is no evenly hovering attention. "The model of the patient as unbiased reporter and the analyst as unbiased listener suggests a kind of naïve realism that is hard to imagine" (p. 25). Ordinary psychoanalysts are naïve. The lenses through which they (and their analysands) see dictate the results of their investigations.

Spence often reminds his readers that Freud craved the mantle of natural scientist; had he not claimed that psychoanalysis requires no world view of its own, since it shares that of science? But, Spence objects, psychoanalysis is a story-telling discipline (also see Schafer, 1996). Analysts should discard the futile search for truth in favour of a coherent story that they develop in the course of treatment. "Narrative truth," writes Spence, "can be defined as the criterion we use to decide when a certain experience has been captured to our satisfaction. . . . Once a given construction has acquired narrative truth, it becomes just as real as any other kind of truth; this new reality becomes a significant part of the psychoanalytic cure" (p. 31).

Spence's "coherent story" should permit the analysand to make sense of his life. Analysts, Spence tells us, are "artists and storytellers." Once they fail to recognize this and confound historical and narrative truth, they grow arrogant and authoritarian, treating their interpretations as the only possible ones, foreclosing the free play of alternatives. We dare not minimize the radicalism of these post-modern revisionists. They do *not* just caution colleagues against overzealous interpretations, *not* just warn them against playing God; *not* just alert analysands that free association is beyond their grasp.

What, then, we ask, do the post-modernists want? They want more. To keep Freudian shibboleths alive is to invite calamitous consequences for the analytic process. As the subtitle of Spence's second book, *The Freudian Metaphor* (1984) shows, the post-modernists demand a new paradigm.

But as Thomas Kuhn, the historian of science who put *paradigm* on the map, pointed out, used without careful modulation that term generates a disastrous subjectivism.

In what follows, I offer a set of criticisms, and suggest the difference it makes to take the linguistic turn with Spence and his allies or to stay with old-fashioned truths.

1. Spence's "narrative truth" is not a truth at all. It is a tactical gambit in the service of persuasion. As rhetoricians have known since the ancients, coherent narration is an effective method joining devices like suspense, metaphors, and a show of authority, for securing assent. Spence repeats "coherence" like an incantation. But his reliance on it neglects a truth well known to students of paranoia: a coherent story is often the hallmark of mental malfunctioning. No wonder that conspiracy theorists rely on discovering a single, secret pattern.

In analysis, a good story may have a certain therapeutic effect, but it must be viewed with deep suspicion. It *points to* a truth, but does not establish it; the fact a researcher stumbles upon by watching a tragedy only gives that source a facilitating role. The prepared mind finds truths almost anywhere; Friedrich August Kekulé's famous discovery of the benzene ring, the structure of the benzene molecule, came to him as he was dozing before the fire and glimpsed whirling little snakes biting their tails. If he had not been a professional chemist, the snakes would have meant nothing to him.

2. Among the casualties of the multiple-truth theory is the fact. Spence alludes to fact only fleetingly, but Schafer gives it more thoroughgoing treatment. Using history as an example, he writes, "Historians and philosophers of history have been arguing for some time that the facts – the bits and pieces of information they assemble into history – become historical evidence only within the narratives developed by individual historians" (1994c, p. 257). And he notes that the "plasticity of clinical facts must never be forgotten." After all, "facts are facts for the time being. They are facts of a certain kind for the time being. They matter for the time being. They are true for the time being" (Schafer, 1994a, p. 1028).

Here is post-modernism in full flower. Had Schafer been content with claiming that clinical facts grow more salient during psychoanalytic exploration, this would be obvious and unobjectionable. But facts do not become facts and go out of business when they have done their duty;

they are among the few eternal verities we can point to in a world of ineluctable change.

In his enthusiastic foreword to Spence's (1984) *The Freudian Metaphor*, the psychologist Jerome Bruner approvingly cites the philosopher Nelson Goodman's aphorism, "Facts are not found, but made." The contrary is true; we virtually drown in facts trivial and significant. T. H. Huxley spoke extravagantly when he said that we must sit before a fact like a little child. But his commitment to empiricism remains the royal road to science, including psychoanalytic science.

It is a virtual truism that facts grow more interesting as they are embedded in a context. Facts have an appetite for interpretation that can be satisfied by relevant clusters of them. Take an instance from history. In 1848, there were 1,500 miles of railroad in Prussia. By itself, this statement conveys little. Would a Prussian engineer who designs railroad lines be cheered by this fact or disheartened? Thin, though, as this lonely fact may be, it is strongly preferable to the assertion that the figure was 800 miles (which would be wrong), that it hovered between 1,200 and 2,000 miles (which would be vague), or that it was a "lot of mileage" (which would be vaguer still).

The fact comes alive in juxtaposition with information from the same family. In 1844, the railroad mileage in Prussia was 500; knowing that, we note that in four years Prussian railroad mileage trebled. This significance is multiplied by related facts such as comparisons with British and French railroad mileage.

Does it matter? Freud thought so; the mind's most imaginative "invention" draws on a "real" experience. And apparently the trust in, or distrust of, facts makes a difference in psychoanalytic therapy. There is clinical distinction between patient A, who draws her account of being sexually molested from phantasy alone, and patient B, whose similar account rests on an experience. (There is little psychoanalytic literature on the subject, but practising psychoanalysts have acknowledged that they find a marked difference.)

3. The passion for the here and now implies disdain for causal inquiry. But slighting causes, even causes hard to come by, is to desert a pivotal element in psychoanalytic science. The logic of psychoanalysis places mind into nature and therefore subject to causal influences. Freud was a loose determinist – not a fatalist – insisting that all mental events are caused. Thus armed, he made sense of slips, dreams, gestures, symptoms, to give meaning to the apparently meaningless.

4. The post-modernists' sour view of truth, reality, and causation rests on a premise they do little to support, treating the analyst as impotent before his patient's or his own styles of thinking and feeling. Their mistakes are irreparable because they fail to recognize that they are not perfect models of objectivity.

In history, the issue of how much desire influences perception has been a subject for debate since the nineteenth century. As teachers of historians we know that students embrace their specialty with diverse traits of character, experiences, and religious or political loyalties. We may expect a Roman Catholic writing a life of Luther to be critical; we may expect the same historian writing a history of the papacy to be sympathetic. A historian traumatized by his experience in the trenches will write a history of the First World War radically different from the one a fanatical militarist would write.

I wonder just whom Schafer has been reading when he ascribes to "many" historians the notion that historical writing is "inherently ideological"; for the most part, "concern with arriving at some single, conclusive version of 'how it really happened' has been left behind in modern thought" (1994c, p. 257). But Schafer is relying on a small minority among historians; Ranke, whom he paraphrases, is not so easily left behind.

True, historians face daunting subjective pressures. Their selection of a subject is highly personal – and revealing. And in our climate of aggressiveness against professional establishments, minorities who have felt left excluded from the story of the past have adopted the post-modern protest by rejecting talk of objectivity as an excuse. One result of seeing professional historians as hopelessly blinkered has been the demand that only like should write the history of like – only women the history of women, only Chicanos the history of Chicanos. But if this were true, the profession would have to close up shop, since to understand the Other is basic to its craft, and only ancient Greeks could write the history of ancient Greece.

Things are not that desperate. It is part of historians' training to recognize points of view and set them aside as much as possible. The success of such recognitions is doubtless limited, but failures will be cruelly called to authors' attention by reviewers – a spur to efforts toward objectivity. The psychoanalyst has no such public controls, but, during candidacy, similar professional guidance. Some analysts refuse to analyse ideologues (Ralph Greenson would not analyse anti-Semites) because they cannot muster the necessary distance. And we know that if an analyst senses unmanageable countertransferences, a consultation with a colleague is in order.

5. Post-modernists sound as though insights into perspectives and other temptations to subjectivity are their discovery. They are not. Goethe had maintained that every perception is already pregnant with theory. In some measure, we see what we seek. Shakespeare has King Henry IV admonish his son, Prince Harry, that "thy wish, Harry, was father to that thought" (*King Henry IV Part 2*, Act IV, Scene 5). The issue is not that nobody encounters the world as an epistemological virgin, but what one can do about it. And post-modernists, throwing all the weight on perceivers and their distortions, are persuaded that nothing can be done except to recognize it.

6. The heart of the post-modern charge against "orthodox" psychoanalysis is that their commitment to "metaphors" like truth and cause makes analysts autocratic and patronizing. Instead of welcoming differing stories that might supply keys to the analysand's past, these positivists hunt for what they will never find because it does not exist: the final truth. The colourful warmth and variety of life inherent in post-modern pluralism wilts, they say, before the old categories.

But are post-modern prescriptions for techniques new? In my training at the Western New England Institute for Psychoanalysis (as "orthodox" an institute as one can find) we were early alerted to the perils of rapid and dogmatic diagnoses. Most analysts worthy of their shingle have learned as candidates, and will confirm in their practice, that the need to revise diagnoses and the need for patience have become part of their tool box.

7. Early in his career as a psychoanalyst, Freud was astonished to find that his case reports read like short stories. But this did not mean that he thought they *were* short stories. Their interest as tales had to do less with his literary secondary revision than with the inherent drama of a human life emerging on his couch. We happen to know from the abundant if fragmentary notes on the Rat Man case that Freud fairly faithfully followed these notes in the published version. And he did not believe – nor have his successors – that good writing is equivalent to proof. In the post-modern canon, if it means anything, "narrativity" is intended as a devastating critique of analysts who, calling their stories true, are puffing literary skill as analytic success. But, then, traditional analysts do not need to be told this.

8. Finally, post-modern psychoanalysts have concentrated on counter-transference. Freud, who almost never alluded to it, was categorically negative: he saw counter-transference as an emotional interference in the analytic

process that the analyst must confront, reduce, if possible eliminate. Analysts no longer take this simplistic view, but see it the way physicians see cholesterol: there is the good kind and the bad kind. And Annie Reich's famous paper on counter-transference dates from 1951 – decades before post-modernism was heard of. Counter-transference can aid the analysis. But thoughtful analysts owe none of this or any other wisdom to their post-modern brethren. Hence I conclude with a saying borrowed from Samuel Johnson: What is true in post-modern thinking about psychoanalysis is not new, what is new in it is not true.

Change in Psychoanalysis: Science, Practice, and the Sociology of Knowledge

GEORGE J. MAKARI

Psychoanalysis has been changing, and so it seems natural and important to consider how and why change takes place in our discipline. Of course, this is not a new question; it has been asked at crucial junctures by psychoanalysts since Freud. And as psychoanalysis grew as a cultural force, others – philosophers of science, sociologists, and historians – have weighed in on the matter. In this paper, I shall survey some of these differing accounts, and reflect upon what these differing perspectives tell us about the nature of the psychoanalytic enterprise.

PSYCHOANALYTIC CHANGE AND SCIENTIFIC KNOWLEDGE

For change to be recognizable it must be measured against a background, a baseline. Perhaps the most common baseline by which change in psychoanalysis has been measured has been by comparison to science. If psychoanalysis is a science, then the patterns of change it manifests should correspond with change in science. But what characterizes change in science? How do individual scientists change theories? By what process does a scientific community adopt as true, or reject as false or anomalous, the changes proposed by an individual scientist? Does communal change occur by cumulative accretion or revolution? These are crucial interrelated questions for those who study the history and philosophy of science.

In contrast to those who thought of science as a continuous and progressive enterprise that via accretion and validation moved forward, Karl

Popper, beginning in the 1930s, articulated a point of view in which discontinuous change marked scientific progress. Popper was in good part motivated by his concern that both Freud and Alfred Adler could easily account for identical phenomena via their quite different theories. Hence, he set out to articulate a scientific epistemology that would show why, unlike Einstein's theory of relativity, psychoanalysis was not a science (Popper, 1962, pp. 34–36). Popper's notion of falsifiability as the demarcation between science and pseudo-science suggested a powerful marker for legitimate scientific progress (Popper, 1959).

Where Popper's ruler held firm, his manner of distinguishing sciences from pseudo-sciences had authority, and those who would examine change in psychoanalysis had to address Popper's use of psychoanalysis as the exemplar of a pseudo-science. It seems hardly refutable to assert with Popper that change in psychoanalysis could not easily or often be linked to falsifiability, testability, and external confirmation. Furthermore, the problem of induction in the creation of psychoanalytic theory has always been a deeply vexing one for the discipline. If such experiential induction was per se unscientific – as Sir Karl would have it – then there could be little hope for much clinically based psychoanalytic theory. This Popperian framework remains a denominator – though often implicit – in some critical appraisals of psychoanalysis (see, for instance, Stone, 1997). For many, the "multiple schools" problem signifies that psychoanalysis has been dominated not by scientific falsification but by ideologies, put forth by charismatic leaders who seduced or cajoled their followers into accepting one set of beliefs over another.

But using Popperian science as a baseline from which to examine change in psychoanalysis is problematic. For not only does the history of psychoanalysis not adhere to Popperian dictums for scientific change, neither do important historical aspects of such ur-sciences as theoretical physics, much less the medical sciences. One of Popper's most important critics has been the philosopher Adolph Grünbaum. Beginning in the 1970s, Grünbaum attacked Popper's use of psychoanalysis as the prime example of an inductive pseudo-science. Popper's contention that psychoanalytic claims were all unfalsifiable, in Grünbaum's view, flew in the face of some of Freud's changes in theory, which Grünbaum argued were responses to adverse empirical data (1984, pp. 104–126). For Grünbaum, however, the testability of aspects of psychoanalytic theory stands in stark contrast to a lack of actual corroboration. Hence, psychoanalytic theory at present exists in a pre-scientific, pre-tested state.

Grünbaum has elicited a number of substantial philosophical responses, but more generally his and Popper's epistemological approach to change in science has increasingly lost ground to a more historical approach. Starting in the early 1960s, the notion that scientific change was purely the result of a logical contest of ideas was seriously challenged. Paul Feyerabend (1962; 1978), Thomas Kuhn (1962; 1977), and others argued that the lawful epistemological accounts of philosophers of science simply did not adequately account for historical change in science. Kuhn viewed change in science as oscillating between relatively quiescent non-progressive periods ("normal science") and periods of revolutionary change. Scientific puzzle solving in the normal phases required the "group commitments" of a "disciplinary matrix" to a "paradigm". These theoretical commitments create a socially ratified and presumed framework. Hence, Kuhn's model of scientific change could explain the not infrequent instances in the history of science, when seemingly unassailable evidence is refused and called anomalous by a scientific community. Unlike Popper, who segregated facts from values and scientific change from the realm of social change, for Kuhn no such clear and categorical distinctions could be historically sustained.

Like Popper, Kuhn also judged psychoanalysis to not qualify fully as science, though he denied that status on different and more forgiving grounds. For Kuhn, psychoanalysis was more of a science in its infancy; it was still a practical craft, with close resemblances to nineteenth century engineering, meteorology, and medicine: "In each of these fields shared theory was adequate only to establish the plausibility of the discipline and to provide a rationale for the various craft rules which governed practice. These rules had proved their use in the past, but no practitioner supposed they were sufficient to prevent recurrent failure. A more articulated theory and more powerful rules were desired, but it would have been absurd to abandon a plausible and badly needed discipline with a tradition of limited success simply because these desiderata were not yet at hand" (Kuhn, 1977, p. 275).

Kuhn's work opened the door to those who would seek to explain scientific change in more sociological and historical terms. I. B. Cohen's (1985) historical analysis proposed four stages to characterize revolutionary change in science (pp. 352–368). Cohen found the Freudian revolution to be marked by all these stages, and hence he credited psychoanalysis with being a typical scientific revolution. Kuhn's work can also be seen as wittingly or unwittingly inviting radically sociologic accounts. Though Kuhn felt such a reading represented a "total misunderstanding" of his work

(1977, p. 321), in his wake sociologists of scientific knowledge have proliferated the view that questions of scientific epistemology are at least also, but perhaps only, questions of social order. For example, in his influential writings on the Scientific Revolution, Steven Shapin (1994; 1996) has made the case that the epistemological claims that were made in this, the archetype of scientific change, rested in good part on the shared beliefs of a community of gentlemen, that is, on a social contract of sorts. Through this lens, changes in psychoanalysis could be seen as no different from scientific change insofar as both primarily are driven by their social function.

With this scant overview, I mean only to illustrate that what constitutes scientific change is a matter of complexity and debate. Many writers who consider change in psychoanalysis do so by easy recourse to a notion of scientific change that is obvious, uncontested, assumed. But no such easy assumptions are warranted given the debates over the nature of scientific change. And the commitment of a commentator to a particular notion of change in science, whether Popperian, Grünbaumian, Kuhnian, Foucauldian, or Shapinean, will in good part shape how psychoanalytic change is appraised. Ironically, this problem is the same problem one faces in evaluating competing psychoanalytic theories.

PSYCHOANALYTIC CHANGE AND THE SOCIOLOGY OF KNOWLEDGE

For other commentators, psychoanalytic change should not be evaluated with regard to science at all, but rather alongside social flux. While psychoanalysis has deeply affected the social and cultural life of this century, sociologists and social historians have argued that changing historical circumstances and cultures were also critical to the development of psychoanalysis (e.g. Homans, 1989; Lasch, 1978; Rieff, 1959; 1966).

From this vantage point, psychoanalytic theories must hold or fail to hold meaning, not just for individual theoreticians and their patients, but also for a broader social world. Freud's topographic theory grew up in a Vienna where sexual liberation and freedom from the church had galvanized a generation; that theory offered a model of mind and a treatment that endorsed such desires for liberation. After the mass destruction of World War I, Freud's structural theory was less sanguine about such liberation, and held within it writings on the death drive and the repetition compulsion, writings that found within the human organism a profoundly conservative, anti-progressive force.

Russell Jacoby (1975) has argued that the advent of neo-Freudian thought was the result of cultural pressures to conform in post-war America (also see McLaughlin, 1998). Self psychology offered the clinician an ideology of utopian liberalism, and grew rapidly in a 1970s American political culture that held similar hopes. Hence, changes in psychoanalytic theory can be read as adaptive ways for psychoanalysis to remain meaningful to a changing culture. In his argument on the social origins of psychoanalysis, Peter Homans has put this position most succinctly, writing "historical transitions, I propose showing, produce psychological transitions" (1989, p. 111). Insofar as psychoanalysis is a theory of human subjectivity, it seems obvious that psychoanalysis must alter as the historical conditions that *in part* constitute such subjectivity change. That does not mean that some biologic and universal struggles may not remain. But in its stronger forms, this perspective would argue that for the most part as history moves, it is the dog, and psychoanalytic theory the tail being wagged.

PSYCHOANALYTIC CHANGE AND PRACTICE

While philosophers, historians, and sociologists have all explained change in psychoanalysis by insights derived from their own disciplines, psychoanalysts have not surprisingly looked at the pressing problems that result from within their work. The notion that theoretical change originates in the consulting room is a dearly held notion in our field, and well it should be. However, there are problems with such a model of change in our theory. To highlight these problems, let us examine one of its most extreme forms, what I have elsewhere called "Great Patient" history (1992). Breuer meets Anna O, Freud meets Elizabeth von R, Dora, and the Ratman. Simply put: change in our theories comes from new observations. Freud, Ferenczi, Abraham, Klein, they are our microbe hunters. These accounts are predicated on a pre-Kantian objective observer, and hence this historiography has lost favour amongst contemporary psychoanalysts, steeped as we are in notions of counter-transference.

An equally one-sided view of the history of change in psychoanalysis puts forth a subjectivist vision that argues that psychoanalysts come up with significant conceptual shifts only via their own internal experiences and desires. All philosophy is veiled autobiography, Nietzsche suggested. Similarly, Freud's repeated use of disguised personal experiences, Kohut's crucial test case of Mr. Z., now widely believed to be the author himself, Adler's focus on organ inferiority and his own history of childhood illness, all of these cases can be seen as examples of psychoanalytic theory developing out of a deep conviction that the theorist holds regarding him/herself.

If the "Great Patient" view of history obscured the analyst's subjective contributions to theoretical change, this subjectivist view obliterates any substantial input from clinical encounters. By this theory, analysts simply apply their theories to their patients, who come with such complicated multifaceted narratives that any analyst can successfully read almost any theory into any "treatable" patient. Within this historiography, there is also a darker history, one populated by demagogues for whom their theory is the only theory. Though such a history appeals to some theoreticians – Adler freely placed his own troubles at the centre of his revisionist theory (e.g., Stepansky, 1983) – and appeals to a contemporary suspicion of authority, it is one that I believe does not do justice to the fact that, for a change in theory to be more than eccentric, it must be accepted by a community of patients and practitioners who are convinced of the utility of the theory.

CHANGE IN A SCIENCE OF SUBJECTIVITY

In each of these views – scientific, sociologic, and clinical/pragmatic – I would suggest that there is no single satisfactory account for how psychoanalysis changes. The difficulty, I believe, lies in part in the nature of psychoanalysis itself. If, as Bruno Latour (1987; 1993) and others have argued, modernity is in part based on a division between the scientific and social worlds, upon knowledge garnered through objective observation and that deemed to be subjective, psychoanalysis can only be an odd hybrid, cohering in part with each, but in full with neither. Consequently, for those who would maintain the purity of science, psychoanalysis was bound for contradiction, paradox, and failure, for it was rife with subjective value-laden contents from its social and historical contexts. For those who would have psychoanalysis be a hermeneutic system of meaning, it is compromised by its scientific claims (e.g., Habermas, 1968). Hence, psychoanalysis has been and is attacked for being both not scientific enough and scientistic. For decades, the purifiers of scientific and social discourse have pulled at this strange hybrid.

In my view, psychoanalytic theory originated as an attempt to create an objective science of subjectivity. There is an obvious paradox in that aim, and maintaining that paradox, it seems to me, is crucial to the discipline. Hence, I strongly believe that extra-clinical testing should be done widely and well, and have no doubt it will impact those scientific statements that we make in psychoanalytic theory. But as Paul Ricouer (1970) has pointed out, by its very nature psychoanalysis cannot be adequately described in quantitative, mathematical, and lawful terms for the very reason that subjectivity cannot fully be accounted for in this manner.

Contemporary psychoanalysis, with its multiple models of mind and psychopathology, contains within it both an ambitious and youthful Kuhnian proto-science, a well as an historically rooted system of meanings and values. Hence, change in psychoanalysis is not, cannot be, homogeneous. Rather, there are some changes in our discipline that reflect the kinds of shifts Kuhn attributed to a proto-science. But psychoanalysis is not just that, and in an attempt to win the authority that is conferred with being found a science, psychoanalysis cannot afford to ignore its "unscientific" domains.

Let us return for a moment to Kuhn, who remains, for me, the most deft theoretician of change in science. For Kuhn, the early development of a field in science is deeply marked by social needs and values; the concepts employed by such a proto-science address problems that are extensively organized by contemporary common sense and prevailing philosophical traditions. Fundamental tenets are not agreed upon, but rather are constantly challenged. With growing maturity, the problems that are worked on are removed from social demands, and become more and more dictated by the "internal challenge to increase the scope and precision of the fit between existing theory and nature" (Kuhn, 1977, pp. 118–119).

Kuhn's model is powerful and exceptionally useful in some domains, and it fits well with some aspects of psychoanalysis. If we study the history of the development of the concept of transference, we find that what began as a theory that was highly organized by external discourses, such as associationism, hypnosis, and nineteenth century theories of illusion, became increasingly a concept that dictated its own internal problems, and provided a technical framework for a great majority of psychoanalysts to pursue a kind of "normal science" (see Makari, 1992; 1994; 1997).

But it would be impossible and undesirable for psychoanalysis to take that same path, to immunize itself from social life as dictated by Kuhn's model for a science. For psychoanalysis, unlike the "pure" sciences, is in the end deeply enmeshed in the pragmatic task of knowing precisely the subjective inner worlds of the members of that social world. While empirical evidence from child developmentalists, psychotherapy researchers, and neurobiologists will increasingly act as the framework for the scientific statements that psychoanalysis includes in its theory, much that we analyse will change with the dance of history and cannot meaningfully become general, lawful, technical, and immune to the social world in a Kuhnian sense.

By distinguishing which claims we make in an empirical register and which are more appropriately contextualized historically, we will be able to more fully understand change in psychoanalysis. For I believe with Strenger (1991) that psychoanalysis should continue to be a forum for proposing empirical hypotheses, as well as offering a net of meanings, an ethic, a way to live in the world. Claims that are framed in causal empirical language may have the potential for more rapid, even revolutionary change with extra-clinical testing. Changes that grow out of a shift in historical context will seem from a scientific perspective to be haphazard, but take meaning through historical analysis. History changes, and one day we are no longer seeing hysterical women with conversion reactions, but rather narcissistic men who feel empty. Our clinical demand structure changes and our theories will shift as well (Friedman, 1988). We as analysts will change too, for psychoanalytic theories rise and fall in part due to the implications these theories have for us as clinicians. Who are you as an analyst, and what do you think you are spending your professional life doing? Liberating people, helping tame their animalistic urges, building better adaptations to the world, healing them – which of these connotations does one aspire to as one is analysing?

A final word about my own history. I trained as a psychoanalyst and became a working historian of psychoanalysis during a period of great turbulence in which the scientific, social, and pragmatic merits of the field have all been under scrutiny. But I had the good fortune of being schooled by psychoanalysts such as Arnold Cooper, who in his writings and teaching anticipated and welcomed rethinking our theories (e.g., Cooper, 1987a; 1987c; 1989b; 1989c). That has been fortunate for his students, for psychoanalysis is changing, or is it our culture, or is it our patients, or is it us? Who is wagging whom? Perhaps one day, a history of this strange hybrid called psychoanalysis will tell.

References

Abraham, K. (1924). A short study of the development of the libido, viewed in the light of mental disorders. In *Selected Papers on Psycho-analysis* (pp. 418–501). New York: Basic Books, 1953.

Akhtar, S. (1989). Narcissistic personality disorder: descriptive feature and differential diagnosis. *Psychiatric Clinics of North America* 12:505–529.

Akhtar, S. (1991). Three fantasies related to unresolved separation-individuation: a less recognized aspect of severe character pathology. In S. Akhtar & H. Parens (Eds.), *Beyond the Symbiotic Orbit: Advances in Separation-Individuation Theory – Essays in Honour of Selma Kramer, M.D.* (pp. 261–284). Hillsdale, NJ: Analytic Press.

Akhtar, S. (1992). *Broken Structures: Severe Personality Disorders and Their Treatment*. Northvale, NJ: Jason Aronson.

Akhtar, S. (1994). Object constancy and adult psychopathology. *International Journal of Psycho-Analysis* 75:441–455.

Akhtar, S. (1996). Someday and if only fantasies: Pathological optimism and inordinate nostalgia as related forms of idealization. *Journal of the American Psychoanalytic Association* 44:723–753.

Akhtar, S. (1999). *Inner Torment: Living Between Conflict and Fragmentation*. Northvale, NJ: Jason Aronson.

Akhtar, S., & Thomson, J. A. (1982). Overview: narcissistic personality disorder. *American Journal of Psychiatry* 139:12–20.

American Psychiatric Association. (1994). *Diagnostic and Statistical Manual of Mental Disorders (DSM-IV)*. (4 ed.). Washington, DC: American Psychiatric Association.

Anderson, S. (1942). *Memoirs*. Chapel Hill: University of North Carolina Press.

Angel, A. (1934). Einige Bemerkungen über den Optimismus. *International Journal of Psycho-Analysis* 20:191–199.

Apel, K. O. (1994). *Le Logos Propre au Langage Humain*. Combas: Editions de l'Eclat.
Arlow, J. (1991). Address to the graduating class of the San Francisco Psychoanalytic Institute. *American Psychoanalyst 25*:15–21.
Arlow, J. (1993). Discussion of Baranger's paper on "The mind of the analyst: from listening to interpretation". *International Journal of Psycho-Analysis 74*:1147–1154.
Arlow, J. (1997). Comments on: toward the improvement of psychoanalytic technique. *Journal of Clinical Psychoanalysis 6*:299–307.
Austin, J. L. (1962). *How to Do Things With Words*. Oxford: Clarendon Press.
Bacal, H. (1990). Does an object relations theory exist in self psychology? *Psychoanalytic Inquiry 10*:197–220.
Bach, S. (1977a). On narcissistic fantasies. *International Review of Psycho-Analysis 4*:281–293.
Bach, S. (1977b). On the narcissistic state of consciousness. *International Journal of Psycho-Analysis 58*:209–233.
Baranger, W., & Baranger, M. (1969). *Problemas del Campo Psicoanalítico*. Buenos Aires: Kargieman.
Bartlett, F. C. (1932). *Remembering: A Study in Experimental and Social Psychology*. New York: Cambridge University Press.
Becker, E. (1973). *The Denial of Death*. New York: Free Press.
Bibring, E. (1953). The mechanism of depression. In P. Greenacre (Ed.), *Affective Disorders* (pp. 13–48). New York: International Universities Press.
Bion, W. R. (1962). *Learning from Experience*. London: Heinemann.
Bion, W. R. (1990). *Brazilian Lectures*. London: Karnac.
Blatt, S., & Ford, T. Q. (1994). *Therapeutic Change: An Object Relations Approach*. New York: Plenum.
Bleuler, E. (1910). Vortrag über Ambivalenz. *ZentralBlatt für Psychanalyse 1*:266.
Block, J. H., & Block, J. (1980). The role of ego-control and ego-resiliency in the organization of behaviour. In W. A. Collins (Ed.), *Minnesota Symposium on Child Psychology: Vol. 13. Development of Cognitive Affect and Social Relations* (pp. 39–101). Hillsdale, NJ: Erlbaum.
Bloom, H. (1973). *The Anxiety of Influence: A Theory of Poetry*. Oxford: Oxford University Press.
Blos, P. (1962). *On Adolescence: A Psychoanalytic Interpretation*. New York: Free Press.
Böhm, T. (1992). Turning points and change in psychoanalysis. *International Journal of Psycho-Analysis, 73*:675–684.
Bond, M., Gardner, S. T., Christian, J., & Sigal, J. J. (1983). Empirical study of self-rated defence styles. *Archives of General Psychiatry 40*:333–338.
Bond, M. P., & Vaillant, J. S. (1986). An empirical study of the relationship between diagnosis and defence style. *Archives of General Psychiatry 43*:285–288.
Bowlby, J. (1969). *Attachment and Loss, Vol. 1: Attachment*. London: Hogarth Press and the Institute of Psycho-Analysis.

Brenner, C. (1979). Depressive affect, anxiety and psychic conflict in the phallic-oedipal phase. *Psychoanalytic Quarterly* 48:177–197.
Brenner, C. (1982). *The Mind in Conflict*. New York: International Universities Press.
Brenner, C. (1994). The mind as conflict and compromise formation. *Journal of Clinical Psychoanalysis* 3:473–488.
Bucci, W. (1985). Dual coding: A cognitive model for psychoanalytic research. *Journal of the American Psychoanalytic Association* 33:571–607.
Buckley, P. (1997). Psychoanalysis and its romantic rebellion. *Journal of the American Psychoanalytic Association* 45:577–587.
Busch, F. (1995). *The Ego at the Center of Clinical Technique*. Northvale, NJ: Jason Aronson.
Calvino, I. (1972). *Invisible Cities*. New York: Harcourt Brace Javanovitch.
Canestri, J. (1993). The logic of Freudian research. In D. Meghnagi (Ed.), *Freud and Judaism* (pp. 117–129). London: Karnac.
Canestri, J. (1994a). *The Analyst Mind: From Listening to Interpretation*. London: IPA Press.
Canestri, J. (1994b). Psychoanalytic Heuristics. In P. Fonagy, A. M. Cooper, & R. S. Wallerstein (Eds.), *Psychoanalysis on the Move: The Work of Joseph Sandler* (pp. 201–216). London: Routledge.
Canestri, J. (1994c). Transformations. *International Journal of Psycho-Analysis* 75:1079–1092.
Cannon, W. B. (1976). The role of hunches in scientific thought. In A. Rothernberg & C. R. Housman (Eds.), *The Creativity Question* (pp. 63–69). Durham, NC: Duke University Press.
Caper, R. (1997). Psychic reality and the analysis of transference. *Psychoanalytic Quarterly* 66:18–33.
Cavell, M. (1988). Interpretation, psychoanalysis and the philosophy of mind. *Journal of the American Psychoanalytic Association* 36:859–879.
Changeux, J. P. (1985). *Neuronal Man: The Biology of Mind* (L. Garey, trans.). Princeton, NJ: Princeton University Press.
Chasseguet-Smirgel, J. (1986). *Sexuality and Mind: The Role of the Father and the Mother in the Psyche*. London: New York Universities Press.
Chomsky, N. (1957). *Syntactic Structures*. The Hague: Harcourt Brace.
Chomsky, N. (1980). *Rules and Representations*. New York: Columbia University Press.
Chused, J. (1996). The therapeutic action of psychoanalysis: abstinence and informative experiences. *Journal of the American Psychoanalytic Association* 44:1047–1071.
Cloninger, C. R., Svrakic, D. M., & Pryzbeck, T. R. (1993). A psychobiological model of temperament and character. *Archives of General Psychiatry* 50:975–990.
Coccaro, E. F., & Kavoussi, R. J. (1997). Fluoxetine and impulsive aggressive behaviour in personality disordered subjects. *Archives of General Psychiatry* 54:1081–1088.

Cohen, I. B. (1985). *Revolution in Science*. Cambridge, MA: Harvard University Press.

Compton, A. (1985a). The concept of identification in the work of Freud, Ferenczi and Abraham. A review and commentary. *Psychoanalytic Quarterly* 54:200–233.

Compton, A. (1985b). The development of the drive object concept in Freud's work, 1905–1915. *Journal of the American Psychoanalytic Association* 33:93–115.

Compton, A. (1986a). The beginnings of the object concept in psychoanalysis. In A. D. Richards & M. S. Willick (Eds.), *Psychoanalysis: The Science of Mental Conflict* (pp. 177–189). Hillsdale, NJ: Analytic Press.

Compton, A. (1986b). Freud: Objects and structure, 1915–1938. *Journal of the American Psychoanalytic Association* 34:561–590.

Compton, A. (1987). Objects and attitudes. *Journal of the American Psychoanalytic Association* 35:609–628.

Compton, A. (1995). Objects and object relationships. In B. E. Moore & B. D. Fine (Eds.), *Psychoanalysis: The Major Concepts* (pp. 433–449). New Haven, CT: Yale University Press.

Compton, A. (1997). *Psychoanalysis, religion, postmodernism, and psychoanalysis as postmodern religion*. Paper presented at the Los Angeles Psychoanalytic Society, Los Angeles, September.

Connolly, M. B., Crits-Christoph, P., Shelton, P. C., Hollon, S., Kurtz, J., & Barber, J. P. (in press). The reliability and validity of a measure of self-understanding of interpersonal patterns.

Cooper, A. M. (1964). The masochistic character. Panel Discussion. *Bulletin of the Association for Psychoanalytic Medicine* 3:39–43.

Cooper, A. M. (1972). *Value systems and ego integration*. Paper presented at the New York State Psychiatric Institute 75th Anniversary Celebration, New York.

Cooper, A. M. (1976). Psychoanalysis and literature. *Bulletin of the Association for Psychoanalytic Medicine* 15:31–34.

Cooper, A. M. (1980). *Some current issues in psychoanalytic techniques*. Paper presented at the the Menninger Foundation, Topeka, Kansas.

Cooper, A. M. (1981a). Narcissism. In S. Arieti, H. Keith, & H. Brodie (Eds.), *American Handbook of Psychiatry* (Vol. 7, pp. 297–316). New York: Basic Books.

Cooper, A. M. (1981b). Research in applied analysis. *Bulletin of the Association for Psychoanalytic Medicine* 20:37–43.

Cooper, A. M. (1982a). Narcissistic disorders within psychoanalytic theory. In L. Grinspoon (Ed.), *Psychiatry 1982: The American Psychiatric Association Annual Review* (pp. 487–497). Washington, DC: American Psychiatric Press.

Cooper, A. M. (1982b). Some persistent issues in psychoanalytic literary criticism. *Psychoanalysis and Contemporary Thought* 5:45–53.

Cooper, A. M. (1983a). Psychoanalytic inquiry and new knowledge. In J. D. Lichtenberg & S. Kaplan (Eds.), *Reflections on Self Psychology* (pp. 19–34). Hillsdale, NJ: Analytic Press.

Cooper, A. M. (1983b). *Some suggestions for the education of psychoanalysts.* Paper presented at the joint meeting of the Colorado Psychiatric Society and the Denver Psychoanalytic Society, Denver, CO.

Cooper, A. M. (1984a). Narcissism in normal development. In M. R. Zales (Ed.), *Character Pathology: Theory and Treatment* (pp. 39–56). New York: Brunner/Mazel.

Cooper, A. M. (1984b). Psychoanalysis at one hundred: beginnings of maturity. *Journal of the American Psychoanalytic Association* 32:245–267.

Cooper, A. M. (1984c). The unusually painful analysis: a group of narcissistic-masochistic characters. In J. E. Gedo & H. G. Pollock (Eds.), *Psychoanalysis: The Vital Issues* (Vol. 2, pp. 45–67). New York: International Universities Press.

Cooper, A. M. (1985a). Difficulties in beginning the candidate's first analytic case. *Contemporary Psychoanalysis* 2:143–150.

Cooper, A. M. (1985b). A historical review of psychoanalytic paradigms. In A. Rothstein (Ed.), *Models of the Mind: Their Relationships to Clinical Work* (pp. 5–20). New York: International Universities Press.

Cooper, A. M. (1985c). Will neurobiology influence psychoanalysis? *American Journal of Psychiatry* 19:1395–1402.

Cooper, A. M. (1986a). Narcissism. In A. P. Morrison (Ed.), *Essential Papers on Narcissism* (pp. 113–143). New York: New York University Press.

Cooper, A. M. (1986b). Some limitations on therapeutic effectiveness: the "burn-out syndrome" in psychoanalysts. *Psychoanalytic Quarterly* 55:576–598.

Cooper, A. M. (1986c). Summary. In A. M. Cooper (Ed.), *The Termination of the Training Analysis: Process, Expectations, Achievements* (pp. 53–57). London: International Psychoanalytical Association.

Cooper, A. M. (1986d). Toward a limited definition of psychic trauma. In A. Rothstein (Ed.), *The Reconstruction of Trauma: Its Significance to Clinical Work* (pp. 41–56). Madison, CT: International Universities Press.

Cooper, A. M. (1987a). Changes in psychoanalytic ideas: transference interpretation. *Journal of the American Psychoanalytic Association* 35:77–98.

Cooper, A. M. (1987b). The changing culture of psychoanalysis. *Journal of the American Academy of Psychoanalysis* 15:283–291.

Cooper, A. M. (1987c). The transference neurosis: a concept ready for retirement. *Psychoanalytic Inquiry* 7:569–585.

Cooper, A. M. (1988a). The narcissistic-masochistic character. In R. A. Glick & D. I. Meyers (Eds.), *Masochism: Current Psychological Perspectives* (pp. 117–138). Hillside, NJ: Analytic Press.

Cooper, A. M. (1988b). Our changing views of the therapeutic action of psychoanalysis: comparing Strachey and Loewald. *Psychoanalytic Quarterly,* 57:15–27.

Cooper, A. M. (1989a). Narcissism and masochism: the narcissistic-masochistic character. *Psychiatric Clinics of North America* 12:541–552.

Cooper, A. M. (1989b). Concepts of therapeutic effectiveness in psychoanalysis: a historical review. *Psychoanalytic Inquiry* 9:4–25.

Cooper, A. M. (1989c). Will neurobiology influence psychoanalysis? In A. M. Cooper, O. Kernberg, & E. Person (Eds.), *Psychoanalysis: Toward the Second Century* (pp. 202–218). New Haven, CT: Yale University Press.

Cooper, A. M. (1990a). The future of psychoanalysis: challenges and opportunities. *Psychoanalytic Quarterly* 59:177–196.

Cooper, A. M. (1990b). *Reconstruction*. Paper presented at the Arden House Faculty Retreat, Columbia University Center for Psychoanalytic Training and Research, New York.

Cooper, A. M. (1991a). Psychoanalysis: the past decade. *Psychoanalytic Inquiry* 11:107–122.

Cooper, A. M. (1991b). The unconscious core of perversion. In G. I. Fogel & W. A. Myers (Eds.), *Perversions and Near Perversions in Clinical Practice* (pp. 17–35). New Haven, CT: Yale University Press.

Cooper, A. M. (1992). *Classics revisited: Eissler's "The effect of the structure of the ego on psychoanalytic technique"*. Paper presented at the American Psychoanalytic Association Winter Meetings, New York, December.

Cooper, A. M. (1993). Psychotherapeutic approaches to masochism. *Journal of Psychotherapy Practice and Research* 2:51–63.

Cooper, A. M. (1996). *Psychoanalysis in the 21st century: unity in plurality*. Paper presented at the 50th anniversary of the Los Angeles Psychoanalytic Society and Institute, Los Angeles, September.

Cooper, A. M. (1997). *Psychoanalytic education: past, present and future*. Paper presented at the Association for Psychoanalytic Medicine, New York, November.

Cooper, A. M. (1998). *The impact on clinical work of the analyst's idealizations and identifications*. Paper presented at the 87th Annual Meeting of the American Psychoanalytic Association, Toronto, Canada.

Cooper, A. M., Eckhardt, R. D., Faloon, W. W., & Davidson, C. S. (1950). Investigation of the aminoaciduria in Wilson's Disease (hepatolenticular degeneration): Demonstration in renal function. *Journal of Clinical Investigation* 29:265–278.

Cooper, A. M., & Frances, A. (1980). The DSM-III controversy: A psychoanalytic perspective. *Bulletin of the Association for Psychoanalytic Medicine* 19:37–43.

Cooper, A. M., & Frances, A. (1981). Descriptive and dynamic psychiatry: a perspective on DSM-III. *American Journal of Psychiatry* 138:1198–1202.

Cooper, A. M., Karush, A., Easser, B. R., & Swerdloff, B. (1962). The evaluation of ego strength. *Bulletin of the Association for Psychoanalytic Medicine* 2:24–30.

Cooper, A. M., Karush, A., Easser, B. R., & Swerdloff, B. (1966). The adaptive balance profile and prediction of early treatment behaviour. In G. Goldman & D. Shapiro (Eds.), *Developments in Psychoanalysis at Columbia University* (pp. 183–214). New York: Hafner.

Cooper, A. M., Kernberg, O., & Person, E. S. (Eds.). (1989). *Psychoanalysis: Toward the Second Century.* New Haven, CT: Yale University Press.

Cooper, A. M., Kernberg, O. F., Schafer, R., & Viederman, M. (1991). *Report of the curriculum review committee.* The Columbia Center for Psychoanalytic Training and Research (unpublished manuscript).

Cooper, A. M., Kravis, N. M., Tomlinson, C., & Makari, G. J. (1995). *History and memory: the second death of Sandor Rado.* Paper presented at the Association for Psychoanalytic Medicine, New York, March.

Cooper, A. M., & Michels, R. (1981). Book review: Diagnostic and Statistical Manual of Mental Disorders, 3rd edition. *American Journal of Psychiatry* 138:128–129.

Cooper, A. M., & Michels, R. (1988). Book review: Diagnostic and Statistical Manual of Mental Disorders, 3rd edition, revised (DSM-III-R). *American Journal of Psychiatry* 145:1300–1301.

Cooper, A. M., & Ronningstam, R. (1992). Narcissistic personality. In A. Tasman & M. Riba (Eds.), *American Psychiatric Press Review of Psychiatry* (Vol. II, pp. 80–97). Washington DC: American Psychiatric Press.

Crick, F. H. C. (1994). *The Astonishing Hypothesis: The Scientific Search for the Soul.* New York: Scribner's.

Crits-Christoph, P., Cooper, A., & Luborsky, L. (1988). The accuracy of therapists' interpretations and the outcome of dynamic psychotherapy. *Journal of Consulting and Clinical Psychology* 56:490–495.

Culioli, A. (1990). *Pour Une Linguistique de l'Enontiation. Operations et Représentations.* (Vol. 1). Paris: Ophrys.

Dahl, H., Teller, V., Moss, D., & Trujillo, M. (1978). Countertransference examples of the syntactic expression of warded-off contents. *Psychoanalytic Quarterly* 47:339–363.

Dalsimer, K. (1986). *Female Adolescence: Psychoanalytic Reflections on Literature.* New Haven, CT, & London: Yale University Press.

Dalsimer, K. (1994). The vicissitudes of mourning: Virginia Woolf and *To the Lighthouse. Psychoanalytic Study of the Child* 49:394–411. New Haven, CT: Yale University Press.

Danon-Boileau, L. (1987). *Le Sujet de l'Enonciation. Psychanalyse et Linguistique.* Paris: Ophrys.

Davidson, D. (1980). *Actions, Reasons, and Causes. Essays on Action and Events.* Oxford: Clarendon Press.

Dawkins, R. (1980). Good strategy or evolutionarily stable strategy? In G. W. Barlow & J. Silverberg (Eds.), *Sociobiology Beyond Nature/Nurture?* (pp. 331–370). Boulder: Westview Press.

Dawkins, R. (1982). *The Extended Phenotype.* Oxford: Oxford University Press.

de Saussure, F. (1911). *Course in General Linguistics.* New York: Philosophic Library, 1959.

de Waal, F. (1996). *Good Natured: The Origins of Right and Wrong in Humans and Other Animals*. Cambridge, MA: Harvard University Press.

de Waal, F., & Lanting, F. (1997). *Bonobo: The Forgotten Ape*. Berkeley: University of California Press.

Dennett, D. C. (1991). *Consciousness Explained*. Boston: Little Brown.

Dennett, D. C. (1995). *Darwin's Dangerous Idea: Evolution and the Meanings of Life*. New York: Simon & Schuster.

DeWitt, K. N., Kaltreider, N., Weiss, D. S., & Horowitz, M. J. (1983). Judging change in psychotherapy: reliability of clinical formulations. *Archives of General Psychiatry* 40:1121–1128.

Donovan, S., & Roose, S. P. (1995). The use of medication during psychoanalysis. *Journal of Clinical Psychiatry* 56:177–179.

Edelman, G. M. (1987). *Neural Darwinism: The Theory of Neuronal Group Selection*. New York: Basic Books.

Edelman, G. M. (1989). *The Remembered Present: A Biological Theory of Consciousness*. New York: Basic Books.

Edelman, G. M. (1992). *Bright Air, Brilliant Fire*. New York: Basic Books.

Edelson, M. (1972). Language and dreams. *Psychoanalytic Study of the Child* 27:203–282. New Haven, CT: Yale University Press.

Edelson, M. (1984). *Hypothesis and Evidence in Psychoanalysis*. Chicago: University of Chicago Press.

Eissler, K. R. (1953). The effect of the structure of the ego on psychoanalytic technique. *Journal of the American Psychoanalytic Association* 1:104–143.

Eliade, M. (1965). *The Two and the One*. New York: Harper Torchbook.

Eliot, T. S. (1930). *Collected Poems*. New York: Harcourt Brace.

Ellis, M. L. (1994). Lesbians, gay men and psychoanalytic training. *Free Association* 32:501–517.

Elman, J. L., Bates, A. E., Johnson, M. H., Karmiloff-Smith, A., Parisi, D., & Plunkett, K. (1996). *Rethinking Innateness: A Connectionist Perspective on Development*. Cambridge, MA: MIT Press.

Emde, R. N. (1988). Development terminable and interminable II. Recent psychoanalytic theory and therapeutic considerations. *International Journal of Psycho-Analysis* 69:283–286.

Erikson, E. H. (1950). *Childhood and Society*. New York: Norton.

Erikson, E. H. (1964). *Insight and Responsibility*. New York: Norton.

Erreich, A. (in press). Frankenstein meets the Wolf Man: a meditation on psychoanalysis and empirical research. In R. Prince (Ed.), *The Death of Psychoanalysis: Murder, Suicide or Rumor Greatly Exaggerated*. Northvale, NJ: Jason Aronson.

Evans Pritchard, E. E. (1937). *Witchcraft, Oracles, and Magic Among the Azande*. Oxford: Clarendon Press.

Fairbairn, W. R. D. (1952a). *An Object-Relations Theory of the Personality*. New York: Basic Books, 1954.

Fairbairn, W. R. D. (1952b). *Psychoanalytic Studies of the Personality*. London: Tavistock.

Faloon, W. W., Eckhardt, R. D., Cooper, A. M., & Davidson, C. S. (1949a). The effects of human serum albumin, mercurial diuretics and low sodium excretion in patients with cirrhosis of the liver. *Journal of Clinical Investigation 28*: 595–602.

Faloon, W. W., Eckhardt, R. D., Davidson, C. S., Murphy, T. L., & Cooper, A. M. (1949b). An investigation of human serum albumin in the treatment of cirrhosis of the liver. *Journal of Clinical Investigation 28*:583–594.

Ferenczi, S. (1922). The further development of an active therapy in psychoanalysis. In *Further Contributions to the Theory and Technique of Psychoanalysis* (pp. 198–216). London: Karnac Books, 1980.

Feyerabend, P. (1962). Explanation, reduction and empiricism. In H. Feigl & G. Maxwell (Eds.), *Scientific Explanation, Space, Time* (Vol. 3, pp. 28–97). Minneapolis: University of Minnesota Press.

Feyerabend, P. (1978). *Science in a Free Society*. Verso: London.

Flaubert, G. (1869). *Sentimental Education* (R. Baldick, Trans.). London: Penguin, 1964.

Flexner, A. (1910). *Medical Education in the United States and Canada (Carnegie Foundation for the Advancement of Teaching, Bulletin 4)*. Boston: Updyke.

Fodor, J. (1983). *The Modularity of Mind: An Essay on Faculty Psychology*. Cambridge, MA: MIT Press.

Folkman, S., & Lazarus, R. (1980). An analysis of coping in a middle-aged community sample. *Journal of Health and Social Behaviour 21*:219–239.

Fónagy, I. (1983). *La Vive Voix. Essais de Psycho-phonétique*. Paris: Payot.

Fox, R. (1967). Totem and Taboo reconsidered. In E. Leach (Ed.), *The Structural Study of Myth and Totemism* (pp. 161–178). London: Tavistock.

Fox, R. P. (1984). The principle of abstinence reconsidered. *International Review of Psycho-Analysis 11*:227–236.

Freud, A. (1936). *The Ego and the Mechanisms of Defence*. New York: International Universities Press, 1946.

Freud, A. (1958). Adolescence. *Psychoanalytic Study of the Child, 13*:255–278. New York: International Universities Press.

Freud, S. (1895). Project for a scientific psychology. *Standard Edition 1*:281–293.

Freud, S. (1899a). Screen memories. *Standard Edition 3*:301–322.

Freud, S. (1900). Die Traumdeutung. *Gesammelte Werke 2 & 3*. Frankfurt: Fischer Verlag, 1942.

Freud, S. (1900a). The interpretation of dreams. *Standard Edition 4 & 5*:1–715.

Freud, S. (1905d). Three essays on the theory of sexuality. *Standard Edition 7*:123–230.

Freud, S. (1907c). The sexual enlightenment of children. *Standard Edition 9*:129–140.

REFERENCES

Freud, S. (1909). Bemerkungen über einen Fall von Zwangsneurose. *Gesammelte Werke* 7:381–467. Frankfurt: Fischer Verlag.
Freud, S. (1909b). Analysis of a phobia in a five-year-old boy. *Standard Edition* 10:1–147.
Freud, S. (1909d). Notes upon a case of obsessional neurosis. *Standard Edition* 10:153–320.
Freud, S. (1910e). The antithetical meaning of primal words. *Standard Edition* 11:153–162.
Freud, S. (1912b). The dynamics of transference. *Standard Edition 12*.
Freud, S. (1913). Totem and taboo. *Standard Edition 13*.
Freud, S. (1914c). On narcissism: an introduction. *Standard Edition* 14:67–104.
Freud, S. (1915a). Observations on transference love. *Standard Edition* 12:157–171.
Freud, S. (1916–1917). Introductory lectures on psycho-analysis. *Standard Edition 15 & 16*:13–477.
Freud, S. (1917e). Mourning and melancholia. *Standard Edition* 14:237–258.
Freud, S. (1919a). Lines of advance in psycho-analytic therapy. *Standard Edition* 17:157–168.
Freud, S. (1920g). Beyond the pleasure principle. *Standard Edition* 18:1–64.
Freud, S. (1921c). Group psychology and the analysis of the ego. *Standard Edition* 18:69–143.
Freud, S. (1923b). The ego and the id. *Standard Edition* 19:1–59.
Freud, S. (1924). The future of an illusion. *Standard Edition* 21:1–56.
Freud, S. (1925d). An autobiographical study. *Standard Edition* 20:7–74.
Freud, S. (1925h). On negation. *Standard Edition* 19:235–242.
Freud, S. (1926d). Inhibitions, symptoms and anxiety. *Standard Edition* 20:77–172.
Freud, S. (1930a). Civilization and its discontents. *Standard Edition* 21:57–146.
Freud, S. (1931a). Libidinal types. *Standard Edition* 21:215–220.
Freud, S. (1933). The dissection of the psychical personality. *Standard Edition* 22:59–60.
Freud, S. (1937c). Analysis terminable and interminable. *Standard Edition* 23:209–253.
Freud, S. (1937d). Constructions in analysis. *Standard Edition* 23:257–269.
Freud, S. (1939a). Moses and monotheism. *Standard Edition* 23:3–137.
Freud, S. (1940a). An outline of psychoanalysis. *Standard Edition* 23:139–208.
Freud, S. (1985). *The Complete Letters of Sigmund Freud to Wilhelm Fliess: 1887–1904*. Cambridge, MA: Harvard University Press.
Freud, S. (1993). *The Complete Correspondence of Sigmund Freud and Ernest Jones: 1908–1939*. Cambridge, MA: Harvard University Press.
Freud, S., & Ferenczi, S. (1993). Letter from Freud to Ferenczi, May 13 1913. In E. Brabant, E. Falzeder, & Giampieri-Deutsch (Eds.), *The Correspondence of Sigmund Freud and Sandor Ferenczi* (Vol. 1, 1908–1914, pp. 485–486). Cambridge, MA: Harvard University Press.

Freud, S., & Jung, C. (1974). *The Freud/Jung Letters* (R. Manheim, Trans.). Princeton, NJ: Princeton University Press.
Friedman, L. (1988). *The Anatomy of Psychotherapy*. Hillsdale, NJ: Analytic Press.
Gabbard, G. O. (1989a). Patients who hate. *Psychiatry* 52:96–106.
Gabbard, G. O. (1989b). Two subtypes of narcissistic personality disorder. *Bulletin of the Menninger Clinic* 53:527–532.
Gabbard, G. O. (Ed.). (1994). *Psychodynamic Psychiatry in Clinical Practice: The DSM-IV Edition*. Washington: American Psychiatric Press.
Gabbard, G. O. (1995). Countertransference: the emerging common ground. *International Journal of Psycho-Analysis* 76:475–485.
Gardner, H. (1985). *The Mind's Best Work*. New York: Basic Books.
Gill, M. M. (1982). *Analysis of Transference, Vol I: Theory and Technique*. New York: International Universities Press.
Gill, M. M. (1994). *Psychoanalysis in Transition: A Personal View*. Hillsdale, NJ: Analytic Press.
Gilligan, C. (1982). *In a Different Voice: Psychological Theory and Women's Development*. Cambridge, MA: Harvard University Press.
Good, M. I. (1998). Screen reconstruction: Traumatic memory, conviction and the problem of verification. *Journal of the American Psychoanalytic Association* 46:149–183.
Gould, S. J. (1980). Is a new and general theory of evolution emerging? *Paleobiology* 6:119–130.
Gould, S. J. (1982). Change in developmental timing as a mechanism of macroevolution. In J. T. Bonner (Ed.), *Evolution and Development. Report of the Dahlem Workshop on Evolution and Development* (pp. 333–346). New York: Springer-Verlag.
Gould, S. J., & Eldredge, N. (1993). Punctuated equilibrium comes of age. *Nature* 366: 223–227.
Gray, P. (1986). On helping analysands observe intrapsychic activity. In A. D. Richards & M. S. Willick (Eds.), *Psychoanalysis: The Science of Mental Conflict. Essays in Honour of Charles Brenner* (pp. 245–262). Hillsdale, NJ: Analytic Press.
Gray, P. (1994). *The Ego and the Analysis of Defence*. Northvale, NJ: Jason Aronson.
Greenberg, J. (1991). *Oedipus and Beyond: A Clinical Theory*. Cambridge, MA: Harvard University Press.
Greenberg, J. R., & Mitchell, S. A. (1983). *Object Relations in Psychoanalytic Theory*. Cambridge, MA: Harvard University Press.
Greenson, R. R., & Wexler, M. (1969). The non-transference relationship in the psychoanalytic situation. *International Journal of Psycho-Analysis* 50:27–39.
Grenyer, B., & Luborsky, L. (1998). Positive versus negative CCRT patterns. In L. Luborsky & P. Crits-Christoph (Eds.), *Understanding Transference – The Core Conflictual Relationship Theme Method* (pp. 55–64). Washington, DC: American Psychological Association.

Grenyer, B. F. (1994). *Mastery Scale I: A Research and Scoring Manual*. Wollongong: University of Wollongong.

Grice, H. P. (1989). *Studies in the Way of Words*. Cambridge, MA: Harvard University Press.

Groopman, L. C., & Cooper, A. M. (1995). Narcissistic personality disorder. In G. O. Gabbard (Ed.), *Treatments of Psychiatric Disorders: The Second Edition* (pp. 2327–2344). Washington, DC: American Psychiatric Press.

Grossman, W. I. (1998). Freud's presentation of 'the psychoanalytic mode of thought' in *Totem and Taboo* and his technical papers. *International Journal of Psycho-Analysis* 6:109–130.

Grünbaum, A. (1984). *The Foundations of Psychoanalysis: A Philosophical Critique*. Berkeley: University of California Press.

Gunderson, J. G., & Ronningstam, E. (1991). Is narcissistic personality disorder a valid diagnosis? In J. O. Oldham (Ed.), *Personality Disorders: New Perspectives on Diagnostic Validity* (pp. 107–119). Washington, DC: American Psychiatric Press.

Haan, N. (1977). *Coping and Defending*. New York: Academic Press.

Habermas, J. (1968). *Knowledge and Human Interest* (J. J. Shapiro, Trans.). Boston: Beacon Press, 1971.

Hamilton, V. (1993). Truth and reality in psychoanalytic discourse. *International Journal of Psycho-Analysis* 74:63–79.

Hartley, D. E., & Strupp, H. H. (1983). The therapeutic alliance: its relationship to outcome in brief psychotherapy. In J. Masling (Ed.), *Empirical Studies of Psychoanalytical Theories* (Vol. 1, pp. 1–37). Hillsdale, NJ: Analytic Press.

Hartmann, H. (1939). *Ego Psychology and the Problem of Adaptation*. New York: International Universities Press, 1958.

Hartmann, H. (1964). *Essays on Ego Psychology*. New York: International Universities Press.

Holland, N. N. (1968). *The Dynamics of Literary Response*. New York: Oxford University Press.

Holzman, P. S., & Schlesinger, H. J. (1972). On becoming a hospitalized psychiatric patient. *Bulletin of the Menninger Clinic* 36:383–406.

Homans, P. (1989). *The Ability to Mourn: Disillusionment and the Social Origins of Psychoanalysis*. Chicago: University of Chicago Press.

Horowitz, M. J. (1988). *Introduction to Psychodynamics: A New Synthesis*. New York: Basic Books.

Horowitz, M. J. (1989). Clinical phenomenology of narcissistic pathology. *Psychiatric Clinics of North America* 12:531–539.

Horvath, A. O., & Simmonds, B. D. (1991). Relation between working alliance and outcome in psychotherapy: a meta-analysis. *Journal of Consulting and Clinical Psychology* 38:139–149.

Humphrey, N. (1986). *The Inner Eye*. London: Faber & Faber.

Hunt, W. (1995). The diffident narcissist: a character-type illustrated in *The Beast in the Jungle* by Henry James. *International Journal of Psycho-Analysis* 76:1257–1267.
Ibsen, H. (1879). *A Doll's House*. In J. McFarlane (Ed.), *The Oxford Ibsen*. Oxford: Oxford University Press.
Jacobs, T. (1973). Posture, gesture, and movement in the analyst: cues to interpretation and countertransference. *Journal of the American Psychoanalytic Association* 21:77–92.
Jacobs, T. (1980). Secrets, alliances, and family fictions: some psychoanalytic observations. *Journal of the American Psychoanalytic Association* 28:21–42.
Jacobs, T. (1986). On countertransference enactments. *Journal of the American Psychoanalytic Association* 34:289–307.
Jacobson, E. (1964). *The Self and the Object World*. New York: International Universities Press.
Jacobson, E. (1971). *Depression. Comparative Studies of Normal, Neurotic, and Psychotic Conditions*. New York: International Universities Press.
Jacoby, R. (1975). *A Critique of Contemporary Psychology from Adler to Laing*. Boston: Beacon Press.
James, W. (1890). *Principles of Psychology*. New York: Henry Holt & Co.
Jones, E. (1925). Mother-right and the sexual ignorance of savages. *International Journal of Psycho-Analysis*, 6:109–130.
Jones, E. (1956). The inception of *Totem and Taboo*. *International Journal of Psycho-Analysis* 37:34–35.
Jones, E. (1957). *Sigmund Freud: Life and Work 1919–1939*. (Vol. 3). London: Hogarth Press.
Jones, E. (1964). The God complex. In E. Jones (Ed.), *Essays in Applied Psychoanalysis* (pp. 244–265). New York: International Universities Press.
Kächele, H., & Thomä, H. (1995). Psychoanalytic process research: method and achievements. In T. Shapiro & R. N. Emde (Eds.), *Research in Psychoanalysis: Process, Development, Outcome* (pp. 109–129). Madison, CT: International Universities Press.
Kagan, J. (1984). *The Nature of the Child*. New York: Basic Books.
Kano, T. (1992). *The Lost Ape*. Stanford, CA: Stanford University Press.
Kant, I. (1781). *The Critique of Pure Reason* (N. Kemp, Trans.). New York: Smith, 1966.
Kanzer, M., & Glenn, J. (Eds.). (1995). *Freud and His Patients*. Northvale, NJ: Jason Aronson.
Kaplan, L. J. (1991). *Female Perversions: The Temptations of Emma Bovary*. New York: Doubleday Anchor.
Kauffman, S. (1993). *The Origins of Order: Self-organisation and Selection in Evolution*. New York: Oxford University Press.
Keeley, L. H. (1996). *War Before Civilisation*. New York: Oxford University Press.

Kernberg, O. F. (1970). Factors in the treatment of narcissistic personality disorder. *Journal of the American Psychoanalytic Association* 18:51–85.
Kernberg, O. F. (1975). *Borderline Conditions and Pathological Narcissism*. New York: Jason Aronson.
Kernberg, O. F. (1980). *Internal World and External Reality: Object Relations Theory Applied*. New York: Jason Aronson.
Kernberg, O. F. (1984). *Severe Personality Disorders: Psychotherapeutic Strategies*. New Haven, CT: Yale University Press.
Kernberg, O. F. (1988). Narcissistic personality disorder. In R. Michels (Ed.), *Psychiatry* (Vol. 1, pp. 1–12). New York: Basic Books.
Kernberg, O. F. (1989). The narcissistic personality disorder and the differential diagnosis of antisocial behaviour. *Psychiatric Clinics of North America* 12:553–570.
Kernberg, O. F. (1991). A contemporary reading of narcissism. In J. Sandler, E. S. Person, & P. Fonagy (Eds.), *Freud's On Narcissism: An Introduction* (pp. 131–148). New Haven, CT: Yale University Press.
Kernberg, O. F. (1992). *Aggression in Personality Disorders and Perversions*. New Haven, CT, & London: Yale University Press.
Kernberg, O. F. (1996). Thirty methods to destroy the creativity of psychoanalytic candidates. *International Journal of Psycho-Analysis* 77:1031–1040.
Kernberg, O. F., Burnstein, E., Coyne, L., Appelbaum, A., Horowitz, L., & Voth, H. (1972). Psychotherapy and psychoanalysis: final report of the Menninger Foundation Psychotherapy Research Project. *Bulletin of the Menninger Clinic* 36:3–275.
Kiell, N. (1988). *Freud Without Hindsight: Reviews of his Work, 1893–1939* (V. Rus & D. Boneau, Trans.). Madison, CT: International Universities Press.
Klein, G. (1976). *Psychoanalytic Theory: An Exploration of Essentials*. New York: International Universities Press.
Klein, G. S., & Schlesinger, H. J. (1949). Where is the perceiver in perceptual theory? *Journal of Personality* 8:32–47.
Klein, M. (1940). Mourning and its relation to manic-depressive states. In *Love, Guilt and Reparation and Other Works 1921–1945* (pp. 344–369). New York: Macmillan, 1984.
Klein, M. (1946a). *Envy and Gratitude and Other Works, 1946–1962*. New York: Delta, 1975.
Klein, M. (1946b). Notes on some schizoid mechanisms. In M. Klein, P. Heimann, S. Isaacs, & J. Riviere (Eds.), *Developments in Psychoanalysis* (pp. 292–320). London: Hogarth Press.
Klein, M. (1952). On observing the behaviour of young infants. In R. Money-Kyrle (Ed.), *The Writings of Melanie Klein* (Vol. 3, pp. 94–121). London: Hogarth, 1975.
Klein, M. (1959). Our adult world and its roots in infancy. In R. Money-Kyrle (Ed.), *The Writings of Melanie Klein* (Vol. 3, pp. 247–263). London: Hogarth Press, 1975.

Koch, K. (1971). *Wishes, Lies, and Dreams: Teaching Children to Write Poetry.* New York: Vintage.

Kohut, H. (1971). *The Analysis of the Self.* New York: International Universities Press.

Kohut, H. (1977). *The Restoration of the Self.* New York: International Universities Press.

Kohut, H., & Wolf, E. S. (1978). The disorders of the self and their treatment: an outline. *International Journal of Psycho-Analysis* 59: 413–426.

Kris, E. (1956). On some vicissitudes of insight in psycho-analysis. In *Selected Papers* (pp. 252–271). New Haven: Yale University Press.

Kroeber, A. L. (1920). *Totem and Taboo*: an ethnologic psychoanalysis. *American Anthropologist* 22:48–55.

Kroeber, A. L. (1939). *Totem and Taboo* in retrospect. *American Journal of Sociology* 55:446–451.

Kuhn, T. S. (1962). *The Structure of Scientific Revolutions.* Chicago: University of Chicago Press.

Kuhn, T. S. (1977). *The Essential Tension: Selected Studies in Scientific Tradition and Change.* Chicago: University of Chicago Press.

Lacan, J. (1956). *The Language of the Self: The Function of Language in Psychoanalysis.* Baltimore, MD: Johns Hopkins Press.

Laplanche, J., & Pontalis, J. B. (1973). *The Language of Psychoanalysis.* New York: Norton.

Lasch, C. (1978). *The Culture of Narcissism: American Life in an Age of Diminishing Expectations.* New York: Norton.

Latour, B. (1987). *Science in Action: How to Follow Scientists and Engineers Through Society.* Cambridge, MA: Harvard University Press.

Latour, B. (1993). *We Have Never Been Modern.* New York: Norton.

Le Vine, R. A. (1991). Gender differences. Interpreting anthropological data. In M. T. Notman & C. Nadelson (Eds.), *Women and Men* (pp. 1–9). Washington, DC: American Psychiatric Press.

Leach, E. (1967). *The Structural Study of Myths and Totemism.* London: Tavistock.

Lester, E. P., & Notman, M. T. (1988). Pregnancy and object relations. *Psychoanalytic Inquiry* 8:196–222.

Lévi-Strauss, C. (1964). *Totemism.* London: Merlin Press.

Lewin, B. D. (1973). *Selected Writings of Bertram D. Lewin.* New York: Psychoanalytic Quarterly.

Lichtenberg, J. (1989a). *Psychoanalysis and Motivation.* Hillsdale, NJ: Analytic Press.

Lichtenberg, J. (1989b). A theory of motivational-functional systems as psychic structures. *Journal of the American Psychoanalytic Association* 37:55–70.

Lloyd Meyer, E. (1996). Changes in science and changing ideas about knowledge and authority in psychoanalysis. *Psychoanalytic Quarterly* 65:158–200.

Loewald, H. W. (1960). On the therapeutic action of psycho-analysis. *International Journal of Psycho-Analysis* 41:16–33.

Loewald, H. W. (1970). Psychoanalytic theory and the psychoanalytic process. In *Papers on Psychoanalysis* (pp. 270–301). New Haven, CT, & London: Yale University Press, 1980.

Loewald, H. W. (1972). Freud's conception of the negative therapeutic reaction, with comments on instinct theory. *Journal of the American Psychoanalytic Association 20*:235–245.

Loewald, H. W. (1980). *Papers on Psychoanalysis*. New Haven, CT: Yale University Press.

Lorenz, K. (1965). *Evolution and Modification of Behaviour*. Chicago: University of Chicago.

Luborsky, L. (1962a). Clinicians judgments of mental health: a proposed scale. *Archives of General Psychiatry 7*:407–417.

Luborsky, L. (1962b). The patient's personality and psychotherapeutic change. In H. Strupp & L. Luborsky (Eds.), *Research in Psychotherapy* (Vol. 2, pp. 115–133). Washington, DC: American Psychological Association.

Luborsky, L. (1977). Measuring a pervasive psychic structure in psychotherapy: the core conflictual relationship theme. In N. Freedman & S. Grand (Eds.), *Communicative Structures and Psychic Structures* (pp. 367–395). New York: Plenum.

Luborsky, L. (1984). *Principles of Psychoanalytic Psychotherapy: A Manual for Supportive-Expressive (SE) Treatment*. New York: Basic Books.

Luborsky, L. (1996). *The Symptom-Context Method: Symptoms as Opportunities for Psychotherapy*. Washington, DC: APA Books.

Luborsky, L. (in press). The context for recurrent symptoms in psychoanalysis.

Luborsky, L., & Crits-Christoph, P. (1998). *Understanding Transference: The Core Conflictual Relationship Theme Method*. (2nd ed.). Washington, DC: American Psychological Association Press.

Luborsky, L., Crits-Christoph, P., Mintz, J., & Auerbach, A. (1988). *Who Will Benefit From Psychotherapy? Predicting Therapeutic Outcomes*. New York: Basic Books.

Luborsky, L., & Diguer, L. (1998). The reliability of the CCRT measure: results from eight samples. In L. Luborsky & P. Crits-Christoph (Eds.), *Understanding Transference – the Core Conflictual Relationship Theme Method* (pp. 97–108). Washington, DC: American Psychological Association.

Luborsky, L., & Spence, D. (1971). Quantitative research on psychoanalytic therapy. In A. E. Bergin & S. L. Garfield (Eds.), *Handbook of Psychotherapy and Behaviour Change* (pp. 408–437). New York: Wiley.

Luborsky, L., Stuart, J., Friedman, S., Seligman, D. A., Bucci, W., Pulver, S., Woody, G., Davison, W. S., Krause, E., & Mergenthaler, E. (in press). A unique collection of completely tape-recorded psychoanalyses as a research resource: the Penn Psychoanalytic Treatment Collection.

Maccoby, E. E. (1998). *The Two Sexes: Growing Up Apart, Coming Together*. Cambridge, MA, & London: Belknap Press.

Mackinnon, D., & Duke, W. F. (1962). Repression. In L. Postman (Ed.), *Psychology in the Making* (pp. 662–744). New York: Knopf.
Mahony, P. (1977). Towards a formalist approach to dreams. *International Review of Psycho-Analysis* 4:83–98.
Mahony, P. (1980). Towards the understanding of translation in psychoanalysis. *Journal of the American Psychoanalytic Association* 28:461–473.
Mahony, P. (1987a). The budding International Association of Psychoanalysis and its discontents: a feature of Freud's discourse. In *Psychoanalysis and Discourse* (pp. 159–192). London: Routledge.
Mahony, P. (1987b). *Psychoanalysis and Discourse*. London: Routledge.
Mahoney, P. (1993). Freud's cases: Are they valuable today? *International Journal of Psycho-Analysis* 74:1027–1035.
Mahony, P. (1994). Psychoanalysis: The writing cure. In A. Haynal & E. Falzeder (Eds.), *100 Years of Psychoanalysis* (pp. 100–120). Geneva: Cahiers Psychiatriques et Institutions Universitaires de Psychiatrie de Genève.
Mahony, P. (1996a). Book review of "Kondordanz du den Gesammelten Werke von Freud". *International Journal of Psycho-Analysis* 77:407–412.
Mahony, P. (1996b). *Freud's Dora: A Psychoanalytic, Historical and Textual Study*. New Haven, CT: Yale University Press.
Makari, G. J. (1991). German philosophy, Freud and the riddle of women. *Journal of the American Psychoanalytic Association* 39:183–215.
Makari, G. J. (1992). A history of Freud's first concept of transference. *International Review of Psycho-Analysis* 19:415–432.
Makari, G. J. (1994). In the eye of the beholder: Helmholtz, post-Kantian perception and Freud's 1900 theory of transference. *Journal of the American Psychoanalytic Association* 42:549–580.
Makari, G. J. (1997). Dora's hysteria and the maturation of Sigmund Freud's transference theory: A new historical interpretation. *Journal of the American Psychoanalytic Association* 45:1061–1096.
Makari, G. J., & Shapiro, T. (1993). On psychoanalytic listening: language and unconscious communication. *Journal of the American Psycho-Analytic Association* 41:991–1019.
Malinowski, B. (1916). Baloma: the spirits of the dead in the Trobriand Island. *Journal of the Royal Anthropological Institute* 46:353–430.
Malinowski, B. (1927). *Sex and Repression in Savage Society*. London: Kegan Paul.
Malinowski, B. (1929). *The Sexual Life of Savages in North-Western Melanesia*. New York: Eugenics Publishing Co.
Mann, M. (1986). *The Sources of Social Power. Vol 1: A History of Power From the Beginning to AD 1760*. Cambridge: Cambridge University Press.
Marcus, E. (1990). Integrating psychopharmacotherapy, psychotherapy, and the mental structure in the treatment of patients with personality disorders and depression. *Psychiatric Clinics of North America* 13:255–263.

Masterson, J. F. (1993). *The Emerging Self: A Developmental, Self and Object Relations Approach to the Treatment of the Closet Narcissistic Disorder of the Self*. New York: Brunner/Mazel.

Maynard Smith, J. (1978). Optimization theory in evolution. *Annual Review of Ecology and Systematics* 9:31–56.

Maynard Smith, J. (1979). Game theory and the evolution of behaviour. *Proceedings of the Royal Society of London* B205:475–488.

Maynard Smith, J. (1989). *Did Darwin Get It Right?* New York: Chapman & Hall.

McLaughlin, W. (1998). Why do schools of thought fail? Neo-Freudianism as a case study in the sociology of knowledge. *Journal of the History of the Behavioral Sciences* 36:113–134.

Mehler, J. A., & Argentieri, S. (1989). Hope and hopelessness: A technical problem? *International Journal of Psycho-Analysis* 70:295–304.

Meltzoff, A. N., & Moore, M. K. (1992). Perception, action and cognition in early infancy. *Annals of Paediatrics* 32:63–77.

Meyers, H. C. (1990). *Major theoretical changes at the Columbia Psychoanalytic Center: 1956 to the present*. Paper presented at the Oral History Workshop of the American Psychoanalytic Association, New York, Winter.

Michels, R. (1994). Psychoanalysis enters its second century. *Annual of Psychoanalysis* 22:37–45.

Mill, J. S. (1869). *The Subjection of Women*. London: Parker.

Milrod, B., Busch, F., Cooper, A., & Shapiro, T. (1997). *Manual for Panic-Focused Psychodynamic Psychotherapy*. Washington, DC: American Psychiatric Press.

Milrod, B., & Shear, M. K. (1991). Dynamic treatment of panic disorder: A review. *Journal of Nervous and Mental Disease* 179:741–3.

Mitchell, S. A. (1988). *Relational Concepts in Psychoanalysis: An Integration*. Cambridge, MA: Harvard University Press.

Modell, A. H. (1993). *The Private Self*. Cambridge, MA: Harvard University Press.

Moos, R. H., & Billings, A. G. (1982). Conceptualizing and measuring coping resources and processes. In L. Goldberger & S. Breznitz (Eds.), *Handbook of Stress: Theoretical and Clinical Aspects* (pp. 212–230). New York: Free Press.

Moran, R. (1988). Making up your mind: self-interpretation and self-constitution. *Ratio (New Series)* 1:137–151.

Morgan, R., Luborsky, L., Crits-Christoph, P., Curtis, H., & Solomon, J. (1982). Predicting the outcomes of psychotherapy by the Penn Helping Alliance Rating Method. *Archives of General Psychiatry* 39:397–402.

Nemeroff, C. B. (1996). The corticotropin-releasing factor (CRF) hypothesis of depression: new findings and new directions. *Molecular Psychiatry* 1:326–342.

Nersessian, E. (1995). Some reflections on curiosity and psychoanalytic technique. *Psychoanalytic Quarterly* 64:113–135.

Nesse, R. M., & Lloyd, A. T. (1992). The evolution of psychodynamic mechanisms. In J. H. Barkow, L. Cosmides, & J. Tooby (Eds.), *The Adapted Mind* (pp. 601–624). New York: Oxford University Press.

Neu, J. (1992). Genetic explanation in *Totem and Taboo*. In R. Wollheim (Ed.), *Freud: A Collection of Critical Essays* (pp. 366–393). Garden City, NY: Anchor Books.

Neubauer, P. (1979). The role of insight in psychoanalysis. *Journal of the American Psychoanalytic Association 27 (Suppl)*:29–40.

Norville, R., Sampson, H., & Weiss, J. (1996). Accurate interpretations and brief psychotherapy outcome. *Psychotherapy Research* 6:16–29.

Notman, M. T., & Nadelson, C. (1991). *A Review of Gender and Behaviour in Women and Men*. Washington, DC: American Psychiatric Press.

Ogden, T. H. (1979). On projective identification. *International Journal of Psycho-Analysis* 60:357–373.

Ogden, T. H. (1994). The concept of interpretative action. *Psychoanalytic Quarterly* 63:219–244.

Olds, D., & Cooper, A. M. (1997). Dialogue with other sciences: opportunities for mutual gain. Guest Editorial. *International Journal of Psycho-Analysis* 78:219–226.

Oyama, S. (1985). *The Ontogeny of Information*. Cambridge: Cambridge University Press.

Paul, R. (1992). Freud's anthropology: a reading of the "cultural books". In E. E. Garcia (Ed.), *Understanding Freud: A Collection of Critical Essays* (pp. 366–393). Garden City, NY: Anchor Books.

Perry, J. C. (1986). Perry's defence mechanism rating scale. In G. E. Vaillant (Ed.), *Ego Mechanisms of Defence* (pp. 253–259). Washington, DC: American Psychiatric Press, 1992.

Person, E. S. (1988). *Dreams of Love and Fateful Encounters: The Power of Romantic Passion*. New York: Norton.

Person, E. S. (1995). *By Force of Fantasy: How We Make Our Lives*. New York: Basic Books.

Peskin, M. M. (1997). Drive theory visited. *Psychoanalytic Quarterly* 66:377–402.

Pinker, S. (1994). *The Language Instinct*. New York: Morrow.

Pinker, S., & Bloom, P. (1992). Natural language and natural selection. In J. H. Barkow, L. Cosmides, & J. Tooby (Eds.), *The Adapted Mind* (pp. 451–493). New York: Oxford University Press.

Plakun, E. M. (1989). Narcissistic personality disorder: a validity study and comparison in borderline personality disorder. *Psychiatric Clinics of North America* 12:603–620.

Plotkin, H. (1998). *Evolution in Mind: An Introduction to Evolutionary Psychology*. Cambridge, MA: Harvard University Press.

Poe, E. A. (1843). The Conqueror Worm. In T. O. Mabbott (Ed.), *The Collected Works of Edgar Allan Poe: Volume 1 – Poems.* Cambridge, MA: Harvard University Press, 1979.
Popper, K. (1959). *The Logic of Scientific Discovery.* London: Routledge & Kegan Paul, 1992.
Popper, K. (1962). *Conjectures and Refutations.* Basic Books: New York.
Posner, M. I., & Raichle, M. E. (1994). *Images of Mind.* New York: Scientific American Library.
Potamianou, A. (1992). *Un Bouclier dans L'Economie des Etats Limites L'Espoir.* Paris: Presses of the University of France.
Pray, M. (1996). Two different methods of analysing defence. In M. Goldberger (Ed.), *Danger and Defence* (pp. 53–106). Northvale, NJ: Jason Aronson.
Proust, M. (1913). *Remembrance of Things Past. Vol. 1, Swann's Way.* (C. K. Scott Moncrieff & T. Kilmartin, Trans.). New York: Vintage Books, 1982.
Racker, H. (1968). *Transference and Countertransference.* New York: International University Press.
Raichle, M. E. (1998). Behind the scenes of functional brain imaging: A historical and physiological perspective. *Proceedings of the National Academy of Sciences of the United States of America* 95:765–772.
Rangell, L. (1997). A unitary theory of psychoanalysis. *Journal of Clinical Psychoanalysis* 6:451–612.
Rapaport, D. (1951). *Organization and Pathology of Thought.* New York: Columbia Universities Press.
Rapaport, D. (1967). *The Collected Papers of David Rapaport.* New York: Basic Books.
Reich, A. (1951). On counter-transference. *International Journal of Psycho-Analysis* 32:25–31.
Reich, W. (1933). *Character Analysis* (V. R. Carfagno, Trans.). (3rd ed.). New York: Farrar, Strauss and Giroux, 1972.
Reik, T. (1937). *Surprise and the Psychoanalyst.* New York: Dutton.
Renik, O. (1993). Analytic interaction: conceptualizing technique in the light of the analyst's irreducible subjectivity. *Psychoanalytic Quarterly* 62:553–571.
Richman, J. A., & Flaherty, J. A. (1988). "Tragic Man" and "Tragic Woman": gender differences in narcissistic styles. *Psychiatry* 51:368–377.
Ricoeur, P. (1970). *Freud and Philosophy: An Essay on Interpretation* (D. Savage, Trans.). New Haven, CT: Yale University Press.
Ricoeur, P. (1978). Image and language in psychoanalysis. In J. Smith (Ed.), *Psychoanalysis and Language* (pp. 293–324). New Haven, CT: Yale University Press.
Rieff, P. (1959). *Freud: The Mind of the Moralist.* New York: Viking Press.
Rieff, P. (1966). *The Triumph of the Therapeutic.* Chicago: University of Chicago.
Roazen, P., & Swerdloff, B. (1995). *Heresy: Sandor Rado and the Psychoanalytic Movement.* Northvale, NJ: Jason Aronson.

Robertson-Smith, W. (1889). *Lectures on the Religion of the Semites*. London: A&C Black.
Robins, L. N. (1966). *Deviant Children Grown-Up: A Sociological and Psychiatric Study of Sociopathic Personality*. Baltimore, MD: Williams and Wilkins.
Roheim, G. (1949). Psychoanalysis and anthropology. In D. Harin (Ed.), *Personal Character and Cultural Milieu* (pp. 565–588). Syracuse, NY: Syracuse University Press.
Ronningstam, E. (1988). Comparing three diagnostic systems for narcissistic personality disorder. *Psychiatry 51*:300–311.
Ronningstam, E., & Gunderson, J. (1989). Descriptive studies on narcissistic personality disorder. *Psychiatric Clinics of North America 12*:585–601.
Rosen, V. H. (1969). Introduction to panel on language and psychoanalysis. *International Journal of Psycho-Analysis 50*:113–116.
Rosen, V. H. (1977). *Style, Character and Language*. New York: Jason Aronson.
Rosenblatt, A. D., & Thickstun, J. T. (1970). A study of the concept of psychic energy. *International Journal of Psycho-Analysis 51*:265–278.
Rosenblatt, A. D., & Thickstun, J. T. (1977). *Modern Psychoanalytic Concepts in a General Psychology. Part 1: General Concepts and Principles. Part 2: Motivation*. New York: International Universities Press.
Rosenblatt, A. D., & Thickstun, J. T. (1994). Intuition and consciousness. *Psychoanalytic Quarterly 63*:696–714.
Rothstein, A. (1997). Panel report: turning points in psychoanalysis. *Journal of the American Psychoanalytic Association 45*:1271–1284.
Russo, N. F. (1991). Reconstructing the psychology of women. In M. T. Notman & C. Nadelson (Eds.), *Women and Men: New Perspectives in Gender Differences* (pp. 43–61). Washington, DC: American Psychiatric Press.
Sandler, J. (1981). Character traits and object relationships. *Psychoanalytic Quarterly 50*:694–708.
Sandler, J. (1989). Toward a reconsideration of the psychoanalytic theory of motivation. In A. M. Cooper, O. F. Kernberg, & E. S. Person (Eds.), *Psychoanalysis: Toward the Second Century* (pp. 91–110). New Haven, CT: Yale University Press.
Sartre, J. P. (1960). *The Transcendence of the Ego* (F. Williams & R. Kirkpatrick, Trans.). New York: Hill and Wang.
Schachter, J. (1984). Abstinence and neutrality: Development and diverse views. *International Journal of Psycho-Analysis 75*:709–720.
Schachter, J., & Luborsky, L. (1998). Who's afraid of psychoanalytic research? Analysts' attitudes towards reading clinical versus empirical research papers. *International Journal of Psycho-Analysis 79*:965–969.
Schafer, R. (1968). *Aspects of Internalisation*. New York: International Universities Press.
Schafer, R. (1976). *A New Language for Psychoanalysis*. New Haven, CT: Yale University Press.

Schafer, R. (1978). *Language and Insight*. New Haven, CT: Yale University Press.
Schafer, R. (1983). *The Analytic Attitude*. New York: Basic Books.
Schafer, R. (1992). *Retelling a Life: Narration and Dialogue in Psychoanalysis*. New York: Basic Books.
Schafer, R. (1994a). The conceptualisation of clinical facts. *International Journal of Psycho-Analysis* 75:1023–1030.
Schafer, R. (1994b). The contemporary Kleinians of London. *Psychoanalytic Quarterly* 63:409–432.
Schafer, R. (1994c). The practice of revisiting classics: an essay on Heinz Hartmann's "Psychoanalysis and Moral Values". *Psychoanalysis and Contemporary Thought* 17:251–286.
Schafer, R. (1995). The evolution of my views on nonnormative sexual practices. In T. Domenici & R. C. Lester (Eds.), *Disorienting Sexuality: Psychoanalytic Reappraisals of Sexual Identities* (pp. 187–202). New York: Routledge.
Schafer, R. (1996). Authority, evidence, and knowledge in the psychoanalytic relationship. *Psychoanalytic Quarterly* 65:236–253.
Schafer, R. (1997a). *The Contemporary Kleinians of London*. Madison, CT: International Universities Press.
Schafer, R. (1997b). *Tradition and Change in Psychoanalysis*. Madison, CT: International Universities Press.
Schlesinger, H. J. (1969). Diagnosis and prescription for psychotherapy. *Bulletin of the Menninger Clinic* 33:269–278.
Schlesinger, H. J. (1970). The place of forgetting in memory functioning. *Journal of the American Psychoanalytic Association* 18:358–371.
Schlesinger, H. J. (1974). Problems in doing research on the therapeutic process in psychoanalysis. *Journal of the American Psychoanalytic Association* 22:3–13.
Schlesinger, H. J. (1978). Developmental and regressive aspects of the making and breaking of promises. In S. Smith (Ed.), *The Human Mind Revisited. Essays in Honour of Karl Menninger* (pp. 21–50). New York: International Universities Press.
Schlesinger, H. J. (1981a). Chapter III. General principles of psychoanalytic supervision; Chapter V. The data: process notes of 14 supervision hours; Chapter XIII. On being the supervisor studied: confessions and observations. In R. Wallerstein (Ed.), *Becoming a Psychoanalyst* (pp. 17–38, 61–118, 283–309). New York: International Universities Press.
Schlesinger, H. J. (1981b). A contribution to a theory of promising: II. Mature and regressive determinants of the keeping of promises. In S. Greenspan & G. Pollock (Eds.), *The Course of Life, Vol 3: Adulthood* (pp. 129–147). Washington, DC: US Government Printing Office.
Schlesinger, H. J. (1981c). The process of empathic response. *Psychoanalytic Inquiry* 1:393–416.

Schlesinger, H. J. (1981d). Resistance as process. In P. Wachtel (Ed.), *Resistance in Psychodynamic and Behavioural Therapies* (pp. 25–44). New York: Plenum.

Schlesinger, H. J. (1988a). Case discussion and position statement. In "The Intrapsychic and Interpersonal Dimensions: An Unresolved Dilemma". *Psychoanalytic Inquiry* 8:524–534.

Schlesinger, H. J. (1988b). A historical overview of conceptions of the mode of therapeutic action of psychoanalytic psychotherapy. In A. Rothstein (Ed.), *How Does Treatment Help? On the Modes of Therapeutic Action of Psychoanalytic Psychotherapy* (pp. 7–27). Madison, CT: International Universities Press.

Schlesinger, H. J. (1990). Supervision and the training analysis: Repetition or collaboration? In M. Meisels & E. R. Shapiro (Eds.), *Tradition and Innovation in Psychoanalytic Education* (pp. 135–140). Hillsdale, NJ: Lawrence Erlbaum.

Schlesinger, H. J. (1992). What does psychoanalysis have to contribute to the understanding of character? *Psychoanalytic Study of the Child* 47:225–234. New Haven, CT: Yale University Press.

Schlesinger, H. J. (1994a). How the analyst listens: the pre-stages of interpretation. *International Journal of Psycho-Analysis* 75:31–37.

Schlesinger, H. J. (1994b). The role of the intellect in the process of defence. *Bulletin of the Menninger Clinic* 58:15–36.

Schlesinger, H. J. (1995a). Facts is facts, or is they? *International Journal of Psycho-Analysis* 76:1167–1177.

Schlesinger, H. J. (1995b). The process of interpretation and the moment of change. *Journal of the American Psychoanalytic Association* 43:662–685.

Schlesinger, H. J. (1995c). Supervision for fun and profit: or how to tell if the fun is profitable. *Psychoanalytic Inquiry* 15:190–210.

Schlesinger, H. J. (1996). The fear of being left half-cured. *Bulletin of the Menninger Clinic* 60:428–448.

Schlesinger, H. J., & Appelbaum, A. H. (in press). When words are not enough. *Psychoanalytic Inquiry*.

Schlesinger, H. J., & Holzman, P. S. (1970). The therapeutic aspects of the hospital milieu: Prescribing an activities programme. *Bulletin of the Menninger Clinic* 34:1–11.

Schur, M. (1966). *The Id and the Regulatory Principles of Mental Functioning*. New York: International Universities Press.

Searle, J. R. (1969). *Speech Acts*. London: Cambridge University Press.

Searle, J. R. (1992). *The Rediscovery of the Mind*. Cambridge, MA: MIT Press.

Seitz, P. (1966). The consensus problem in psychoanalytic research. In L. Gottschalk & A. Auerbach (Eds.), *Methods of Research in Psychotherapy* (pp. 209–225). New York: Appleton-Century-Crofts.

Sellars, W. (1956). *Empiricism and the Philosophy of Mind. Vol. 1*. Minneapolis: University of Minnesota Press.

Shapin, S. (1994). *A Social History of Truth: Civility and Science in Seventeenth Century England*. Chicago: University of Chicago Press.

Shapin, S. (1996). *The Scientific Revolution*. Chicago: University of Chicago Press.

Shapiro, T. (1970). Interpretation and naming. *Journal of the American Psychoanalytic Association* 18:399–421.

Shapiro, T. (1971). Symbol formation (report of colloquium). *American Imago* 28:195–215.

Shapiro, T. (1977). Oedipal distortions in severe character pathologies: developmental and theoretical considerations. *Psychoanalytic Quarterly* 46:559–579.

Shapiro, T. (1986). Sign, symbol and structural theory. In A. D. Richard & M. S. Willick (Eds.), *Psychoanalysis: The Science of Mental Conflict – Essays in Honour of Charles Brenner* (pp. 107–125). Hillsdale, NJ: Analytic Press.

Shapiro, T. (1988). Language, structure and psychoanalysis. In T. Shapiro (Ed.), *The Concept of Structure in Psychoanalysis* (pp. 339–358). New York: International Universities Press.

Shapiro, T. (1995). *Psychoanalysis as conversation*. Paper presented at the 39th congress of the International Psychoanalytic Association, San Francisco.

Shulman, R. G. (1996). Interview with Robert G. Shulman. *Journal of Cognitive Neuroscience* 8:474–480.

Shulman, R. G., Blamire, A. M., Rothman, D. L., & McCarthy, G. (1993). Nuclear magnetic resonance imaging and spectroscopy of human brain function. *Proceedings of the National Academy of Sciences of the United States of America* 90:3127–3133.

Shulman, R. G., & Rothman, D. L. (1998). Interpreting functional imaging studies in terms of neurotransmitter cycling. *Proceedings of the National Academy of Sciences of the United States of America* 95:11993–11998.

Shulman, R. G., Rothman, D. L., & Hyder, F. (1999). Stimulated changes in localized cerebral energy consumption under anesthesia. *Proceedings of the National Academy of Sciences of the United States of America* 96:3245–3250.

Sibson, N. R., Dhankhar, A., Mason, G. F., Rothman, D. L., Behar, K. L., & Shulman, R. G. (1998). Stoichiometric coupling of brain glucose metabolism and glutamatergic neuronal activity. *Proceedings of the National Academy of Sciences of the United States of America* 95:316–321.

Siever, L. J., & Davis, K. L. (1991). A psychobiological perspective on the personality disorders. *American Journal of Psychiatry* 148:1647–1658.

Silberschatz, G., Sampson, H., & Weiss, J. (1986). Testing pathogenic beliefs versus seeking transference gratifications. In J. Weiss & H. Sampson (Eds.), *The Psychoanalytic Process: Theory, Clinical Observation and Empirical Research* (pp. 256–266). New York: Guilford Press.

Slavin, M. O., & Kriegman, D. (1992). *The Adaptive Design of the Human Psyche: Psychoanalysis, Evolutionary Biology, and the Therapeutic Process*. New York: Guilford Press.

Solms, M. (1997). What is consciousness? *Journal of the American Psychoanalytic Association* 45:681–703.
Sophocles. (1970). *Oedipus Tyrannus* (L. Berkowitz & T. Brunner, Trans.). New York: Norton.
Spector, J. J. (1972). *The Aesthetics of Freud: A Study in Psychoanalysis and Art*. London: Allen Lane.
Spence, D. (1984). *The Freudian Metaphor*. New York: Norton.
Spence, D. P. (1982a). *Narrative Truth and Historical Truth. Meaning and Interpretation in Psychoanalysis*. New York/London: Norton.
Spence, D. P. (1982b). Narrative truth and theoretical truth. *Psychoanalytic Quarterly* 51:43–69.
Spence, D. P. (1994). The special nature of psychoanalytic facts. *International Journal of Psycho-Analysis* 75:915–925.
Spence, D. P. (1998). Rain forest or mud field. *International Journal of Psycho-Analysis* 79:643–647.
Spence, D. P., Dahl, H., & Jones, E. E. (1993). Impact of interpretation on associative freedom. *Journal of Consulting and Clinical Psychology* 61:395–402.
Sperber, D., & Wilson, D. (1986). *Relevance*. Oxford: Blackwell.
Stanford, C. B. (1996). The ecology of wild chimpanzees: implications for the evolutionary ecology of pliocene hominids. *American Anthropologist* 98:96–113.
Stepansky, P. (1983). *In Freud's Shadow: Adler in Context*. Hillsdale, NJ: Analytic Press.
Sterba, R. (1934). The fate of the ego in analytic therapy. *International Journal of Psycho-Analysis* 15:117–126.
Stern, D. N. (1985). *The Interpersonal World of the Infant: A View from Psychoanalysis and Developmental Psychology*. New York: Basic Books.
Stoller, R. J. (1975). *Perversion: The Erotic Form of Hatred*. New York: Pantheon.
Stoller, R. J. (1976). Primary femininity. *Journal of the American Psychoanalytic Association* 24 (Supplement 5):59.
Stoller, R. J. (1985). *Observing the Erotic Imagination*. New Haven, CT: Yale University Press.
Stolorow, R. D. (1997). Review of "A dynamic systems approach to the development of cognition and action". *International Journal of Psycho-Analysis* 78:620–623.
Stone, A. (1997). Where will psychoanalysis survive? *Harvard Magazine Jan-Feb*: 35–39.
Stone, M. H. (1986). Borderline personality disorder. In R. Michels & J. O. Cavenart (Eds.), *Psychiatry* (Vol. 1, pp. 1–18). New York: Basic Books.
Stone, M. H. (1993). Aetiology of borderline personality disorders: Psychobiological factors contributing an underlying irritability. In J. Paris (Ed.), *Borderline Personality Disorder*. Washington, DC: American Psychiatric Press.
Strenger, C. (1991). *Between Hermeneutics and Science: An Essay on the Epistemology of Psychoanalysis*. Madison, CT: International Universities Press.

Sullivan, H. S. (1940). *Conceptions of Modern Psychiatry*. New York: Norton.
Suomi, S. J. (1995). Influence of attachment theory on ethological studies of biobehavioural development in nonhuman primates. In S. Goldberg, R. Muir, & J. Kerr (Eds.), *Attachment Theory: Social, Developmental and Clinical Perspectives* (pp. 185–230). Hillsdale, NJ: Analytic Press.
Svrakic, D. M., Whitehead, C., Pryzbeck, T. R., & Cloninger, C. R. (1993). Differential diagnosis of personality disorders by the seven-factor model of temperament and character. *Archives of General Psychiatry 50*:991–999.
Symons, D. (1987). If we're all Darwinians, what's the fuss about? In C. B. Crawford, M. Smith, & D. Krebs (Eds.), *Sociobiology and Psychology* (pp. 121–146). Hillsdale, NJ: Lawrence Erlbaum.
Tartakoff, H. (1966). The normal personality in our culture and the Nobel Prize complex. In R. M. Lowenstein, L. M. Newman, M. Schur, & A. J. Solnit (Eds.), *Psychoanalysis: A General Psychology* (pp. 222–252). New York: International Universities Press.
Taylor, C. (1992). *The Ethics of Authenticity*. Cambridge, MA: Harvard University Press.
Teller, V., & Dahl, H. (1995). What psychoanalysis needs is more empirical research. In T. Shapiro & R. N. Emde (Eds.), *Research in Psychoanalysis: Process, Development, Outcome* (pp. 31–49). Madison, CT: International Universities Press.
Thelen, E., & Smith, L. (1994). *A Dynamic Systems Approach to the Development of Cognition and Action*. Cambridge, MA: MIT Press.
Thomas, A., & Chess, S. (1977). *Temperament and Development*. New York: Brunner/Mazel.
Thomas, A., & Chess, S. (1984). Genesis and evolution of behavioral disorders: from infancy to early adult life. *American Journal of Psychiatry 141*:1–9.
Tobak, M. (1989). Lying and the paranoid personality (letter to editor). *American Journal of Psychiatry 146*:125.
Tooby, J., & Cosmides, L. (1992). The psychological foundations of culture. In J. H. Barkow, L. Cosmides, & J. Tooby (Eds.), *The Adapted Mind* (pp. 19–136). New York: Oxford University Press.
Trivers, R. (1971). The evolution of reciprocal altruism. *Quarterly Review of Biology 46*:35–57.
Trivers, R. L. (1974). Parental–offspring conflict. *American Zoologist 14*:249–264.
Tuckett, D. (1993). Some thoughts on the presentation and discussion of the clinical material of psychoanalysis. *International Journal of Psycho-Analysis 74*:1175–1189.
Tuckett, D. (1998). Evaluating psychoanalytic papers: towards the development of common standards. *International Journal of Psycho-Analysis 79*:431–448.
Tuckett, D., Boulton, C. O., & Williams, A. (1985). *Meetings Between Experts: An Approach to Sharing Ideas in Medical Consultations*. London: Tavistock Publications.

Vaillant, G. E. (1977). *Adaptation to Life*. Boston, MA: Little Brown.
Viederman, M. (1976). The influence of the person of the analyst on structural change: a case report. *Psychoanalytic Quarterly 45*:231–249.
Viederman, M. (1983). The psychodynamic life narrative: a psychotherapeutic intervention useful in crisis situations. *Psychiatry 46*:236–246.
Viederman, M. (1984). The active dynamic interview and the supportive relationship. *Comprehensive Psychiatry 25*:147–157.
Viederman, M. (1986). Personality change through life experience (I): a model. *Psychiatry 49*:204–217.
Viederman, M. (1989). Personality change through life experience (III): two creative types of response to object loss. In D. Dietrich & P. Shabad (Eds.), *The Problem of Loss and Mourning: Psychoanalytic Perspectives* (pp. 187–212). Madison, CT: International Universities Press.
Viederman, M. (1991). The impact of the real person of the analyst on the psychoanalytic cure. *Journal of the American Psychoanalytic Association 39*:451–489.
Viederman, M. (1994). The uses of the past and the actualisation of a family romance. *Journal of the American Psychoanalytic Association 42*:469–489.
Viederman, M. (1995). The reconstruction of a repressed sexual molestation fifty years later. *Journal of the American Psychoanalytic Association 43*:1169–1195.
Viederman, M. (1998). Reconstruction and veridicality. *Journal of the American Psychoanalytic Association 46*:551–556.
Viederman, M., & Blumberg, H. (1993). Anatomy of a consultation: a teaching method. *General Hospital Psychiatry 15*:183–199.
Volkan, V. D. (1973). Transitional fantasies in the analysis of a narcissistic personality. *Journal of the American Psychoanalytic Association 21*:351–376.
Volkan, V. D. (1982). Narcissistic personality disorder. In J. O. Cavenar & H. K. H. Brodie (Eds.), *Critical Problems in Psychiatry* (pp. 332–350). Philadelphia, PA: J.B. Lippincott.
Wallace, E. R. (1983). *Freud and Anthropology: A History and Reappraisal*. New York: International Universities Press.
Wallerstein, R. S. (1986). *Forty-two Lives in Treatment: A Study of Psychoanalysis and Psychotherapy*. New York: Guilford Press.
Wax, M. L. (1990). Malinowski, Freud and Oedipus. *International Journal of Psycho-Analysis 17*:47–60.
Weber, M. (1923). *Economy and Society*. New York: Bedminster Press, 1968.
Wittgenstein, L. (1958). *Lectures and Conversation*. Berkeley and Los Angeles, CA: University of California Press.
Wolfenstein, M. (1969). How is mourning possible? *Psychoanalytic Study of the Child 21*:92–123. New York: International Universities Press.

Woody, G., McLellan, A. T., Luborsky, L., O'Brien, C., Blaine, J., Fox, S., Herman, I., & Beck, A. T. (1984). Psychiatric severity as a predictor of benefits from psychotherapy: the Veterans Administration–Penn Study. *American Journal of Psychiatry 141*:1172–1177.

Wrangham, R., & Peterson, D. (1996). *Demonic Males: Apes and the Origin of Human Violence*. Boston & New York: Houghton Mifflin.